DOUBLING
AND INCEST / REPETITION
AND REVENGE

DOUBLING
AND INCEST / REPETITION
AND REVENGE

*A Speculative Reading
of Faulkner*

Expanded Edition

John T. Irwin

THE JOHNS HOPKINS UNIVERSITY PRESS
Baltimore and London

Originally published, 1975
Expanded edition, 1996
05 04 03 02 01 00 99 98 97 96   5 4 3 2 1

"*Knight's Gambit*: Poe, Faulkner, and the Tradition of the Detective Story"
originally appeared in *Faulkner and the Short Story*, and "Horace Benbow and
the Myth of Narcissa" originally appeared in *Faulkner and Psychology*,
copyright © 1992 and 1994 by the University Press of Mississippi.

The Johns Hopkins University Press
2715 North Charles Street
Baltimore, Maryland 21218-4319
The Johns Hopkins Press Ltd., London

Library of Congress Cataloging-in-Publication Data will be found at the
end of this book.

A catalog record for this book is available from the British Library.

ISBN 0-8018-5231-5 (pbk.)

For Alicia,
far away
in Buenos Aires

"I believe that every word a writing man writes is put down with the ultimate intention of impressing some woman that probably don't care anything at all for literature, as is the nature of women."
—Dawson Fairchild, in Faulkner's *Mosquitoes*

Contents

PREFACE TO THE EXPANDED EDITION / *Doubling and Incest / Repetition and Revenge: A Speculative Reading of Faulkner* was first published in the fall of 1975 and has remained in print for the past twenty years. Earlier this year, when the Johns Hopkins Press proposed a new printing of the book with a revised cover, I suggested that it be made an expanded edition, by adding as appendixes two essays I had written on Faulkner in the early 1990s, both of which were related to the book's subject. The essays were delivered at the annual Faulkner and Yoknapatawpha Conference at the University of Mississippi in 1990 and 1991.

The first, "*Knight's Gambit*: Poe, Faulkner, and the Tradition of the Detective Story," examines Faulkner's self-conscious manipulation of detective story structures in the tradition originated by Poe's Dupin stories, an inquiry with implications for Quentin's and Shreve's detective work in *Absalom, Absalom!* The second, "Horace Benbow and the Myth of Narcissa," focuses on Horace Benbow as a transitional figure in the development of a single character structure whose earlier incarnation is Quentin Compson and whose later is Gavin Stevens, a character structure that forms the backbone of Faulkner's major fiction.

Both essays appeared in magazines, the former in *The Arizona Quarterly* and the latter in *American Literature*, and I wish to thank their respective editors, Edgar Dryden and Cathy Davidson, for publishing them. The essays were also included in the volumes of papers from the two Faulkner conferences published by the University of Mississippi Press, and I want to express my appreciation to the editors of the volumes and the organizers of the conference—Evans Harrington, Ann J. Abadie, Donald M. Kartiganer, and Doreen Fowler.

Doubling and Incest was my first book, and it has a special place in my affections. I still subscribe to the interpretation of Faulkner's fiction it contains, particularly where that interpretation has been expanded or modified by the two subsequent essays. I can only hope that in its new form the book will find a new generation of readers who, like myself, are admirers of our greatest modern American fiction writer.

Baltimore, July 1995

INTRODUCTION / There is something that writers of introductions seldom say but that readers should never forget: an introduction, though it is read first, is written last. Consequently, an introduction is always also a conclusion; it should be read once at the beginning of the book and once again at the end. That act of rereading the introduction at the end is an embodiment of one of the things that this book is about, for in that act one must experience a repetition-in-difference whereby an earlier event (the original reading of the introduction) reread in light of a later event (the reading of the text) is at once constituted as different and yet the same. Introductions are also, insofar as books are the alter egos of their authors, acts of autocriticism, a looking back of the self at the self. That is another thing that this book is about. Finally, an introduction is often, as well, an inquiry into the origins of the book that it precedes—an attempt to explain why the book is as it is by telling where it came from. That inquiry into the origins of the book is another of the subjects of *this* book, and it is as good a starting point as any for this introduction.

Let me try, then, to recall as best I can, in light of the book's final form, its beginning, since in matters like these it is only in light of a final form that we can ever recognize a beginning. One day after teaching Faulkner to a group of undergraduates, I was suddenly struck by the relationship of the story that Quentin Compson tells in *Absalom, Absalom!* to his own story as we know it from *The Sound and the Fury.* The more I thought about it, the more I began to realize that in the relationship between these two books through the figure of Quentin Compson I had found a key to the structure out of which Faulkner's best work is written, for I saw that in that intertextual oscillation between the story a narrator tells and his own story Faulkner was evoking the oscillating relationship between a writer and his book, evoking it as a kind of incestuous doubling in which the writer, through an oblique repetition, seeks revenge against time.

From that point on, the story of the origin of my book is essentially a litany of the names of people who allowed me to bore them with the endless repetition of my ideas about Faulkner. First of all, there was Larry Holland, who with his customary good grace and intelligence listened to my fiftieth recital as if it were the first and made helpful suggestions on each occasion. There was Paul Olson, who introduced me to Ernest Jones's work on the fantasy of the reversal of generations and to the writings of Guy Rosolato. There was Harry Sieber, who over a period of years kept me up to date on the works of many European critics and finally badgered me into taking them seriously even though my field was American literature, with its traditional rejection of European influences. In the spring of 1974 I delivered part of this study as a paper at the Johns Hopkins Philological Association. In the months immediately preceding and following that meeting, I discussed the paper frequently with the two people whose attention and response to its arguments had the greatest influence on the final form of the book—Alicia Borinsky and Jeffrey Mehlman. Not that they necessarily agreed with my ideas about Faulkner, or about anything else (indeed, we were often in fundamental disagreement, particularly in our interpretations of Freud), but that that disagreement allowed me to test certain ideas and to try to discover the floating boundaries of my own critical position. That those boundaries were and are floating doesn't greatly disturb me, since it has been my observation that the price one pays for having clear, distinct ideas is to have very few ideas.

The discussions with Alicia Borinsky and Jeffrey Mehlman, which usually took place at lunch, were often three-sided tennis matches in which texts from Latin American, French, and American literature were batted back and forth between the not-so-fixed poles of Nietzsche and Freud. One of the recurring questions that Jeffrey Mehlman asked about my juxtaposition of texts by Faulkner and Freud concerned what I understood the relationship between Freud's psychoanalytic writings and Faulkner's novels to be—did I think, for example, that Freud's insights explained Faulkner's books, that is, explained the psychology of the characters or of the author? My answer to that question was no, and thus the book that follows is not what many people would consider to be psychoanalytic criticism. And if by "explained" one meant "explained away," then the answer was emphatically no. In juxtaposing Faulkner and Freud or Faulkner and Nietzsche, my aim was not to explain or reduce or simplify Faulkner's novels but to make them more problematic, richer and more complex. At the same time I realized that the reciprocal nature of such a juxtaposition would render the works of Freud and Nietzsche more problematic as well.

My feeling about the "truth" of Freud's writings is that his works are in themselves as problematical as any speculative philosophic writing, and in this book my interest in Freud is centered in those areas—like repetition or the death instinct—where Freud is at his most metapsychological, at his most philosophical, and thus at his closest to a philosopher like Nietzsche who always thought of himself as a kind of philological psychologist. My sense of the relationship between Faulkner, Freud, and Nietzsche is that they were writers who addressed themselves to many of the same questions, and that at numerous points their works form imaginative

2

analogues to one another. If the critical discourse in this book is able to oscillate across Faulkner's novels to evoke a structure that exists in the interstices between those novels, then one should not be surprised to find that that oscillation can be extended to reveal the existence of that structure beyond Faulkner's work as well—in the interstices between his writings and the work of writers like Freud and Nietzsche who shared his preoccupations, for the structure that is created by Faulkner's writing simultaneously creates that writing, at once in and beyond, contained and container.

It is precisely because I understand Faulkner, Freud, and Nietzsche to be related specifically as *writers* that I treat the works of all three as literary texts whose implications are ultimately philosophical. That action is not, of course, as arbitrary as it sounds: in the case of Freud, for example, it is not just that his psychoanalytic writings frequently involve the analysis of a literary text, as in the essay on the uncanny, but that the whole psychoanalytic enterprise is one of linguistic analysis—what is analyzed is language, the means of that analysis is language, and what is discovered is that the unconscious is structured like a language. Indeed, what else could such a process discover? To say that the process is tautological is not, of course, to discredit it in any way. It is the process of translation, the process of discovering the different ways in which one says the same about the Same. And what endeavor could be more philosophical than that? The analyst who listens while a patient repeats again and again the story or stories of his life is simply trying to understand the relationship between the narrator and the story or stories that he tells, trying to decipher a hidden story by analyzing the variations among the patent translations of that story, trying to discover the laws of condensation, distortion, substitution that govern the different oblique repetitions of that same hidden story. And it is, I think, not unjustified to say that the motive force of those repetitions is, in a very real sense, an oblique revenge against time, for if revenge means trying to get even, then in light of Freud's economic model for psychic energy exchanges and the principle of constancy, those repetitions are attempts to stabilize or equalize a tension, attempts "to get even" in terms of energy levels for an insult or affront to the psychic apparatus. But because of the irreversibility of the flow of time, the insult or affront can never be gotten at directly, and the reversal, the flowing back or discharge of energy that equalizing or "getting even" demands, always involves an oblique attempt to get even with that irreversibility of time that has rendered the original affront immune to direct action. One might say that the purpose and point of those narrations, and perhaps of all narration, is to use the temporal medium of narration to take revenge against time, to use narration to get even with the very mode of narration's existence in a daemonic attempt to prove that through the process of substitution and repetition, time is not really irreversible. One might add that this is the very essence of tragedy, for I take it that all tragedies are in a sense revenger's tragedies—actions in which the central figure (or the audience observing him) comes to the tragic awareness that, because of the irreversibility of time, man in time can never get even, indeed, comes to understand that the whole process of getting even is incompatible with time. The two chief factors in that awareness are the foredoomed aspirations to power inherent in the very workings of the memory and the unalterability of the effects of the past. In this connection let me juxtapose two facts whose relationship, if it is not clear now, will, I trust, become clear in the course of the book: first, that Freud found the paradigm for that central complex in the psychic life in the most famous of the Greek tragedies, and second, that Nietzsche began his career as a writer with *The Birth of Tragedy from the Spirit of Music* and then closed the circle in his most ambitious work, *Thus Spoke Zarathustra,* when he maintained that "the bridge to the highest hope" is "that man be delivered from revenge," specifically from "the spirit of revenge" against the "it was" of time.

In dealing with Freud's writings as literary/philosophical texts, I have tried to present certain structures like the Oedipus complex, the death instinct, and the repetition compulsion in what I understand to be their classically Freudian form, devoid of later clinical revision. I have done this because my approach to these structures is, in part, historical as well as literary and philosophic. In confining myself to the writings of first-generation psychoanalysts like Freud, Rank, Jones, and Stekel, I have tried to evoke the general understanding of certain major psychoanalytic structures contemporary with the writing of Faulkner's novels. Further, whatever the truth of external correspondence that Freud's writings possess in terms of clinical practice, I am more interested in them as written texts, interested in their truth of internal coherence as works of literature, since for the *reader* of Freud's work, it is only as written texts that that work exists—texts in which a patient's story is presented, and then by an active repetition in the form of a linguistic analysis is transformed into another story, different and yet the same, a story whose implications are invariably philosophic. My one exception to the procedure of historical reconstruction was in the use of Guy Rosolato's work on the transformation of the Oedipal triangle into the three generations of patrilinearity. In that instance, however, it was not a case of a clinical revision but of a philosophic expansion specifically addressed to the linguistic ground of psychoanalysis, for

4

Rosolato's study is a textual analysis of two Biblical stories (the sacrifices of Isaac and of Jesus) to discover in the mechanism of substitution and sacrifice, as applied to the Oedipal triangle, the very origin of the mediation that is language.

The appropriateness of using texts from Freud and Nietzsche to provide imaginative analogues for Faulkner's work derives in part from the fact that the three writers are linked by a chain of denied influence. As Freud denied the influence of Nietzsche, so Faulkner denied the influence of Freud. According to his biographer Ernest Jones, Freud, during meetings of the Vienna Psycho-Analytic Society in 1908 at which Nietzsche's writings were discussed, "related, as he did on several other occasions, how he had found the abstractness of philosophy so unsympathetic that he gave up studying it. Nietzsche had in no way influenced his ideas. He had tried to read him, but found his thought so rich that he renounced the attempt. . . . He several times said of Nietzsche that he had a more penetrating knowledge of himself than any other man who ever lived or was ever likely to live."[1] In one of the conferences that he gave at the University of Virginia, Faulkner said, "What little of psychology I know the characters I have invented and playing poker taught me. Freud I'm not familiar with."[2] Yet in his second novel, *Mosquitoes* (1927), two of the characters, in discussing the psychology of a third character, talk about Freud and Havelock Ellis, and the substance of their conversation shows that if the author of the novel was not familiar with Freud, his characters certainly were. In an interview, Faulkner said, "Everybody talked about Freud when I was in New Orleans, but I have never read him."[3] Indeed, the very fact that Faulkner had never read Freud would mean that in those conversations in New Orleans he could have absorbed many ideas whose ultimate derivations from Freud he would not have been aware of. In reply to a question about Faulkner's knowledge of Freud and Jung, his close friend Phil Stone said in an interview, "He wouldn't read Freud. I tried to get him to. I taught *at* him, but he wouldn't listen. He wasn't interested in psychology."[4] It seems less likely that Faulkner was uninterested in psychology than that he had learned enough about Freud's ideas to want to avoid the threat to his own creative energy and enterprise that might be posed by a sense of his own work having been anticipated by Freud's. Suffice it to say that whatever the extent of Freud's influence on Faulkner's novels, at some point the similarities in their work seemed great enough (either to Faulkner himself or to readers who questioned him about those similarities) to make a denial of that influence seem worthwhile.

Perhaps the most obvious difficulty that the reader will confront in the following book, and for which the introduction should prepare him, concerns its mechanical format, or more precisely, its lack of a mechanical format, for the book is one long essay without chapter divisions or mechanical breaks. The lack of division is the result of the book's not having been written in logical units. Rather, its structure is the product of a continuing act of deferment and accumulated tension. As I look back on the writing, I suppose that, stylistically, I was trying to weave a kind of seamless garment, and that that was necessary because the structure that I was trying to reveal exists only as a whole, exists not as the sum of its elements, not by the simple addition of those elements, but rather through the simultaneous multiplication of every element by every other element. What I tried to evoke was a kind of synergism in which the structure in its irreducible wholeness is infinitely more than simply the sum of its parts, for, strictly speaking, *considered as structure, as a continuous system of differences,* it has no parts, no independently meaningful, logically separable units. To speak of the *elements* of the structure is simply to speak of various limited perspectives of the whole, and to say that this structure in Faulkner's work is intertextual and its meaning interstitial is simply to evoke the effort to see the structure from all of its various perspectives at once, to see the structure as epistemologically created by the simultaneous interaction of all of its individually limited perspectives, its *elements.* And it is precisely the impossibility of seeing the structure from all sides at once that allows us to take a further step, allows us to see why structures are always virtual, always *to-be-known,* or more exactly, always *to-be-inferred.* As Lévi-Strauss says, a structure is a virtual object whose shadow alone is real. Some of the perspectival elements of the structure that I am concerned with in Faulkner are spatial and temporal doubling, spatial and temporal incest, narcissism, the Oedipus complex, the castration complex, repetition, sameness and difference, recollection, repression, revenge, substitution, reversal, sacrifice, and mediation. And it is not simply that every element is simultaneously present to and interacting with every other element, it is that every element, *considered in its relationship to every other element in the structure,* is simultaneously present to and interacting with every other element. I realized that in order to make *that* structure declare itself, in order to make it appear in the light, I would need the critical equivalent of an integral and differential calculus, since what I would have to show in my text was how every element was simultaneously affecting and being affected by all the other elements.

At one point I simply had to ask myself if I thought that it was possible to present a holistic, simultaneous structure in the temporal, successive medium of written discourse. My answer was, "Of course not"—not if by "present" one meant "explain." But it seemed to me that I could come as close as possible to presenting that structure by trying to embody it in the structure of my own text. The model that I used as a starting point for that attempt was the musical, motival structure of Lévi-Strauss's *The Raw and the Cooked.* In order to achieve the multiple counterpointing effect that is the great strength of that method, I had to try to create within my text a kind of multidimensional imaginative space in which there existed the possibility of simultaneously placing every element side by side with every other element. Or rather, what I needed was to create an imaginative space in which there could be a superposition or interpenetration of every element by every other element, a space in which every element could be simultaneously folded into every other element. And the reason for this is that in the structure it is not simply a case of every element simultaneously interacting with every other element, but rather that by that simultaneous interaction the elements mutually create one another, mutually constitute themselves *as elements in a holistic structure.* Let me take as a simplified model the binary opposition left and right. Obviously, they are not logically separable units. They are always implicit in one another (one thinks of Freud's essay on the antithetical sense of primal words); the concept of one without the other is meaningless. Nor is there any question of priority, of which came first, for if they don't both come into existence together, then neither comes into existence, because it is precisely by means of the opposition, the tension, the difference between them that they mutually constitute one another. It is just this concept of mutually constitutive opposites linking any two given positions in the Oedipal triangle that underlies my treatment of reversibility and oscillation in the text; and when the closed Oedipal triangle is, by a substitution, transformed into the open-ended three generations of patrilinearity, the binary opposition of difference and the linking unity of sameness are embodied in the mediation of language and the transmission of the name. And yet the mutually constitutive character of the tensions in the structure that I was trying to embody in my text was more complicated still.

The way that I tried, stylistically in my own book, to embody that holistic structure was by continually refusing to let my text come to intermediate conclusions—the kind of conclusions that one would have in chapters. Of course, each of the elements of the structure had to be introduced in succession, but the stylistic solution to the problem of embodying a structural whole in this manner was to introduce each element and then hold it in suspension while another element was introduced that was in turn held in suspension, and so on, until all the elements had been suspended in a homogeneous medium, a medium constructed to allow optimal fluidity in the association of elements by the reader. I realize now that in this procedure I was unconsciously guided by work that I had done earlier on Hart Crane's "logic of metaphor,"—specifically, on the way in which Crane dissolves syntax in order to create within the poem a fluid linguistic medium in which the reader is led to manipulate metaphoric vehicles in a kind of controlled free association, a technique that Crane called "the dynamics of inferential mention." My attempt to achieve in this book an optimal fluidity in the association of elements by the reader is nowhere near as radical as Crane's. Indeed, the way that the reader will experience this procedure during most of the book, or perhaps during his entire first reading of the book, is as a deferment of meaning: he will feel that elements are being presented to him whose exact point, whose relationship to one another and to the novels, is continually being withheld, continually being deferred. That is necessary because, until all the elements can be simultaneously suspended in the imaginative space of the text, their relationship to one another and to the novels will not appear, for that relationship and the elements themselves *as the related* are only constituted by the interaction of all of them at once.

There is a further reason why this continual deferment of meaning as embodied in my text is appropriate to a treatment of Faulkner's novels, for Faulkner himself seems to have understood the oscillating relationship between a narrator and his story, between a writer and his book, as embodying "the always deferredness" of meaning—as a kind of Freudian *Nachträglichkeit,* in which the act of narration, as a recollection and reworking, produces a story that almost makes sense but not quite, yet whose quality of *almost* being meaningful seems to indicate, seems to promise, that meaning has only been temporarily deferred and that some future repetition of the story, some further recollection and reworking, will capture that ultimate meaning. Clearly, that seems to have been Faulkner's sense of the writing of *The Sound and the Fury.* He said that he began it as a short story told from the point of view of one character, but that wasn't right, so he told it again from the point of view of another character, but that wasn't right either, and then he told it again from the point of view of a third, which still wasn't right, so finally he told it from his own point of view, and when that turned out not to be right, turned out to be partial and incomplete, he stopped. And just as clearly in *Absalom,* Quentin realizes that his narration of the story of the Sutpens is an answer that doesn't answer—an answer that puts the answerer in question. One might say that Faulkner's modern classical sense, his sense of the tragic absurd, is not the sense of the meaningless but of the almost meaningful—the sense of the meaningful as the always deferred. Indeed, I have the feeling that it is this quality of the always deferred that characterizes as well the structure that I have tried to present in my text, and that consequently there is no possibility of presenting that structure but only its effects. It is as if in some past that never existed the structure was deferred to some future that will never exist, as if the structure is both before and after without ever having been here and now. (One might almost say that this sense of the always deferred, this sense of a before and after that has never been, and can never be, here and now is precisely what Freud meant, on the deepest level, by the Unconscious.) Or, if you want a spatial image, it is as if the structure were one of those black holes in space that, because it absorbs light but never emits it, can never appear in the light but can only be known by its warping or disjointing effect on the things that do appear in the light and on the light itself. But in order to infer this structure from its effects, from its afterimages, one must have a set of elements large enough to understand what constitutes a warp across those elements.

For a good part of my text, then, things simply have to be kept up in the air, and that process of keeping things up in the air, of keeping elements in suspension, does not favor mechanical breaks and is without logical divisions. Indeed, it may seem at some points in the text as if a paragraph is never going to end and at other points as if a sentence has been hijacked in midcourse by one of Faulkner's compulsive-obsessive narrators. Those long, complex paragraphs and sentences are not the result of prolixity or of willful obscurity, but rather of an attempt to achieve a kind of radical brevity, an attempt to put as many elements into as close a physical contiguity as possible. And if at certain points in the text I start to sound like one of Faulkner's compulsive-obsessive narrators, it is at least in part to evoke Faulkner's own sense that narration *is* compulsion, narration *is* obsession. In fact, I would have liked to have written this book in one long unpunctuated sentence, or perhaps one long unbroken paragraph. As it is, I have had to be satisfied with a process of continually holding the elements in suspension to try to create a multidimensional imaginative space in which every element could be folded into every other element, thus allowing the discourse to move with great ease from element to element, from element to novel, from novel to novel, from fiction to psychology, from psychology to philosophy to history and back again, continually oscillating, continually sweeping back and forth in an unbroken arc in order to paint, as on a radar screen by a pulse and an afterimage, a holistic structure. Since my approach is intertextual and the structure interstitial, I sought an analogously in-between form for my own text—a "neither/nor" form like the novella in fiction: neither novel nor short story, but permitting the scope of a novel with the unified impact of a short story. So my text, neither book nor essay, seeks to combine the scope of the former with the striking force of the latter. And if at points the attempt to achieve a radical brevity (a strict economy of force) leads to a certain density in the text, yet that very brevity should, in compensation, encourage a rereading of the text.

At times in my text it may seem to the reader that, after a series of arguments preparatory to some broad inference, there is a sudden swing away from drawing the inference. My reason for that procedure was my sense that there were multiple (and often contrary) inferences to be drawn, that I could not draw all of them even if I wanted to, and that only to draw some would simply be reductive, would arrest thought rather than provoke it, and so I swung away in a new, though related, direction, leaving the reader to draw as few or as many inferences as the text seemed to warrant and his attention would suggest. For example, at one point I discuss the oscillating active/passive relationship between the self and the double and at another point characterize this as a master/slave relationship—do I then need to discuss the connection between doubling, Nietzsche's concept of the will to power, and Freud's interpretation of sadomasochism, or will the reader make that connection on his own? Or when I refer to Freud's denial of Nietzsche's influence, his denial that Nietzsche had preceded him, do I need to make the connection between that denial and the triangular relationship between Nietzsche, Freud, and Lou Andreas-Salomé, or point out its Oedipal significance? Part of what I mean by calling this study "a speculative reading" is just that process of refusing to voice what the text has clearly been leading up to, so as to cause further thought rather than preempt it in a conclusion. I have tried in this manner to build into my text the same kind of fruitful in-between space that exists among Faulkner's novels and between his writings and those of Nietzsche and Freud. It is precisely because my method is inferential, because a holistic structure is only available to inference, that my attempt at embodiment must provoke inference. Should I at this point draw the inferential connection between inference and deferred action? Or will the reader do that? To my way of thinking, a good book should be like *the* Good Book; it should be parabolic—though it is a text addressed to the many, it should always be in search of the few. The other part of what I mean by calling this study "a speculative reading" I leave to the etymological reader to determine.

As one final preparation for the text that follows, let me outline within American literature a partial genealogy of Faulkner's ancestors in the use of (or use by) the structure that I have been discussing. This genealogy is, of course, retrospective; it exists as a genealogy only in light of Faulkner's work and thus can only be fully understood on rereading this introduction at the end of the text. As an epigraph for this genealogy I choose a sentence from Emerson's *Nature:* "One after another his victorious thought comes up with and reduces all things, until the world becomes at last only a realized will,—the double of the man"—an epigraph that during the course of this genealogy will be turned upside down. To start, I would point to Poe's double stories as the polar opposite of that epigraph—not just the obvious double stories like "William Wilson" but the less obvious ones like "The Murders in the Rue Morgue," where the detective Dupin, whom the narrator describes as "a double Dupin—the creative and the resolvent," discovers the murderer, an animal with a human shape, by realizing that if man has a double nature, if he is half animal, then the murderer, whom the witnesses describe as speaking a foreign, unintelligible tongue, might in fact be an animal mistaken for a man.

The most important of Poe's double stories for the purposes of this genealogy is that brief masterpiece that caps the series of incestuous male/female doublings that runs through "Berenice," "Morella," and "Ligeia"—I refer, of course, to "The Fall of the House of Usher" (1839). In this story the doubling is part of a substitutive Oedipal triangle: Roderick Usher, his twin sister Madeline, and the narrator, who describes himself as being almost like a brother to Roderick. At the crucial point in the tale when Roderick is about to be overwhelmed by his own fear, the narrator reads him the story of a hero who slays a dragon (the fear of death, the animal, the monstrous, the unconscious) and wins a brazen shield (like the one that Athena gave Perseus in order to slay the Medusa)—the shield of self-reflection that is both end and means, both prize and weapon, and that symbolizes the self-reflective distance of the narrative act of Poe's tale. But that enabling, self-reflective distance Roderick cannot achieve. The apparition of his sister returned from the crypt frightens him to death, the narrator flees the mansion, and the House of Usher (both building and family) collapses into the narcissistic mirroring pool. In *Absalom* that collapse of the house and the family, the destruction of the mansion containing the white half brother and the black half sister, is accomplished when Clytie sets the house on fire.

From Poe's double stories I would draw a line of genealogical descent to Mark Twain's *Pudd'nhead Wilson* (1894). Twain said of the novel's composition that it "was not one story, but two stories tangled together; and they obstructed and interrupted each other at every turn and created no end of confusion and annoyance."[5] The original story concerned the foreign twins Angelo and Luigi Capello: "One was a little fairer than the other, but otherwise they were exact duplicates" (p. 43). Angelo, the blond twin, is soft-spoken, mild-mannered, and a teetotaler, while Luigi, the brunet twin, is fiery and quick to take offense, and has killed a man to protect his brother's life. "Tangled together" with the story of the light and dark twins is the story of Thomas à Becket Driscoll and Valet de Chambre, the former white and free, the latter black and a slave, who as infants are switched in their cradles by the slave Roxy, so that her son Valet de Chambre will be raised as the white master and the real Tom Driscoll raised as a slave. As the dark twin, Luigi, saved his brother's life, so the real Tom in his role as the black servant saves the false Tom from drowning when they are boys.

The real Valet de Chambre is the product of miscegenation between Roxy and Colonel Cecil Burleigh Essex. At one point when Roxy's son has refused, out of cowardice, to fight a duel with the dark twin, Luigi, Roxy tells him, "Thirty-one parts o' you is white, en on'y one part nigger, en dat po' little one part is yo' *soul*. 'Tain't wuth savin'; 'tain't wuth totin' out on a shovel en throwin' in de gutter. You has disgraced yo' birth. What would yo' pa think o' you? It's enough to make him turn in his grave" (p. 123). Twain continues, "The last three sentences stung Tom into a fury, and he said to himself that if his father were only alive and in reach of assassination his mother would soon find that he had a very clear notion of the size of his indebtedness to that man, and was willing to pay it up in full, and would do it too, even at risk of his life..." (pp. 123–24). Later, the false Tom has a chance to act out his desire for revenge against his white father when, during the course of a robbery, he is surprised by his father-surrogate Judge York Driscoll (the uncle of the real Tom), and murders the Judge. Significantly, during the robbery the false Tom is disguised as a black woman. Because of previous trouble between Judge Driscoll and the foreign twins, Angelo and Luigi are accused of his murder. At this point Pudd'nhead Wilson, the twins' lawyer, turns detective, and by means of a fingerprint on the murder weapon not only brings the real murderer to light and frees the twins but also discovers the master/slave reversal of the white and black infants and restores the real Tom Driscoll to his inheritance. (Twain's description of the plight of the real Tom, who has been raised as a black and is then suddenly transformed into a white, reminds us of one of those Faulknerean characters like Joe Christmas or Charles Etienne de Saint Velery

Bon, who spend their lives caught between two worlds.) Wilson is able to solve the mystery and restore order because, like an analyst, he is able to bring to light, to raise to the level of consciousness and then interpret, a latent trace, a hidden writing. He calls the reproductions of the fingerprints that he produces in court "pantagraphs," and he says, "These marks are his signature, his physiological autograph, so to speak, and this autograph cannot be counterfeited, nor can he disguise it or hide it away, nor can it become illegible by the wear and mutations of time" (p. 192). Wilson's ability as a reader of hidden writing had been established earlier in the book when he examined Luigi's palm and mapped out his "character and disposition, his tastes, aversions, proclivities, ambitions, and eccentricities" (p. 90), as well as his past history, even to the point of revealing that Luigi had killed someone. The false Tom, who witnesses this demonstration, says, "Why, a man's own hand is his deadliest enemy! Just think of that—a man's own hand keeps a record of the deepest and fatalest secrets of his life . . ." (p. 91).

For an author, a man who is always using his hand to write, it can only seem of the deepest significance that a man's palm bears the history of his life in a hidden writing that is signed with the latent autograph of his fingerprint. One thinks of Twain's short humorous piece "An Encounter with an Interviewer" in which the writer is questioned by a newspaperman. Noticing a picture on the wall, the interviewer asks if it is the writer's brother, and when Twain replies that it is his brother Bill, "poor old Bill," the interviewer asks,

Q. Why? Is he dead, then?

A. Ah! well, I suppose so. We never could tell. There was a great mystery about it.

Q. That is sad, very sad. He disappeared, then?

A. Well, yes, in a sort of general way. We buried him.

Q. *Buried* him! *Buried* him, without knowing whether he was dead or not?

A. Oh, no! Not that. He was dead enough.

Q. Well, I confess that I can't understand this. If you buried him, and you knew he was dead—

A. No! no! We only thought he was.

Q. Oh, I see! He came to life again?

A. I bet he didn't.

Q. Well, I never heard anything like this. *Somebody* was dead. *Somebody* was buried. Now, where was the mystery?

A. Ah! that's just it! That's it exactly. You see, we were twins—defunct and I—and we got mixed in the bathtub when we were only two weeks old, and one of us was drowned. But

13

we didn't know which. Some think it was Bill. Some think it was me.

Q. Well, that *is* remarkable. What do *you* think?

A. Goodness knows! I would give whole worlds to know. This solemn, this awful mystery has cast a gloom over my whole life. But I will tell you a secret now, which I have never revealed to any creature before. One of us had a peculiar mark—a large mole on the back of his left hand; that was *me*. *That child was the one that was drowned!*[6]

It is pure Poe filtered through Twain. One can only wonder whether the distinguishing mark on the hand was really a mole or a spot of ink.

From *Pudd'nhead Wilson* the genealogical line of descent runs to Henry James's "The Jolly Corner" (1908). The story has its autobiographical basis in James's 1904 trip to America and his reactions to the changes in New York City. In the story, Spencer Brydon returns to New York after a thirty-three-year absence in Europe and is appalled by "the differences, the newnesses, the queernesses, above all the bignesses" of his native place. There were the familiar "ugly things of his far-away youth"—"these uncanny phenomena placed him rather, as it happened, under the charm; whereas the 'swagger' things, the modern, the monstrous...were exactly his sources of dismay."[7] Brydon's reason for returning is "to look at his 'property' " (p. 194), two houses, one the family home, "the jolly corner," the other "not quite so 'good' " (p. 195), in the process of being modernized for rental. As Brydon involves himself in the business of his "property," he becomes more and more obsessed with the question of what he would have become if he had not gone to Europe but had remained in New York and gone into business: "It was mere vain egoism, and it was moreover...a morbid obsession. He found all things come back to the question of what he personally might have been, how he might have led his life and 'turned out,' if he had not so, at the outset, given it up" (p. 203). Discussing this obsession with his friend Alice Staverton, for whom he feels a strange attraction because "of *their* common, their quite far-away and antediluvian social period and order," he says that he originally left for Europe "almost in the teeth" of his "father's curse" (p. 204), and he adds, "It comes over me that I had then a strange *alter ego* deep down somewhere within me, as the full-blown flower is in the small tight bud, and that I just took the course, I just transferred him to the climate, that blighted him for once and for ever" (p. 204). Alice tells him that she believes in that flower: "I feel it would have been quite splendid, quite huge and monstrous" (p.

205). And he replies, "Monstrous above all! . . . and I imagine, by the same stroke, quite hideous and offensive" (p. 205). Earlier, in explaining Alice Staverton's strange attraction for Brydon, James had said that "with her precious reference, above all, to memories and histories into which he could enter, she was as exquisite for him as some pale pressed flower . . ." (p. 197). In both cases James probably has the same flower in mind—the common flower of double stories, the narcissus—the same flower that Benjy Compson holds in his hand at the end of *The Sound and the Fury*. Brydon tells Alice that he has led "a selfish frivolous scandalous life" (p. 205), and she says about his obsession with his alter ego, ". . . you don't care for anything but yourself" (p. 206). Brydon replies, "*He* isn't myself. He's the just so totally other person. But I do want to see him. . . . And I can. And I shall" (p. 206).

In his obsession with this other self, Brydon has come to believe that his alter ego lurks in the family home, that he roams through it at night, and so every night Brydon roams through the house as well, in pursuit of his double. Brydon's search through the dark rooms and hallways of the family home becomes a search through the "dim passages" (p. 198) and hidden compartments of his own psyche. At one point, he describes the house as being like "an Egyptian tomb," for "his parents and his favorite sister, to say nothing of other kin, in numbers, had run their course and met their end there" (p. 203). But what begins as a search soon turns into a hunt, with the alter ego like a "beast of the forest" fleeing Brydon (p. 210). Presently, however, the expected reversal occurs, and Brydon, from being the pursuer, becomes the pursued. Returning to the house after an absence of three nights, he has the impression "of being definitely followed, tracked at a distance carefully taken and to the express end that he should the less confidently, less arrogantly, appear to himself merely to pursue. It worried, it finally broke him up, for it proved, of all conceivable impressions, the one least suited to his book. He was kept in sight while remaining himself—as regards the essence of his position—sightless, and his only recourse then was in abrupt turns, rapid recoveries of ground" (p. 212). The final confrontation is not long in coming. Entering the house one evening, he suddenly senses that his alter ego is waiting for him on one of the upper floors: "I've hunted him till he has 'turned': that, up there, is what has happened—he's the fanged or antlered animal brought at last to bay" (p. 213). Brydon experiences "a prodigious thrill," a "duplication of consciousness" that gives him "a sensation more complex than had ever before found itself consistent with sanity" (pp. 213–14). Since his alter ego has decided to make a stand, Brydon must try "to measure by how much more he himself might now be in peril of fear; so rejoicing that he could, in another form, actively inspire that fear, and simultaneously quaking for the form in which he might passively know it" (p. 214).

As Brydon is wandering through one of the upper floors, he suddenly experiences the kind of "start that often attends some pang of recollection, the violent shock of having ceased happily to forget" (p. 216), for he notices that a door that he had left open on a previous passage has subsequently been closed, and he realizes that it is a challenge from his alter ego, posing "the question of courage" (p. 218). The "blank face of the door" seems to say "Show us how much you have!" (p. 218). He stands wondering whether or not to open the door and then realizes that "to think . . . , as he stood there, was, with the lapsing moments, not to have acted! Not to have acted—that was the misery and the pang—was even still not to act . . ." (p. 218). Rendered passive by fear, Brydon flees the closed door, rushes to another part of the house, and throws open a window, but then, with a shock, senses that because of his surrender his alter ego may now take the offensive, and that "*should* he see the door open, it would all too abjectly be the end of him" (p. 222). It "would mean that the agent of his shame . . . was once more at large and in general possession; and what glared him thus in the face was the act that this would determine for him. It would send him straight about to the window he had left open, and by that window, be long ladder and dangling rope as absent as they would, he saw himself uncontrollably insanely fatally take his way to the street" (p. 222). So Brydon flees again, descending the stairs and heading for the front door. Evoking the descent of the self into the narcissistic pool, James describes the vestibule at the foot of the stairs as "the bottom of the sea" (p. 223) and adds that it is paved with "the marble squares" of Brydon's childhood. Waiting for Brydon in the shadows of the vestibule is his alter ego. As his other self stands there with his hands covering his face, Brydon notices that one of the hands is mutilated; two fingers are missing. Suddenly, Brydon's double begins to advance, and the hands fall away: "Horror, with the sight, had leaped into Brydon's throat . . . for the bared identity was too hideous as *his* . . . the face was the face of a stranger. It came upon him nearer now, quite as one of those expanding fantastic images projected by the magic lantern of childhood . . ." (pp. 225–26). As his double advances, Brydon falls back and then faints.

The spot on which Brydon confronts his double has been the object of special comment at various points in the story—the vestibule with its floor of "large black-and-white squares" that Brydon "remembered as the admiration of his childhood and that had then made in him, as he now saw, for the growth of an early conception of style" (p. 209). It is on "these marble squares of his childhood," these "old black-and-white slabs" (p. 227), that Brydon is found lying unconscious the next morning. Considering the biographical resonances of the story—James's own obsession with what he would have been if he had stayed in America—one can be fairly certain that those "black-and-white squares" that made "for the growth of an early conception of style" have less to do with Brydon than with James himself. For we recognize what those squares are; they are the black-and-white squares on which a writer must always encounter his other self in the growth of a personal style—the black squares of print on the white squares of the page. One might remark as well that the alter ego's mutilated hand is another detail with biographical resonances, evoking James's sense of the writer as non-participant, as passive observer—the sense of the writer, as one of Faulkner's characters says, as eunuch.

Brydon is discovered in the morning by Alice Staverton. She had come looking for him because during the night Brydon's other self had appeared to her in a dream, the same even to the distinguishing detail of the mutilated right hand, and she knew that this was a sign that he had appeared to Brydon as well. She had seen Brydon's double in a dream once before:

> "And when this morning I again saw I knew it would be because you had—and also then, from the first moment, because you somehow wanted me. *He* seemed to tell me of that. So why," she strangely smiled, "shouldn't I like him?"
>
> It brought Spencer Brydon to his feet. "You 'like' that horror—?"
>
> "I could have liked him. And to me," she said, "he was no horror. I had accepted him."
>
> " 'Accepted'—?" Brydon oddly sounded.
>
> "Before, for the interest of his difference—yes. And as *I* didn't disown him, as *I* knew him—which you at last, confronted with him in his difference, so cruelly didn't, my dear—well, he must have been, you see, less dreadful to me...." (pp. 231–32)

Brydon and his double, the "black stranger," are simply two-thirds of a triangle, whose other member, Alice Staverton, is attracted to both aspects of Brydon, and who, by an act of acceptance and transference, presumably frees Brydon from the narcissistic obsession with his alter ego.

From James the line of descent runs to Robinson Jeffers's narrative poem "Tamar" (1924), the story of the destruction of the Cauldwell family. One day while they are swimming in a pool,

Tamar Cauldwell and her brother Lee commit incest. The narcissistic implications are clear. The pool is described as a "dark mirror."[8] When Lee dives into the water, Jeffers says that "he drowned his body / In the watery floor under the cave of foliage, / and heard her sobbing" (p. 116). When Lee surfaces, Tamar calls to him:

"Lee.
We have stopped being children; I would have drowned myself;
If you hadn't taught me swimming—long ago—long ago, Lee—
When we were children." "Tamar, what is it, what is it?"
"Only that I want . . . death. You lie if you think
Another thing." (p. 116)

They then make love "like drowning folk brought back / By bitter force to life" (p. 117), and afterward Lee asks his sister, "What shall I do? Go away? Kill myself, Tamar?" (p. 117). Tamar replies, "O brother, brother, / Mine and twice mine" (p. 117). Tamar's words suggest, of course, the doubling of relationships in brother-sister incest, but there is another doubling of which Tamar is not aware. From her Aunt Jinny Cauldwell, an idiot, and her Aunt Stella Moreland, a medium, Tamar learns that her father, David Cauldwell, had committed incest with his sister Helen years before, and Tamar's incest with her brother now seems merely a fated repetition of that earlier incident. Tamar thinks, "It makes me nothing, / My darling sin a shadow and me a doll on wires" (p. 121). The spirit of Helen speaks through Stella, and Tamar engages in a battle of wills with Helen that reveals that Tamar's incestuous desire for her brother was really a desire for her father. At one point, Tamar, naked, tempts her father and says,

"Is the echo louder than the voice,
I have surpassed her,
Yours was the echo, time stands still, old man, you'll learn
when you have lived at the muddy root
Under the rock of things; all times are now, to-day plays on
last year and the inch of the future
Made in the first morning of the world. You named me for
the monument in a desolate graveyard,
Fool, and I say you were deceived, it was out of me that
fire lit you and your Helen, your body
Joined with your sister's
Only because I was to be named Tamar and to love my
brother and my father.
I am the fountain." (pp. 153–54)

To taunt her father, Tamar

> caught the mirror from its fastening
> And held it to him, reverse. "Here is her picture, Helen's
>   picture, look at her, why is she always
> Crying and crying?" When he turned the frame and looked,
>   then Tamar: "See that is her lover's . . . ."

> The old man turned the
> glass and gazed at the blank side, and turned it
> Again face towards him, he seemed drinking all the vision
>   in it . . .

> Then the old man sobbing, "It is not easy
> To be old, mocked, and a fool." And Tamar, "What, not
>   yet, you have not gone mad yet? Look, old fellow.
> These rags drop off, the bandages hid something but I'm
>   done with them. See . . . I am the fire
> Burning the house." "What do you want, what do you
>   want?" he said, and stumbled toward her, weeping.
> "Only to strangle a ghost and to destroy the house . . ." (p. 155)

When Tamar becomes pregnant by her brother Lee, she seduces her boyfriend, Will Andrews, to protect her brother, but when Lee decides to leave for the war and become an aviator, Tamar, out of jealousy, lies to both Lee and Will Andrews to set them against each other. Sensing the impending destruction of his family, David Cauldwell says,

> ". . . we know we are damned, why
> should He speak? The book
> Is written already . . . ."

> "You needn't have any fear,
> old father,
> Of anything to happen after to-morrow," Tamar answered,
>   "we have turned every page
> But the last page, and now our paper's so worn out and tissuey
>   I can read it already
> Right through the leaf, print backwards."   (p. 164)

In the final encounter, David, Lee, and Will Andrews are gathered in Tamar's bedroom; egged on by Tamar, Andrews knocks Lee down, and Lee stabs him. Exulting in her triumph, Tamar says, "I have my three lovers / Here in one room, none of them will go out, / How can

19

I help being happy?" (p. 179). While the fight is going on, the idiot, Aunt Jinny, sets the building on fire, and the House of Cauldwell is totally consumed. At one point, Tamar had thought that "life is always an old story, repeating itself always like the leaves of a tree / Or the lips of an idiot" (p. 143).

From "Tamar" the line of descent runs directly to Faulkner. The preceding genealogy could, of course, have included scores of works from American literature and other literatures as well, but with the outlines drawn, the reader can supply many of those other instances for himself. Certainly, in the use of (and use by) the structure with which this study is concerned, Faulkner's work represents the high point in twentieth-century American literature. The figure of Quentin Compson—the narrator locked in an incestuous, suicidal struggle with his dark twin, the story—is the shadow that falls in one form or another across the works of most postwar American novelists; it is a presence, a pervasive influence that the novelist who aspires to major status must come to terms with. This suicidal, incestuous struggle between the writer and the other self of his book has had a profound influence as well on postwar American poetry; there, however, the pervasive presence has not been Faulkner but Hart Crane. One might almost define the difference between American novelists and poets since the Second World War in terms of this struggle by saying that though novelists drink heavily and drive fast in the fog, it is the poets who actually step in front of the car.

Let me conclude this introduction by acknowledging two final debts (one personal, one regional) that I owe in the composition of this book. My understanding of Faulkner's work is due in large measure to the influence on my thinking of the writings of John Bricuth, even to the extent of my considering *Doubling and Incest / Repetition and Revenge* as the second point in a larger work of triangulation, whose first point is Bricuth's book *The Heisenberg Variations,* and whose third point is my book *American Hieroglyphics,* now being completed. The regional debt is, obviously, to the South, since no one born in the South in this century and interested in literature can avoid, at some time or other, confronting the very personal significance of Faulkner's work to an understanding of his own way of life. In my case, I have something like a dual perspective. I was born in Texas—the land to which Faulkner's villains and ne'er-do-wells traditionally flee after chalking GTT on their doors. My mother's family has been there since the days of the Republic. My father was from New York City. My mother's ancestors fought in the Confederate army, my father's father fought in the Union navy. My maternal great-grandfather burned the ships he owned rather than let them be used by the Union navy, and then after the war he claimed that they had been burned by the Yankees and he tried to recover damages from the Federal government. I have an aunt in Texas who says that she was thirty years old before she learned that "damn Yankee" wasn't one word. I have an uncle in New York who once asked that same aunt if the picture of Sam Houston hanging on our dining-room wall was a picture of General Grant. To which she replied, "Yes," and then motioning to the picture of Robert E. Lee hanging beside it, said, "And I suppose you think that's General Sherman." I never felt myself so surely a Southerner as when I first lived in the North, and perhaps it was my dual perspective that allowed me to associate that act of self-definition through a constitutive opposition to my new surroundings with the act of self-definition that the Southern writer performs through a deep-seated ambivalence to his homeland. Certainly, that ambivalence is at the core of Faulkner's work. To anyone who doesn't understand this, I can only say what Quentin said to Shreve, "You would have to be born there." Yet clearly, part of the greatness of Faulkner's writing is that with his evocation of the South, to understand that creative ambivalence to the homeland, one doesn't have to be born there. In transforming the local into the universal, Faulkner presented us with a place where we have all lived, and where some of us come from.

Doubling and Incest /
Repetition and Revenge

But he wouldn't want his sister to marry one.

The epigraph to this essay is a reference to the racial slur
that goes, "I don't have anything against Negroes, but I
wouldn't want my sister to marry one." Its implied argument is that integration leads to miscegenation, and that
miscegenation is a threat to the purity of white women
and an affront to the manhood of their protectors—their
fathers and brothers. In Faulkner's *Absalom, Absalom!*
Henry Sutpen kills his half brother Charles Bon, who is
part black, to prevent Bon from marrying their sister
Judith. At one point in the narrative Bon, in a mixture of
despair and grief at his father's refusal to acknowledge him
as his son, replies to Henry's declaration *"You are my
brother"* with the taunt *"No I'm not. I'm the nigger that's
going to sleep with your sister. Unless you stop me, Henry."*[1] In the story of the Sutpens the threat of miscegenation between Bon and Judith is also a threat of brother-
sister incest, and it is another brother, Henry, who acts to
stop these threats. This archetype of the brother who must
kill to protect or avenge the honor of his sister pervades
Absalom, Absalom! It occurs, first of all, in the very title
of the novel. In the Old Testament (2 Sam. 13), Absalom,
one of David's sons, kills his brother Amnon for raping
their sister Tamar. The archetype presents itself again in
Quentin Compson, the principal narrator of *Absalom.*
From *The Sound and the Fury* we know that Quentin is in
love with his own sister Candace and that he is tormented
by his inability to play the role of the avenging brother
and kill her seducer. Of the many levels of meaning in
Absalom, the deepest level is to be found in the symbolic
identification of incest and miscegenation and in the relationship of this symbolic identification both to Quentin
Compson's personal history in *The Sound and the Fury*

and to the story that Quentin narrates in *Absalom, Absalom!*

There are, of course, four narrators in the novel—Quentin, his father, his roommate Shreve, and Miss Rosa Coldfield—but of these four certainly Quentin is the central narrator, not just because he ends up knowing more of the story than do the other three, but because the other three only function as narrators in relation to Quentin. When Mr. Compson or Shreve or Miss Rosa Coldfield tell what they know or conjecture of the Sutpens' story, they are talking, either actually or imaginatively, to Quentin. One reason that the voices of the different narrators sound so much alike is that we hear those voices filtered through the mind of a single listener: Quentin's consciousness is the fixed point of view from which the reader *overhears* the various narrators, Quentin included. Since Quentin is the principal narrative consciousness in *Absalom,* and since the story of the Sutpens contains numerous gaps that must be filled by conjecture on the part of the narrators, it is not surprising that the narrative bears a striking resemblance to Quentin's own personal history and that of his family. Quentin uses his own experience of family life in a small Southern town to try to understand the motives for events in the story of Thomas Sutpen and his children, particularly that central enigmatic event to which the narration continually returns—the murder of Charles Bon by his best friend, Henry Sutpen. This is not to imply that the factual similarities between the stories of the Sutpen and Compson families are a product of Quentin's imagination, but to point out that, given these similarities of fact, Quentin as creative narrator could easily presume similarity of motivation. It is a mutual process in which what Quentin knows of the motivations in his own family life illuminates the story of the Sutpens and, in turn, the events in the Sutpens' story help Quentin to understand his own experiences.

That the story Quentin narrates resembles his own story has been noted by critics, but they have considered this parallel to be of secondary importance. Richard Poirier says that Quentin may see in the murder of Charles Bon "a distorted image of his own failure in *The Sound and the Fury* to defend the honor of his sister, Caddy, and of the incest which he claims to have committed. . . . But it is well to remember that Quentin's interest in Sutpen's story transcends any reference he finds in it for such personal problems, which, after all, we are acquainted with only from observing his activity outside the context of *Absalom, Absalom!* Had Quentin assumed the luxury of treating the Sutpen story merely as an objectification of some personal obsession, the total effect of the novel would have partaken of the overindulgent and romantic self-dramatization of Rosa's soliloquy."[2] Poirier's assumption that Quentin's personal history, because it is contained in another novel, is therefore inapplicable to *Absalom* seems to be a particularly inappropriate principle to apply to the works of a writer like Faulkner, whose novels are parts of a single continuing story. Faulkner did not need to make Quentin Compson a narrator of *Absalom,* nor did he need to involve the Compson family in the story of the Sutpens. The fact that he did both indicates that what we know of Quentin Compson and his family from *The Sound and the Fury* is somehow material to the meaning of Sutpen's story. When Faulkner, in one of the conferences he gave at the University of Virginia, was asked whether the central character in *Absalom* was Sutpen or Quentin, he replied that Sutpen was the central figure but that the novel was "incidentally the story of Quentin Compson's hatred of the bad qualities in the country he loves."[3] And on

27

another occasion, in commenting on the relationship of Quentin's personal history to the story of the Sutpens, Faulkner remarked that "every time any character gets into a book no matter how minor, he's actually telling his biography—that's all anyone ever does, he tells his own biography, talking about himself, in a thousand different terms, but himself. Quentin was still trying to get God to tell him why, in *Absalom, Absalom!* as he was in *The Sound and the Fury*" (p. 275). Poirier's contention that Quentin's narrative act is an attempt to avoid merely objectifying a personal obsession, an attempt to avoid becoming like Rosa Coldfield in her narration, ignores the fact that for Quentin the objectification of subjective contents is an effort to give a personal obsession a more than personal significance.

To what extent, then, does the story that Quentin tells in *Absalom* resemble his own life story in *The Sound and the Fury?* We noted first of all that Quentin's failure to kill Candace's seducer and thus fulfill the role of protective brother has its reverse image in Henry's murder of Bon to safeguard the honor of their sister. Also, Quentin's incestuous love for Candace is mirrored by Bon's love for Judith. That Quentin identifies with both Henry, the brother as protector, and Bon, the brother as seducer, is not extraordinary, for in Quentin's narrative they are not so much two separate figures as two aspects of the same figure. Quentin projects onto the characters of Bon and Henry opposing elements in his own personality—Bon represents Quentin's unconsciously motivated desire for his sister Candace, while Henry represents the conscious repression or punishment of that desire. This separation of the unacceptable elements from the acceptable elements in the self, this splitting of Quentin's personality into a bad half and a good half, with the subsequent tormenting of the good half by the bad and the punishment of the bad half by the good, involves a kind of narrative bipolarity typical of both compulsion neurosis and schizophrenia. The split is the result of the self's inability to handle ambivalence, in this case, Quentin's failure to reconcile his simultaneous attraction to and repulsion by the incestuous desire for his sister. The solution is primitive and effective: one simply splits the good-bad self into two separate people. Indeed, at the very beginning of the novel when he first visits Miss Rosa, Quentin is presented as a divided self: ". . . he would listen to two separate Quentins now—the Quentin Compson preparing for Harvard in the South, the deep South dead since 1865 and peopled with garrulous outraged baffled ghosts, listening, having to listen, to one of the ghosts which had refused to lie still even longer than most had, telling him about old ghost-times; and the Quentin Compson who was still too young to deserve yet to be a ghost, but nevertheless having to be one for all that, since he was born and bred in the deep South the same as she was—two separate Quentins now talking to one another in the long silence of notpeople, in notlanguage . . ." (p. 9). If at points during the narrative Quentin divides his personality between the characters of Bon and Henry, at other points Henry and Bon merge into one figure by exchanging roles. For example, though Henry ends up as the avenging brother, yet, as Mr. Compson says, "it must have been Henry who seduced Judith, not Bon: seduced her along with himself . . ." (p. 99). And though Bon dies playing the role of the dark seducer, yet he offers to give up Judith and never trouble the Sutpens again if his father will only acknowledge his existence. When Sutpen ignores him, Bon's deliberate provoking of Henry amounts almost to a suicidal self-punishment.

Clearly, the relationship between Henry and Bon is a form of doubling: the hero-worshiping Henry imitates Bon's manners, speech, and dress, while Bon (as Shreve conjectures) looks at Henry and thinks "not *there but for the intervening leaven of that blood which we do not have in common is my skull, my brow, sockets, shape and angle of jaw and chin and some of my thinking behind it, and which he could see in my face in his turn if he but knew to look as I know but there, just behind a little, obscured a little by that alien blood whose admixing was necessary in order that he exist is the face of the man who shaped us both out of that blind chancy darkness which we call the future; there—there—at any moment, second, I shall penetrate by something of will and intensity and dreadful need, and strip that alien leavening from it and look not on my brother's face whom I did not know I possessed and hence never missed, but my father's, out of the shadow of whose absence my spirit's posthumeity has never escaped*" (p. 317). On another occasion Bon, debating this family resemblance with himself, divides into two voices that reflect Quentin's own splitting: "one part of him said *He has my brow my skull my jaw my hands* and the other said *Wait. Wait. You cant know yet. You cannot know yet whether what you see is what you are looking at or what you are believing*" (p. 314). That last remark is an apt description as well of Quentin's relationship to the story of Charles Bon, for it is impossible for us to tell whether many of the things that Quentin says about Bon are what he knows or what he simply believes.

In the doubling between Bon and Henry, Bon plays the role of the shadow—the dark self that is made to bear the consciously unacceptable desires repudiated by the bright half of the mind. Throughout the novel, Bon is identified with the image of the shadow. Mr. Compson speaks of Bon's "impenetrable and shadowy character. Yes, shadowy: a myth, a phantom: something which they engendered and created whole themselves; some effluvium of Sutpen blood and character, as though as a man he did not exist at all" (p. 104). Miss Rosa calls Bon "a shadow with a name" (p. 146). And she says that "he had left no more trace" in her sister's house than if "he had been but a shape, a shadow" (p. 149). At one point, Quentin and Shreve's reconstruction of Bon's character is described as "the creating of this shade whom they discussed (rather, existed in)" (p. 316). The contrast between Bon's role as the dark self and Henry's as the bright self is made particularly clear in Bon's imagined appraisal of his younger brother: *"this flesh and bone and spirit which stemmed from the same source that mine did, but which sprang in quiet peace and contentment and ran in steady even though monotonous sunlight, where that which he bequeathed me sprang in hatred and outrage and unforgiving and ran in shadow"* (p. 318). Realizing that Quentin projects his own unacceptable impulses onto Bon as the shadow self, we understand the deeper significance of the imagery that Quentin employs in imagining the final confrontation between the brothers. Bon and Henry ride up to the house, one falls behind or one draws ahead, they face each other and speak, *"Dont you pass the shadow of this post, this branch, Charles; and I am going to pass it, Henry"* (p. 133). And when Quentin unwillingly accompanies Rosa Coldfield out to the Sutpen place to discover the secret of the old dark house, he approaches the rotting gate posts and looks apprehensively about, "wondering what had cast the shadow which Bon was not to pass alive" and "wishing that Henry were there now to stop Miss Coldfield and turn them back" (p. 364).

Bon serves as the shadow self of Quentin by acting within Quentin's narrative as the shadow self of Henry. That Henry vicariously satisfies his own desire for his sister Judith by identifying himself with her lover is first suggested by Mr. Compson. He says that Henry pleaded his friend's suit better than Bon could himself, "as though it actually were the brother who had put the spell on the sister, seduced her to his own vicarious image which walked and breathed with Bon's body" (p. 107). And he comments, ". . . perhaps this is the pure and perfect incest: the brother realizing that the sister's virginity must be destroyed in order to have existed at all, taking that virginity in the person of the brother-in-law, the man whom he would be if he could become, metamorphose into, the lover, the husband; by whom he would be despoiled, choose for despoiler, if he could become, metamorphose into the sister, the mistress, the bride. Perhaps that is what went on, not in Henry's mind but in his soul" (p. 96). Clearly, the relationship between Henry and Bon is ambivalent—that characteristic love/hate between the bright and the dark selves. Mr. Compson says that Henry loved Bon (p. 96) and that Bon "not only loved Judith after his fashion but he loved Henry too and . . . in a deeper sense than merely after his fashion. Perhaps in his fatalism he loved Henry the better of the two . . ." (p. 108). Indeed, Mr. Compson suggests that Bon's marriage to Judith would have represented a vicarious consummation of the love between Bon and Henry. Yet between the two there is a veiled antagonism as well. Bon's dark Latin sensibility is galled by Henry's clodhopper Puritanism. When Bon and Henry are in New Orleans, Bon gradually reveals the existence of his octoroon mistress to prevent Henry, with his shocked provincial morality, from challenging him to a duel, for, as Bon sardonically remarks, he would have to give Henry the choice of weapons and he would prefer not to fight with axes. And later, in an imagined conversation, Henry tells Bon, "I used to think that I would hate the man that I would have to look at every day and whose every move and action and speech would say to me, I have seen and touched parts of your sister's body that you will never see and touch: and now I know that I shall hate him and that's why I want that man to be you . . ." (p. 328).

As Otto Rank has pointed out in his classic study of doubling, the brother and the shadow are two of the most common forms that the figure of the double assumes. Rank locates the origin of doubling in narcissism, specifically in that guilt which the narcissistic ego feels at "the distance between the ego-ideal and the attained reality."[4] In this case the ego's towering self-love and consequent overestimation of its own worth lead to the guilty rejection of all instincts and desires that don't fit its ideal image of itself. The rejected instincts and desires are cast out of the self, repressed internally only to return externally personified in the double, where they can be at once vicariously satisfied and punished. The double evokes the ego's love because it is a copy of the ego, but it evokes the ego's fear and hatred as well because it is a copy with a difference. It is this element of sameness with a difference that gives the figure of the double that quality of the uncanny which we will discuss later in relation to the repetitive structure of doubling. The difference that the ego senses in the double is the implicit presence of the unconscious and particularly that form of unconsciousness which the narcissistic ego finds most offensive to its self-esteem—death. In the myth, Narcissus sees his image reflected in the water; he recognizes the image as himself, yet sees that it is shadowed on a medium whose fluidity, whose lack of differentiation, whose anarchy continually threaten to dissolve the unity of that image at the very moment that the medium itself seems to supply the force to sustain that image. What Narcissus sees is that unified image of his conscious life buoyed up from moment to moment by a medium whose very constitution, in relation to the ego, seems, paradoxically, to be dissolution and death. Rank points out that in myth and literature the appearance of the double is often a harbinger of death and that just as often the ego attempts to protect itself by killing the double, only to find that this is "really a suicidal act" (p. 79). It is in the mechanism of narcissistic self-love that Rank finds the explanation for that "denouement of madness, almost regularly leading to suicide, which is so frequently linked with pursuit by the double . . ." (p. 74). In this mechanism, the ego does not so much fear death as find unbearable "the *expectation* of the unavoidable destiny of death . . ." (p. 77). Rank quotes Wilde's Dorian Gray: "I have no terror of Death. It is only the *coming* of Death that terrifies me" (p. 77). Or as Poe's Roderick Usher says, "In this unnerved—in this pitiable condition—I feel that the period will sooner or later arrive when I must abandon life and reason together, in some struggle with the grim phantasm, Fear." Roderick is driven mad by the image of his own fate which he sees in the progressive physical dissolution of his twin sister Madeline, and he is literally frightened to death when Madeline, whom he has prematurely buried in an unconscious attempt at self-defense, returns from the tomb as a figure of death-in-life. The narrator succinctly remarks that Roderick fell "a victim to the terrors he had anticipated." Rank notes that "the normally unconscious thought of the approaching destruction of the self—the most general example of the repression of an unendurable certainty—torments these unfortunates with the conscious idea of their eternal inability to return, an idea from which release is only possible in death. Thus we have the strange paradox of the suicide who voluntarily seeks death in order to free himself of the intolerable thanatophobia" (pp. 77–78). There is as well about the suicidal murder of the double a suggestion of the *liebestod,* as if the only way that the ego could be joined with the beloved yet fearful other self is by a reflexive death in which the ego plunges itself into the otherness of the unconscious evoked by the double.

Both the narcissistic origin of doubling and the scenario of madness leading to the suicidal murder of the double help to illuminate the internal narrative of Quentin Compson's last day given in *The Sound and the Fury* and in turn to illuminate the story he tells in *Absalom*. In the fictive time of the novels, Quentin and Shreve's joint narration, which occupies the last half of *Absalom,* takes place in January 1910, and Quentin's suicide occurs six months later on June 2, 1910, but the account of that suicide is given in a novel that appeared seven years before *Absalom*. Since we already know Quentin's end when we observe his attempt in *Absalom* to explain the reason for Bon's murder, we not only participate in that effort but also engage at the same time in an analogous effort of our own to explain Quentin's murder of himself. And it is only when we see in the murder of Bon by Henry what Quentin saw in it—that Quentin's own situation appears to be a repetition of the earlier story—that we begin to understand the reason for Quentin's suicide. And this whole repetitive structure is made even more problematic by the fact that the explanation which Quentin gives for Bon's murder (that Bon is black, i.e., the shadow self) may well be simply the return of the repressed—simply an unconscious projection of Quentin's own psychic history. Quentin's situation becomes endlessly repetitive insofar as he constantly creates the predecessors of that situation in his narration of past events. And to escape from that kind of repetition, one must escape from the self.

Like Narcissus, Quentin drowns himself, and the internal narrative of his last day, clearly the narrative of someone who has gone insane, is dominated by Quentin's obsessive attempts to escape from his shadow, to "trick his shadow," as he says. When Quentin leaves his dormitory on the morning of his death, the pursuit begins: "The shadow hadn't quite cleared the stoop. I stopped inside the door, watching the shadow move. It moved almost perceptibly, creeping back inside the door, driving the shadow back into the door. . . . The shadow on the stoop was gone. I stepped into the sunlight, finding my shadow again. I walked down the steps just ahead of it."[5] Later, standing by the river, he looks down: "The shadow of the bridge, the tiers of railing, my shadow leaning flat upon the water, so easily had I tricked it that it would not quit me. At least fifty feet it was, and if I only had something to blot it into the water, holding it until it was drowned, the shadow of the package like two shoes wrapped up lying on the water. Niggers say a drowned man's shadow was watching him in the water all the time" (p. 109). Like Narcissus staring at his image in the pool, Quentin stares at his shadow in the river and, significantly, makes a reference to Negroes in relation to that shadow. I say "significantly" because at crucial points during Quentin's last day this connection between the shadow and the Negro recurs, most notably on the tram ride down to the river when Quentin sits next to a black man: "I used to think that a Southerner had to be always conscious of niggers. I thought that Northerners would expect him to. When I first came East I kept thinking You've got to remember to think of them as coloured people not niggers, and if it hadn't happened that I wasn't thrown with many of them, I'd have wasted a lot of time and trouble before I learned that the best way to take all people, black or white, is to take them for what they think they are, then leave them alone. That was when I realised that a nigger is not a person so much as a form of behavior; a sort of obverse reflection of the white people he lives among" (p. 105). If, in Quentin's mind, blacks are the "obverse reflection" of whites, if they are like shadows, then in Quentin's narrative projection of his own psychodrama in *Absalom,* Charles Bon's role as the dark seducer, as the shadow self, is inevitably linked with Bon's Negro blood. Further, since Quentin's own shadow has Negro resonances in his mind, it is not surprising that on the day of his suicide Quentin, who is being pursued by his shadow, is told by one of the three boys that he meets walking in the country that he (Quentin) talks like a colored man, nor is it surprising that another of the boys immediately asks the first one if he isn't afraid that Quentin will hit him.

If Quentin's determination to drown his shadow represents the substitutive punishment, upon his own person, of the brother seducer (the dark self, the ego shadowed by the unconscious) by the brother avenger (the bright self, the ego controlled by the superego), then it is only appropriate that the events from Quentin's past that obsessively recur during the internal narrative leading up to his drowning are events that emphasize Quentin's failure as both brother avenger and brother seducer in relation to his sister Candace—failures which his drowning of himself is meant to redeem. On the one hand, Quentin is haunted by his inability to kill Candace's lover Dalton Ames and by his further inability to prevent Candace from marrying Herbert Head, whom he knows to be a cheat. But on the other hand, he is equally tormented by his own failure to commit incest with his sister. In this connection it is significant that one of the obsessive motifs in the narrative of Quentin's last day is the continual juxtaposition of Quentin's own virginity to his sister's loss of virginity: "In the South you are ashamed of being a virgin. Boys. Men. They lie about it. Because it means less to women, Father said. He said it was men invented virginity not women. Father said it's like death: only a state in which the others are left and I said, But to believe it doesn't matter and he said, That's

37

what's so sad about anything: not only virginity, and I said, Why couldn't it have been me and not her who is unvirgin and he said, That's why that's sad too; nothing is even worth the changing of it" (p. 97).

In Quentin's world young men lose their virginity as soon as possible, but their sisters keep their virginity until they are married. The reversal of this situation in the case of Quentin and Candace makes Quentin feel that his sister has assumed the masculine role and that he has assumed the feminine role. Quentin's obsessive concern with Candace's loss of virginity is a displaced concern with his own inability to lose his virginity, for, as both novels clearly imply, Quentin's virginity is psychological impotence. Approaching manhood, Quentin finds himself unable to assume the role of a man. Consider his failure as the avenging brother when he encounters Dalton Ames on the bridge— Ames whom Quentin has earlier associated with the figure of the shadow (pp. 173, 174). He tells Ames to leave town by sundown or he will kill him. Ames replies by drawing a pistol and demonstrating his marksmanship. He then offers the pistol to Quentin:

> youll need it from what you said Im giving you this one because youve seen what itll do
> to hell with your gun
> I hit him I was still trying to hit him long after he was holding my wrists but I still tried then it was like I was looking at him through a piece of coloured glass I could hear my blood and then I could see the sky again and branches against it and the sun slanting through them and he holding me on my feet
> did you hit me
> I couldn't hear
> what
> yes how do you feel
> all right let go
> he let me go I leaned against the rail   (p. 180)

Later, sick and ashamed, Quentin thinks, "I knew he hadnt hit me that he had lied about that for her sake too and that I had just passed out like a girl . . ." (p. 181). Quentin, by rejecting the use of the pistol with its phallic significance and thus avoiding the necessity of risking his life to back up his words, relinquishes the masculine role of avenging brother and finds suddenly that in relation to the seducer he has shifted to a feminine role. Struggling in Ames's grasp, Quentin faints "like a girl," and Ames, because he sees the sister in the brother, refuses to hurt Quentin and even lies to keep from humiliating him.

Quentin's failure of potency in the role of avenging brother is a repetition of an earlier failure in the role of brother seducer. On that occasion, Quentin had gone looking for Candace, suspecting that she had slipped away to meet Dalton Ames, and he found her lying on her back in the stream: ". . . I ran down the hill in that vacuum of crickets like a breath travelling across a mirror she was lying on her back in the water her head on the sand spit the water flowing about her hips there was a little more light in the water her skirt half saturated flopped along her flanks to the waters motion in heavy ripples going nowhere . . ." (p. 168). Forcing Candace to get out of the water, Quentin begins to question her about Ames, only to find that the questioning suddenly turns to the subject of his own virginity:

> Caddy you hate him dont you
> she moved my hand up against her throat her heart was hammering there . . .
> Yes I hate him I would die for him I've already died for him I die for him over and over again everytime this goes . . .
> poor Quentin
> she leaned back on her arms her hands locked about her knees
> youve never done that have you
> what done what
> that what I have what I did
> yes yes lots of times with lots of girls
> then I was crying her hand touched me again and I was

crying against her damp blouse then she lying on her back
looking past my head into the sky I could see a rim of white
under her irises I opened my knife

do you remember the day damuddy died when you sat
down in the water in your drawers

yes

I held the point of the knife at her throat

it wont take but a second just a second then I can do mine I
can do mine then

all right can you do yours by yourself

yes the blades long enough benjys in bed by now

yes

it wont take but a second Ill try not to hurt

all right

will you close your eyes

no like this youll have to push it harder

touch your hand to it . . .

but she didnt move her eyes were wide open looking past
my head at the sky

Caddy do you remember how Dilsey fussed at you because
your drawers were muddy

dont cry

Im not crying Caddy

push it are you going to

do you want me to

yes push it

touch your hand to it

dont cry poor Quentin . . .

what is it what are you doing

her muscles gathered I sat up

its my knife I dropped it

she sat up

what time is it

I dont know

she rose to her feet I fumbled along the ground

Im going let it go

I could feel her standing there I could smell her damp
clothes feeling her there

its right here somewhere

let it go you can find it tomorrow come on

wait a minute I'll find it

are you afraid to

here it is it was right here all the time

was it come on . . .

> its funny how you can sit down and drop something and
> have to hunt all around for it   (pp. 169–72)

Candace says that she has died for her lover many times,
but for the narcissistic Quentin the mention of sexual
death evokes the threat of real death, the feared dissolution of the ego through sexual union with another, the
swallowing up of the ego in the instinctual ocean of the
unconscious. And Quentin, tormented by his virginity, by
his impotence ("poor Quentin youve never done that have
you"), can only reply to Candace's sexual death by offering a real *liebestod*. He puts his knife to his sister's throat
and proposes that they be joined forever in a murder/
suicide—a double killing that represents the equivalent,
on the level of brother/sister incest, of the suicidal murder
of the brother seducer by the brother avenger. For if
the brother-seducer/brother-avenger relationship represents
doubling and the brother/sister relationship incest, then
the brother/brother relationship is also a kind of incest and
the brother/sister relationship a kind of doubling. In at
least one version of the Narcissus myth (Pausanias 9.31.6),
Narcissus is rendered inconsolable by the death of his
identical twin sister, and when he sees himself reflected in
the water he transfers to his own image the love that he
felt for his dead twin. In this light, consider once again the
image that begins the scene: Quentin says, "I ran down the
hill in that vacuum of crickets like a breath travelling
across a mirror she was lying on her back in the water. . . ." The narcissistic implication is that his sister lying
on her back in the stream is like a mirror image of himself,
and indeed, one of the recurring motifs in Quentin's internal narrative is the image of his sister in her wedding dress
running toward him out of a mirror (pp. 96, 100). Further,
Quentin says that Ames was always "looking at me
through her like through a piece of coloured glass . . ." (p.
193).

It would appear that for Quentin the double as a male figure is associated with the shadow and the double as a female figure is associated with the mirror image. If so, then his suicide represents the attempt to merge those two images. During his walk in the country on the afternoon of his death, Quentin senses the nearness of a river and suddenly the smell of water evokes a memory of his desire for his sister and his desire for death:

> The draft in the door smelled of water, a damp steady breath. Sometimes I could put myself to sleep saying that over and over until after the honeysuckle got all mixed up in it the whole thing came to symbolise night and unrest I seemed to be lying neither asleep nor awake looking down a long corridor of grey halflight where all stable things had become shadowy paradoxical all I had done shadows all I had felt suffered taking visible form antic and perverse mocking without relevance inherent themselves with the denial of the significance they should have affirmed thinking I was I was not who was not was not who.
> I could smell the curves of the river beyond the dusk and I saw the last light supine and tranquil upon tide-flats like pieces of broken mirror. . . . Benjamin the child of. How he used to sit before that mirror. Refuge unfailing in which conflict tempered silenced reconciled. (pp. 188–89)

The image of Benjamin, Quentin's idiot younger brother, staring at himself in a mirror, locked forever in mental childhood, is a forceful evocation of the infantile, regressive character of narcissism, and it is in light of that infantile, regressive character that we can understand Quentin's drowning of himself in the river as an attempt to merge the shadow and the mirror image. Quentin's narcissism is, in Freudian terms, a fixation in secondary narcissism, a repetition during a later period in life (usually adolescence) of that primary narcissism that occurs between the sixth and the eighteenth months, wherein the child first learns to identify with its image and thus begins the work that will lead to the constitution of the ego as the image of the self and the object of love. The fixation in secondary narcissism in which the ego at a later period is recathected as the *sole* object of love condemns the individual to an endless repetition of an infantile state. This attempt to make the subject the sole object of its own love, to merge the subject and the object in an internal love union, reveals the ultimate goal of all infantile, regressive tendencies, narcissism included: it is the attempt to return to a state in which subject and object did not yet exist, to a time before that division occurred out of which the ego sprang—in short, to return to the womb, to reenter the waters of birth. But the desire to return to the womb is the desire for incest. Thus, Quentin's narcissism is necessarily linked with his incestuous desire for his sister, for as Otto Rank points out, brother-sister incest is a substitute for child-parent incest—what the brother seeks in his sister is his mother.[6] And we see that the triangle of sister/ brother avenger/brother seducer is a substitute for the Oedipal triangle of mother/father/son. Quentin's drowning of his shadow, then, is not only the punishment, upon his own person, of the brother seducer by the brother avenger, it is as well the union of the brother seducer with the sister, the union of Quentin's shadow with his mirror image in the water, the mirror image of himself that evokes his sister lying on her back in the stream. The punishment of the brother seducer by the brother avenger is death, but the union of the brother seducer and the sister is also death, for the attempt to merge the shadow and the mirror image results in the total immersion of both in the water on which they are reflected, the immersion of the masculine ego consciousness in the waters of its birth, in the womb of the feminine unconscious from which it was originally differentiated. By drowning his shadow, Quentin is able simultaneously to satisfy his incestuous desire and to punish it, and as we noted earlier it is precisely this simultaneous satisfaction and punishment of a repressed desire that is at the core of doubling. For Quentin, the incestuous union and the punishment of that union upon his own person can be accomplished by a single act because both the union and its punishment are a *liebestod,* a dying of the ego into the other.

In the confrontation between Quentin and Candace at the stream, this linking of sexual desire and death centers for Quentin around the image of Candace's muddy drawers and the death of their grandmother, "Damuddy." The image recalls an incident in their childhood when, during their grandmother's funeral, they had been sent away from the house to play. Candace goes wading in the stream, and when Quentin and Versh tell her that she'll get a whipping for getting her dress wet, she says that she'll take it off to let it dry, and she asks the black boy Versh to unbutton the back:

> "Dont you do it, Versh." Quentin said.
> "Taint none of my dress." Versh said.
> "You unbutton it, Versh." Caddy said, "Or I'll tell Dilsey what you did yesterday." So Versh unbuttoned it.
> "You just take your dress off." Quentin said. Caddy took her dress off and threw it on the bank. Then she didn't have on anything but her bodice and drawers, and Quentin slapped her and she slipped and fell down in the water.   (pp. 37–38)

Candace splashes water on Quentin, an act that in retrospect is sexually symbolic, and Quentin's fear that now they will both get a whipping destroys his attempt to play the role of the protective brother. Shifting from an active to a passive role, Quentin sees Caddy take charge and lead the children back to the house while he lags behind, taunted by Caddy. When they reach the house, Caddy climbs the tree outside the parlor window to see the funeral, and at that point the image of her muddy drawers seen by the children below is fused with the image of Damuddy's death. It is significant that Quentin's obsessive linking of these two images (his sexual desire for his sister and death) involves the repetition, in each case, of the same word—the word "muddy" in Candace's "muddy drawers" and "Damuddy's" funeral, for the threat that sexual union poses to the bright, narcissistic ego is, in Quentin's mind, associated with the image of mud—soft, dark, corrupt, enveloping—the image of being swallowed up by the earth. In the scene where Candace interrupts an abortive sexual encounter in the barn between Quentin and a girl named Natalie ("a dirty girl like Natalie," as Candace says), Quentin retaliates by jumping into the hog wallow and then smearing his sister with mud:

> *She had her back turned I went around in front of her. You know what I was doing? She turned her back I went around in front of her the rain creeping into the mud flatting her bodice through her dress it smelled horrible. I was hugging her that's what I was doing. . . .*
> *I dont give a damn what you were doing*
> *You dont you dont I'll make you I'll make you give a damn. She hit my hands away I smeared mud on her with the other hand I couldn't feel the wet smacking of her hand I wiped mud from my legs smeared it on her wet hard turning body hearing her fingers going into my face but I couldn't feel it even when the rain began to taste sweet on my lips. . . .*
> *We lay in the wet grass panting the rain like cold shot on my back. Do you care now do you do you*
> *My Lord we sure are in a mess get up. Where the rain touched my forehead it began to smart my hand came red away streaking of pink in the rain. Does it hurt*
> *Of course it does what do you reckon*
> *I tried to scratch your eyes out my Lord we sure do stink we better try to wash it off in the branch . . .* (pp. 155–57)

Later, when Quentin identifies with his sister's lover Dalton Ames and imagines Ames and Candace making "the beast with two backs" (p. 167), the image of Quentin and Candace smeared with mud from the hog wallow metamorphoses into the image of the swine of Eubuleus—the swine that are swallowed up into the earth when Hades

45

carries Persephone down to be the queen of the dead. And a variant of this image occurs in Quentin's last internal monologue before he drowns himself when he imagines the clump of cedars where Candace used to meet her lovers: "Just by imagining the clump it seemed to me that I could hear whispers secret surges smell the beating of hot blood under wild unsecret flesh watching against red eyelids the swine untethered in pairs rushing coupled into the sea . . ." (p. 195).

Since Quentin's incestuous desire for his sister is synonymous with death, it is no surprise that in the scene by the branch, where Quentin puts his knife to his sister's throat and offers to kill her and then himself, their conversation parodies that of sexual intercourse:

> will you close your eyes
> no like this youll have to push it harder
> touch your hand to it . . .
> push it are you going to
> do you want me to
> yes push it
> touch your hand to it

It is a mark of the brilliance and centrality of this scene that its imagery evokes as well the reason for that fear which continually unmans Quentin whenever he tries to assume the masculine role. When Quentin puts his knife to his sister's throat, he is placing his knife at the throat of someone who is an image of himself, thereby evoking the threat of castration—the traditional punishment for incest. The brother seducer with the phallic knife at his sister's throat is as well the brother avenger with the castrating knife at the brother seducer's throat—the father with the castrating knife at the son's penis. The fear of castration fixes Quentin in secondary narcissism, for by making sexual union with a woman synonymous with death, the castration fear prevents the establishment of a love object outside the ego. Quentin's fear of castration is projected onto the figure of his sister, incest with whom would be punished by castration. Thus in her encounters with Quentin, Candace becomes the castrator. When Candace tells him to go ahead and use the knife, his fear unmans him; he drops the phallic knife and loses it, and when he tells Candace that he will find it in a moment, she asks, "Are you afraid to?" Recall as well that in the scene at the hog wallow Candace says that she tried to scratch Quentin's eyes out. Having failed in the masculine role of brother seducer in relation to Candace, Quentin shifts to a passive, feminine role, and Candace assumes the active, masculine role. It is a shift like the one that Quentin undergoes when he fails in the masculine role of brother avenger in relation to the seducer Dalton Ames; Quentin immediately assumes a feminine role, fainting like a girl in Ames's grasp. Indeed, brooding on that fear of risking his life that caused him to reject Ames's offer of the phallic pistol, Quentin thinks, "And when he put Dalton Ames. Dalton Ames. Dalton Ames. When he put the pistol in my hand I didn't. . . . Dalton Ames. Dalton Ames. Dalton Ames. If I could have been his mother lying with open body lifted laughing, holding his father with my hand refraining, seeing, watching him die before he lived" (p. 99).

The explanation for this shifting from a masculine to a feminine role is to be found in the son's ambivalence toward his father in the castration complex. On the one hand, there is an aggressive reaction of the son toward the castrating father, a desire for the father's death, a desire to kill him. But on the other hand, there is a tender reaction, a desire to renounce the object that has caused the father's anger, to give up the penis and thus to retain the father's love by assuming a passive, feminine role in relation to him—in short, to become the mother in relation to the father.[7] In this second situation (the tender, passive reaction) the fear of castration turns into a longing for castration, and since, as Freud points out, the fear of death is an analogue of the fear of castration (S.E., 20:130), this transformation of the castration fear into a desire for castration within the incest scenario has as its analogue, within the scenario of narcissistic doubling, that fear of death that becomes a longing for death—the paradox, as Rank says, of a thanatophobia that leads to suicide. What the fear of castration is to incest the fear of death is to doubling, and as the fear of castration and the fear of death are analogues, so too are incest and doubling. We need only recall in this connection that the characteristic doubling scenario of madness leading to suicide often includes incidents of self-mutilation, for self-mutilation is simply a partial form of self-destruction. During the walk in the country that Quentin takes on the day of his suicide, he stops on a bridge and looks down at his shadow in the water and remembers,

> Versh told me about a man mutilated himself. He went into the woods and did it with a razor, sitting in a ditch. A broken razor, flinging them backward over his shoulder the same motion complete the jerked skein of blood backward not looping. But that's not it. It's not not having them. It's never to have had them then I could say O That That's Chinese I dont know Chinese. And Father said it's because you are a virgin: dont you see? Women are never virgins. Purity is a negative state and therefore contrary to nature. It's nature is hurting you not Caddy and I said That's just words and he said So is virginity and I said you dont know. You cant know and he said Yes. On the instant when we come to realise that tragedy is second-hand.
>
> Where the shadow of the bridge fell I could see down for a long way, but not as far as the bottom.   (pp. 134–35)

In a real or imagined conversation with his father, bits of which recur during his internal narrative, Quentin confesses that he and Candace have committed incest, and he seeks a punishment, he says, that will isolate himself and his sister from the loud world. When his father asks him if he tried to force Candace to commit incest, Quentin re- es, "i was afraid to i was afraid she might" (p. 195). It is f in seeking to be punished for incest, to be castrated, ntin would have proof that his masculinity had ever n potent enough to constitute a threat to the father; ation would constitute the father's acknowledgment e son's manhood. The similarity between Quentin's tion and Charles Bon's becomes clearer, for Bon's decision to go ahead and commit incest by marrying his half sister Judith is motivated less by his love for Judith than by his desire to force his father to acknowledge his existence, and when Bon learns that the reason that Sut- pen refuses to acknowledge him is that he is black, then it becomes the desire to force Sutpen to acknowledge his manhood, even if that acknowledgment means forcing his father to kill him through his surrogate, Henry. It is as if Bon, realizing that he will never have his father's love in any normal sense, seeks to have that love in an inverse sense through a *liebestod* with that substitute for the father, the avenging brother. Henry's murder of his half brother, the dark double, is an incestuous love-death. And the paradox of Bon's solution is that in order to force his father to acknowledge his masculinity in this manner Bon must submit to being feminized. He must assume a passive role in relation to Sutpen and Henry: he announces his intention to marry Judith, knowing the danger involved, but he does not kill Sutpen or Henry; rather, he offers his own pistol to Henry in a scene that reminds us of Dalton Ames's offer of his pistol to Quentin:

> Now it is Bon who watches Henry; he can see the whites of Henry's eyes again as he sits looking at Henry with that expression which might be called smiling. His hand vanishes beneath the blanket and reappears, holding his pistol by the barrel, the butt extended toward Henry.
> —Then do it now, he says. . . .

49

—You are my brother.

—No I'm not. I'm the nigger that's going to sleep with your sister. Unless you stop me, Henry.

Suddenly Henry grasps the pistol, jerks it free of Bon's hand stands so, the pistol in his hand, panting and panting. . . .

—Do it now, Henry, he says.

Henry whirls, in the same motion he hurls the pistol from him and stoops again, gripping Bon by both shoulders, panting.

—You shall not! he says. —You shall not! Do you hear me? . . .

—You will have to stop me, Henry. (pp. 357–58)

But while Quentin rejects the pistol, never to use it, Henry rejects it only to use it later to kill Bon. Indeed, one has been prepared for Bon's ultimate feminization by references at various points in the novel to a certain feminine quality in him, as when Quentin and Shreve theorize that Henry must have learned from Bon "how to lounge about a bedroom in a gown and slippers such as women wore, in a faint though unmistakable effluvium of scent such as women used, smoking a cigar almost as a woman might smoke it, yet withal such an air of indolent and lethal assurance that only the most reckless man would have gratuitously drawn the comparison" (p. 317). The result of Henry's murder of his black half brother is the kind of regression that one would expect from the suicidal murder of the double: Henry ends his life hidden in the womb of the family home where, helpless as a child, he is nursed by his black half sister Clytie. In a way, Henry's end repeats the fate of his maternal grandfather who at the beginning of the Civil War nailed himself into the attic of his home and who, though cared for by his daughter Rosa, eventually starved himself to death.

Clearly, for Quentin the triangle of Candace, Dalton Ames, and himself appears as a repetition of the earlier triangle of Judith, Bon, and Henry, and in both triangles the danger of castration that lies at the core of narcissistic doubling is evoked by the woman's name. In the Apocrypha, Judith decapitates the Assyrian general Holofernes. In his essay "The Taboo of Virginity," Freud, commenting on Hebbel's drama *Judith und Holofernes,* says, "Judith is one of those women whose virginity is protected by a taboo. Her first husband was paralysed on the bridal night by a mysterious anxiety and never again dared to touch her. 'My beauty is like belladonna,' she says. 'Enjoyment of it brings madness and death.' " And of Judith's murder of Holofernes, Freud remarks, "Beheading is well-known to us as a symbolic substitute for castrating" (S.E., 11: 207). Candace's name recalls the incident in the Acts of the Apostles (8:26–40) when Philip meets the eunuch of Queen Candace of Ethiopia:

> ... and, behold, a man of Ethiopia, an eunuch of great authority under Candace queen of the Ethiopians, who had the charge of all her treasure, and had come to Jerusalem for to worship, was returning, and sitting in his chariot read Esaias the prophet. Then the Spirit said unto Philip, Go near, and join thyself to this chariot. And Philip ran thither to him, and heard him read the prophet Esaias, and said, Understandest thou what thou readest? And he said, How can I, except some man should guide me? And he desired Philip that he would come up and sit with him. The place of the scripture which he read was this, He was led as a sheep to the slaughter; and like a lamb dumb before his shearer, so opened he not his mouth: In his humiliation his judgment was taken away: and who shall declare his generation? for his life is taken from the earth. And the eunuch answered Philip, and said, I pray thee, of whom speaketh the prophet this? of himself, or of some other man?

When Philip clarifies the text, the eunuch asks to be baptized, and Philip and the eunuch descend together into the water. Quentin's incestuous desire for his sister and the disabling fear of castration that she embodies for him have made Quentin in effect Candace's eunuch—impotent with his sister and yet obsessed with preventing her from making love to other men. As we suggested earlier, Quentin's brother Benjy is in certain respects a double of Quentin—in his arrested, infantile state, in his obsessive attachment to Candace, in his efforts to keep Candace from becoming involved with anyone outside the family, Benjy is a copy of Quentin, and when their brother Jason has Benjy gelded for attempting to molest a little girl, Benjy's physical condition doubles Quentin's psychological impotence, acting out the fate of the brother seducer at the hands of the brother avenger. Jason is, of course, named after his and Quentin's father.

In the Biblical account of Philip's baptism of the eunuch of Queen Candace, the detail of Philip and the eunuch's descent together into the water is worth noting, for when Quentin kills himself by descending into the river to join his shadow, there is in his internal narrative a religious significance attached to the act. Quentin wonders whether his bones will rise from the water at the general resurrection, a resurrection for which baptism makes one a member of the elect. Quentin thinks, "And I will look down and see my murmuring bones and the deep water like wind, like a roof of wind, and after a long time they cannot distinguish even bones upon the lonely and inviolate sand. Until on the Day when He says Rise only the flatiron would come floating up" (p. 99). And again later, "And maybe when He says Rise the eyes will come floating up too, out of the deep quiet and the sleep, to look on glory" (p. 135). The date of Quentin's section of *The Sound and the Fury* is June 2, 1910, while the dates of the other three sections of the novel are April 6, 7, and 8, 1928, that is, Good Friday, Holy Saturday, and Easter Sunday. As Quentin's suicide is associated in his mind with the image of the general resurrection, so the dating of the other sections in the novel associates Quentin's death with Christ's death and resurrection, establishing for Quentin's suicidal murder of the brother seducer by the father-surrogate a religious context in which the archetypal son sacrifices his life to appease the anger of the archetypal father. As the dates of three of the sections have a liturgical significance, so too does the date of the fourth section: June 2, the day of Quentin's drowning, is the feast day of St. Erasmus (also known as St. Elmo), who is the patron saint of sailors, particularly of sailors caught in a storm, and thus the saint whose special care it is to prevent drownings.[8]

In *As I Lay Dying* (1930), the novel that Faulkner published immediately after *The Sound and the Fury*, the triangle of a mentally unbalanced brother, a promiscuous sister, and a seducer recurs. Darl Bundren discovers that his sister Dewey Dell has made love to her boyfriend Lafe, and Dewey Dell thinks, ". . . then I saw Darl and he knew. . . . and I said 'Are you going to tell pa are you going to kill him?' without the words I said it and he said 'Why?' without the words. And that's why I can talk to him with knowing with hating because he knows."[9] Dewey Dell is pregnant, and when Doc Peabody comes out to be at her mother's deathbed, Dewey Dell tells herself that the doctor could help her out of her trouble if he only knew: "I would let him come in between me and Lafe, like Darl came in between me and Lafe . . ." (p. 57). The implication at various points in the novel is that there exists, at least on Darl's part, an incestuous attachment between brother and sister, an attachment that represents for Darl a displacement of his love for his mother Addie. In a fantasy that is the reverse of the scene in which Quentin puts his knife to Candace's throat, Dewey Dell, riding into town with Darl, thinks, "The land runs out of Darl's eyes; they swim to pinpoints. They begin at my feet and rise along my body to my face, and then my dress is gone: I sit naked on the seat above the unhurrying mules, above the travail. *Suppose I tell him to turn. He will do what I say. Dont you know he will do what I say?* Once I was waked with a black void rushing under me. I could not see. I saw Vardaman rise and go to the window and strike the knife into the fish, the blood gushing, hissing like steam but I could not see. *He'll do as I say. He always does. I can persuade him to anything. You know I can. Suppose I say Turn here.* That was when I died that time. *Suppose I do. We'll go to New Hope. We wont have to go to town.* I rose and took the knife from the streaming fish still hissing and I killed Darl" (p. 115).

When at the end of the novel Darl is being taken to the state asylum, one of the two guards accompanying him must ride backwards in the railroad coach (so that the guards are facing each other), and Darl thinks, "One of them had to ride backward because the state's money has a face to each backside and a backside to each face, and they are riding on the state's money which is incest. A nickel has a woman on one side and a buffalo on the other; two faces and no back. I dont know what that is. Darl had a little spy-glass he got in France at the war. In it it had a woman and a pig with two backs and no face. I know what that is" (p. 244). The image of "a woman and a pig with two backs and no face" recalls Quentin's fantasy of Candace and Ames making love: "*. . . running the beast with two backs and she blurred in the winking oars running the swine of Euboeleus running coupled within how many Caddy*" (p. 167). And the image of the coin with "two faces and no back" balanced against the image of the two guards facing each other evokes the psychic splitting, the doubling, that has taken place in Darl's personality. This doubling is clear from the very start of the section in which Darl describes his departure for the asylum, for Darl talks about himself in the third person, and then the first-person Darl carries on a dialogue with this other self:

> Darl has gone to Jackson. They put him on the train, laughing down the long car laughing, the heads turning like the heads of owls when he passed. "What are you laughing at?" I said.
>
> "Yes yes yes yes yes."
>
> ... "Is it the pistols you're laughing at?" I said. "Why do you laugh?" I said. "Is it because you hate the sound of laughing?"
>
> ... Darl is our brother, our brother Darl. Our brother Darl in a cage in Jackson where, his grimed hands lying light in the quiet interstices, looking out he foams.
>
> "Yes yes yes yes yes yes yes yes." (pp. 243–44)

We should at this point make a clear distinction between the spatial aspect of doubling—the way in which one person can be a spatial repetition of another person who is his contemporary—and the temporal aspect of doubling— the way in which one person later in time recognizes another person earlier in time as a double of himself and thus sees his own condition as a fated repetition of that earlier life, or the way in which one pair of doubles later in time repeats another pair of doubles earlier in time. An indication of how interested Faulkner was in the temporal aspect of doubling at the period when he wrote *The Sound and the Fury* is to be found in the novel that he published in the same year, *Sartoris* (1929). *Sartoris* is the story of two pairs of brothers named John and Bayard Sartoris, three generations apart. The first pair goes off to fight in the Civil War; Bayard is killed and John returns. John has a son named Bayard Sartoris II, who in turn has a son named John Sartoris II, who in turn has twin sons named John Sartoris III and Bayard Sartoris III. The twins go off to fight in the First World War, and this time John is killed and Bayard returns. At home, Bayard marries a girl who, the novel implies, was in love with Bayard's dead twin brother and who unconsciously seeks, by marrying the surviving twin, to regain her lost love. Predictably enough, the girl's name is Narcissa. Bayard, however, is so haunted by the death of his twin brother that he launches into a series of self-destructive acts and finally manages to duplicate his brother's death by killing himself in a plane crash—killing himself on the very day that his son is born.

We learn from another book, *The Unvanquished* (1938), that besides the doubling of the two pairs of brothers in the Sartoris family there is as well a repetition of incest episodes. John Sartoris, the surviving brother of the first pair, returns home after the Civil War to live with, and eventually marry, his cousin Drusilla Hawk, and his son Bayard II, at the age of twenty-four, has an incestuous, though unconsummated, affair with Drusilla, who is both his stepmother and his cousin. During the period when Drusilla is living with John Sartoris prior to their marriage, Drusilla's mother writes letters begging her to stop disgracing Southern womanhood by her conduct. One of the letters is delivered to the Sartoris place by Mrs. Compson, presumably the great-grandmother of Quentin and Candace, and in this letter Drusilla's mother says that she hopes that Mrs. Compson has "been spared the sight of her own daughter if Mrs. Compson had one flouting and outraging all Southern principles of purity and womanhood that our husbands had died for,"[10] since, as the letter implies, Mrs. Compson, in delivering the message to Drusilla, was not spared the sight of Mrs. Hawk's daughter doing just that. It is a nice touch of irony when one considers Quentin's obsession in *The Sound and the Fury* with the "flouting and outraging" of "all Southern principles of purity and womanhood" by Mrs. Compson's great-granddaughter Candace.

In *The Unvanquished* when Sartoris's son, Bayard II, is

twenty years old and just beginning to be attracted to his stepmother, he and Drusilla, while walking in the garden one evening, discuss his father's ruthless conduct in rebuilding Jefferson after the war, and Bayard compares his father to Thomas Sutpen who has been equally ruthless in his dream of rebuilding a lost world. Bayard remarks of Sutpen that "he lost everything in the War like everybody else, all hope of descendants too (his son killed his daughter's fiancé on the eve of the wedding and vanished)" (p. 255). When Sartoris is himself killed by his former partner Redmond, and Bayard returns from college to avenge his father's death, Drusilla, in a scene filled with sexual overtones, gives Bayard his father's dueling pistols to accomplish the revenge, implying that her love will be the reward for his courageous action: "She faced me, she was quite near; again the scent of the verbena in her hair seemed to have increased a hundred times as she stood holding out to me, one in either hand, the two duelling pistols. 'Take them, Bayard,' she said, in the same tone in which she had said 'Kiss me' last summer, already pressing them into my hands, watching me with that passionate and voracious exaltation, speaking in a voice fainting and passionate with promise: 'Take them. I have kept them for you. I give them to you. . . . Do you feel them? the long true barrels true as justice, the triggers (you have fired them) quick as retribution, the two of them slender and invincible and fatal as the physical shape of love?' " (p. 273). But, as one would expect from other scenes in Faulkner where one person offers a pistol to another, Bayard rejects his father's dueling pistols, having decided that he will face his father's killer unarmed and either be killed or drive Redmond out of town by the sheer moral force of his presence. It seems likely, however, that on a deeper level Bayard's willingness to risk his own life to avenge his father's death is a displaced attempt to confront the vengeance due another wrong done to the father, an effort on Bayard's part to face the punishment for his own sin of desiring his father's wife and thus for the implicit sin of desiring his father's death. It is worth noting that the punishment for the active, masculine sin of desiring the stepmother and unconsciously desiring the death of the father involves the son's willingness to assume a passive, feminine role in relation to his father's killer, who in this scenario would act as a substitute for the father. Bayard, unarmed, allows Redmond to fire his pistol at him twice. If Redmond had killed Bayard, the avenging of the father would have been accomplished by the feminization of the son. But Bayard's courage unmans Redmond, and the characteristic shifting of roles occurs: Bayard assumes the active, masculine role and Redmond the passive, feminine role; Redmond drops his pistol and leaves town. By defeating Redmond, Bayard seems to have avenged his father's death, but another interpretation is even more likely: by defeating the man who killed his father, Bayard has proved himself a better man than his father; he has supplanted that overpowering, debilitating image of the father in the life of the son by psychically doing away with the threatening father-surrogate. In defeating his father's killer, Bayard is symbolically killing his father, and when Bayard confronts Redmond, the man who actually did what Bayard had unconsciously desired to do as an implicit part of his incestuous desire for his stepmother, i.e., kill his father, Bayard confronts a double of himself. It is a theme that Faulkner never tires of reiterating: by courageously facing the fear of death, the fear of castration, the fear of one's own worst instincts, one slays the fear; by taking the risk of being feminized, by accepting the feminine elements in the self, one establishes one's masculinity. And it is by allowing the fear of death, of castration, of one's own instincts, of being feminized, to dominate the ego that one is paralyzed, rendered impotent, unmanned, as in the case of Quentin. Considering *Sartoris* and *The Unvanquished* in relation to *Absalom* and *The Sound and the Fury,* one cannot help but be struck by how closely linked doubling and incest, narcissism and the castration complex are in Faulkner's imagination, and by how these twin structures bind together the lives of the three principal families in the novels—the Compsons, Sartorises, and Sutpens—so that incidents in one family story will almost inevitably be doubled by incidents in one of the other family stories.

In examining the temporal aspect of doubling, we must keep in mind as well the temporal aspect of incest—the way in which incidents of incest or of incestuous attach- ment recur at intervals within the same family or within the three related families. For Faulkner, doubling and incest are both images of the self-enclosed—the inability of the ego to break out of the circle of the self and of the individual to break out of the ring of the family—and as such, both appear in his novels as symbols of the state of the South after the Civil War, symbols of a region turned in upon itself. Thus, the temporal aspects of doubling and incest evoke the way in which the circle of the self- enclosed repeats itself through time as a cycle, the way that the inability to break out of the ring of the self and the family becomes the inability of successive generations to break out of the cyclic repetition of self-enclosure. In one of his conferences at the University of Virginia, Faulk- ner was asked if "the miscegenation and incest of Roth Edmonds in 'Delta Autumn' complete a cycle of incest and miscegenation begun by old McCaslin," and Faulkner re- plied, "Yes, it came home. If that's what you mean by complete a cycle, yes, it did" (p. 277). The cycle began in 1833 when Carothers McCaslin had a son, Terrel, by his black daughter Thomasina. Eunice, Thomasina's mother, drowned herself because of this outrage. From then on, the white and black branches of the family are fatally enmeshed, and when Roth Edmonds has a baby by a black girl who he does not know is his cousin he unwittingly completes one cycle of incest and miscegenation only to begin another cycle in the same act. Uncle Ike's sense of the situation is less that something has ended than that something has started all over again. Indeed, by a renunciation of his inheritance, a renunciation that permanently alienated his wife and thus rendered him childless, Uncle Ike had tried to free himself and his family from just such a generative affront that would continue to bind white and black together in an endless cycle of guilt and retribution.

This sense of a cyclic repetition within whose grip individual free will is helpless presents itself in Faulkner's novels as the image of the fate or doom that lies upon a family. Certainly, it would be difficult to think of two words used more often in *The Sound and the Fury* and *Absalom* than "fate" and "doom." In the genealogy that Faulkner appended to *The Sound and the Fury,* he begins with the Indian chief Ikkemotube from whom the first Compson got his land—Ikkemotube, whose name was translated into English as "Doom" (p. 3). Of Candace, Faulkner says, "Doomed and knew it, accepted the doom without either seeking or fleeing it. Loved her brother despite him, loved not only him but loved in him that bitter prophet and inflexible corruptless judge of what he considered the family's honor and its doom, as he thought he loved but really hated in her what he considered the frail doomed vessel of its pride and the foul instrument of its disgrace; not only this, she loved him not only in spite of but because of the fact that he himself was incapable of love, accepting the fact that he must value above all not her but the virginity of which she was custodian and on which she placed no value whatever" (p. 10). And of Candace's daughter Quentin: "Fatherless nine months before her birth, nameless at birth and already doomed to be unwed from the instant the dividing egg determined its sex" (p. 19). Her uncle Quentin's whole narrative in *The Sound and the Fury* is simply a prolonged struggle between his sense of fate and his exertions of will, while in *Absalom,* Faulkner makes it clear that Sutpen's hubris called down a destroying fate upon his descendants. Bon, in pursuit of some acknowledgment from his father, is presented as the archetypal fatalist, while Mr. Compson says that Henry knew that he was "doomed and destined to kill" Bon (p. 91). And when Rosa Coldfield describes Sutpen's first sight of her sister Ellen in church, she says it was "as though there were a fatality and curse on our family and God Himself were seeing to it that it was performed and discharged to the last drop and dreg. Yes, fatality and curse on the South and on our family as though because some ancestor of ours had elected to establish his descent in a land primed for fatality and already cursed with it, even if it had not rather been our family, our father's progenitors, who had incurred the curse long years before and had been coerced by Heaven into establishing itself in the land and the time already cursed" (p. 21).

This feeling that an ancestor's actions can determine the actions of his descendants for generations to come by compelling them periodically to repeat his deeds is the form that the fate or doom of a family takes in Faulkner. Often in his novels the actions of a grandparent preempt the life of a grandchild. One thinks immediately of *Light in August* (1932), where the three principal characters—Hightower, Joanna Burden, and Joe Christmas—have had their destinies determined by the lives of their grandfathers. Hightower originally came to Jefferson because his grandfather was accidentally killed there during a cavalry raid in the Civil War, and he remains in Jefferson even after his disgrace because he is somehow doomed to relive in his imagination every evening at twilight the entrance of his grandfather's cavalry troop into the town. That instant in time, that transitory moment of lost grandeur, has been arrested and preserved by being spatialized in Hightower's imagination, acquiring the status of a painting or of equestrian statuary, and that image has in turn arrested the flow of time in Hightower's life, compelling him to circle back every evening and relive, in the contemplation of that image, his grandfather's death. Joanna Burden has remained by herself in her family home in Jefferson, rather than return to live with her relatives in the North, because her grandfather and brother were shot down on the streets of Jefferson by Colonel John Sartoris, and she will not give the townspeople the satisfaction of thinking that they were finally able to run the Burdens out of town. Joe Christmas's life is, of course, set in its path when his maternal grandfather Doc Hines, who has murdered Joe's father, leaves Joe on the steps of the orphanage and then takes a job at the orphanage to watch the child and make sure that God's curse on Joe, who is the product of miscegenation, is carried out. It is Hines who seals Joe's fate at the end of the novel by inciting the townspeople to lynch his grandson, telling them that Joe is not a Mexican but a black. When Joe is on the run after setting Joanna Burden's house on fire, he approaches Mottstown, where, unknown to him, his grandfather is living; at this point the image of the circle that is a cycle makes its most explicit appearance: ". . . he is entering it again, the street which ran for thirty years. It had been a paved street, where going should be fast. It had made a circle and he is still inside of it. Though during the last seven days he has had no paved street, yet he has travelled further than in all the thirty years before. And yet he is still inside the circle. 'And yet I have been further in these seven days than in all the thirty years,' he thinks. 'But I have never got outside that circle. I have never broken out of the ring of what I have already done and cannot ever undo.' "[11] As Hightower, Joanna Burden, and Joe Christmas resemble one another in the relationship of their lives to the lives of their grandfathers, so their own lives become enmeshed: Joe kills Joanna Burden and is in turn castrated and killed in Hightower's home.

This motif of a grandchild whose destiny is determined by the life of his grandfather is present as well in *The Sound and the Fury*. In one of the conferences at the University of Virginia, Faulkner said that the decay of the Compson family began with Quentin's grandfather General Compson, who had been a failed brigadier general in the Civil War and who put the first mortgage on the Compson property (p. 3). And in the appendix to *The Sound and the Fury*, Faulkner remarked that from the time of General Compson on, a Compson was doomed to "fail at everything he touched save longevity or suicide" (p. 7). What Faulkner called that "basic failure" that began with General Compson was transmitted to Quentin by his father as a problem *in* time and a problem *of* time. This temporal dilemma makes its appearance at the very start of Quentin's narrative on the day of his death: "When the shadow of the sash appeared on the curtains it was between seven and eight oclock and then I was in time again, hearing the watch. It was Grandfather's and when Father gave it to me he said, Quentin, I give you the mausoleum of all hope and desire; it's rather excruciating-ly apt that you will use it to gain the reducto absurdum of all human experience which can fit your individual needs no better than it fitted his or his father's. I give it to you not that you may remember time, but that you might forget it now and then for a moment and not spend all your breath trying to conquer it. Because no battle is ever won he said. They are not even fought. The field only reveals to man his own folly and despair, and victory is an illusion of philosophers and fools" (p. 95). Before Quentin leaves his room that morning, he twists the hands off his grandfather's watch, the watch that in its passage from generation to generation symbolizes both the transmission of General Compson's failure and defeatism and the burden of remembering a past that paralyzes the present. We might note as an aside that in the decaying, aristocratic families like the Sartorises and Compsons, the given names of the male descendants tend to alternate between two possibilities from generation to generation—between John and Bayard in the Sartoris family and between Quentin and Jason in the Compson family. This alternation is one mark of the inbred character of these families and of the way that the locked-in repetition of traditional patterns has made them unable to cope with changing times. One sign of the mongrel vigor and adaptability of the family that supplants the Compsons and Sartorises is that no member of the Snopes family has a given name that is the same as any other member of that family.

It is tempting to speculate that this motif of a grandfather's life that is repeated in the life of his grandson is a variant of what the psychoanalyst Ernest Jones has called "the phantasy of the reversal of generations." Jones points out that there is a fantasy common among small children that when they grow up and their parents grow old, the children "will become the parents and their parents the children."[12] Jones continues, "The logical consequence of the phantasy, which the imagination at times does not fail to draw, is that the relative positions are so completely reversed that the child becomes the actual parent of his parents. . . . Another way of stating this conclusion is that the child becomes identified with his grandfather, and there are many indications of this unconscious identification in mythology, folk-lore, and custom. . . . The custom of naming children after their grandparents is extremely widespread in both civilised and uncivilised races; among many it is not merely a common habit, but an invariable rule" (p. 409). Indeed, there are primitive peoples who believe "that the grandfather has returned in the person of the child" (p. 409).

Jones suggests that the principal origin of the reversal fantasy is the belief in personal immortality: "Neither the child's mind nor the adult unconscious can apprehend the idea of personal annihilation. . . . This narcissistic conviction of personal immortality extends to persons loved or respected by the ego, so that when such a person disappears it is assumed that it can only be for a time, and that he will surely be seen again, either in this world or the next. To the primitive mind the former place of reappearance is the more natural; hence our children, just like adult savages, imagine that when an old person dies he will shortly reappear as a new-born child" (p. 410).

It is significant that Otto Rank proposes a similar origin for doubling—the narcissistic belief in the immortality of the self. In his essay on the uncanny, Freud summarizes Rank's conclusions: ". . . the 'double' was originally an insurance against the destruction of the ego, an 'energetic denial of the power of death,' as Rank says; and probably the 'immortal' soul was the first 'double' of the body. This invention of doubling as a preservation against extinction has its counterpart in the language of dreams, which is fond of representing castration by a doubling or multiplication of a genital symbol. The same desire led the Ancient Egyptians to develop the art of making images of the dead in lasting materials. Such ideas, however, have sprung from the soil of unbounded self-love, from the primary narcissism which dominates the mind of the child and of primitive man. But when this stage has been surmounted, the 'double' reverses its aspect. From having been an assurance

65

of immortality, it becomes the uncanny harbinger of death" (S.E., 17:235). Rank notes that for primitive man the earliest image of the immortal self was his shadow—the shadow which departs with the death of the grandfather but returns with the birth of the grandson. It would seem, then, that in the reversal fantasy we have the archetypal form of the temporal aspect of doubling.

As ambivalence is central to the fully developed figure of the double in that the double in its final form is at once the image of the beloved ego and the image of the feared and hated dissolution of the ego, so Jones points out that ambivalence is also central to the origin of the reversal fantasy—specifically, the child's ambivalence toward his parents. On the one hand, the child's love for his parents takes the form of a parental impulse to care for them as they have cared for him; on the other hand, his hostility toward them expresses itself in a fantasy in which they will be under his power in the same way that he is now under theirs. Jones observes that the most important consequence of the reversal fantasy "is the way in which it determines the later attitude of the individual towards children, especially his or her own," because there "always takes place some transference from a person's parent to the child of the corresponding sex" (p. 411). Thus, a child's personality is "moulded, or distorted, not only by the effort to imitate its parents, but by the effort to imitate its parent's ideals, which are mostly taken from the grandparent of the corresponding sex" (p. 411). Jones notes that "the social significance of this should be apparent in regard to the transmission of tradition," but he adds that one must "take into account the reaction of the child, which may be either positive or negative; that is, the child may either accept the transference or rebel against it, in the latter case developing character traits of exactly the opposite kind to those it sought to implant" (p. 411). The relevance of the reversal fantasy to Quentin's situation becomes even more obvious when we consider the fantasy's relationship to the castration complex. As Jones expresses it: "A experiences in childhood, and possibly also later, hostile impulses directed against his father B, and fears that his father will punish (e.g., castrate) him for them in the appropriate talion manner. When A grows up, he fears to have a son, C, lest C, the unconscious equivalent of B, will carry out this punishment on him. There is a double reason, it is true, for this fear: he fears his son C, not only as a re-incorporation of B, but also as a separate individual, his son, feeling from his own experience that sons always tend to hate their fathers. We doubtless have here the deepest reason for the constant identification of grandson with grandfather; both are equally feared by the father, who has reason to dread their retaliation for his guilty wishes against them. There are many examples of this situation in mythology. Thus, Zeus did actually carry out on his father Cronos the very injury of castration that the latter had effected on his own father, Uranos; so Uranos is avenged by his re-incarnation, Zeus" (p. 412).

Clearly, in Quentin's relationship with his father there is a form of role reversal at work. With Sutpen and Henry, generations contemporary with Quentin's grandfather and father respectively, it is the father who exhorts the reluctant son to protect his sister's honor, but with Mr. Compson and Quentin it is the son who exhorts the reluctant father to avenge his daughter's honor. Quentin tries to assume the role of the father in relation to his own father, thus becoming in a sense his own grandfather. Mr. Compson would, then, transfer onto Quentin the resentment that he harbored against his own father for the failure and defeatism that General Compson passed on to him. As Mr. Compson's father was a failed general, so Mr. Compson is a failed lawyer—an alcoholic nihilist who revenges himself on his father for that psychological castration that has left him with the feeling that nothing can be done, by passing on to his son that same sense of inescapable failure, defeat, and impotence. For Mr. Compson, Quentin is at once the reincorporation of his own castrating father and the son who resents Mr. Compson's psychological castration of him in the same way that Mr. Compson resented his psychological castration by General Compson. In Quentin's case, the instruments of this castration are time and tradition. When Quentin graduates from high school, his father gives him his grandfather's watch, calling it "the mausoleum of all hope and desire." He gives him the timepiece, he says, not that he might remember time but that he might forget it, for time cannot be conquered and the battle only reveals man's own folly and despair—hardly the kind of exhortation to dare and accomplish great things that one would expect a father to give his son on graduation day. As Quentin recalls at one point in his internal narrative, "Father said a man is the sum of his misfortunes. One day you'd think misfortune would get tired, but then time is your misfortune Father said. A gull on an invisible wire attached through space dragged. You carry the symbol of your frustration into eternity" (p. 123). If a man is the sum of his misfortunes and if time is his misfortune, then a man is not one who exerts his will and does things but one to whom things simply happen inevitably in the irresistible flow of time, a man is essentially impotent. And it is precisely against this sense of man's impotence in the grip of time that Quentin struggles.

I suggested earlier that when Quentin seeks to be punished by his father for allegedly committing incest with Candace, he is, paradoxically, seeking castration as a proof that his masculinity had ever been of sufficient potency to constitute a threat to the father, and I related this to Charles Bon's similar effort to force his father to acknowledge his existence and his manhood, even if that meant forcing his father to kill him through his surrogate, Henry. Yet in examining Quentin's relationship with his father, we find that his efforts to play an active, masculine role, even to the point of being castrated, are inevitably linked with his efforts to force his father to play a masculine role as well, the role of the castrator, the role which his father refused to play in relation to the seducer Dalton Ames. Quentin can be a man only if the person who is his model for manhood, his father, can be a man also. The question of Quentin's masculinity, then, becomes preeminently a question of the tradition of masculinity in his family—a temporal problem in which Quentin's struggle against his own psychological impotence is at the same time an effort to reverse the trend of generations within his family. By an act of his will, Quentin attempts to produce a similar act of will on his father's part and thus to reverse the will of time within whose grip, according to his father, man is essentially helpless. For Quentin, the psychological problem that has made him impotent (the castration complex whose origin is generation) becomes merged with the problem of whether man, in relation to the flow of time, can ever be anything but helpless, passive, and impotent, and to solve the former problem he must solve the latter. The question of whether Quentin can assume an active, masculine role is essentially the historical question of whether any male descendant of the Compson family after General Compson can avoid repeating the General's failure and defeatism and avoid passing it on to the next generation.

The crux, then, of Quentin's problem is repetition, the temporal form of doubling, for it is those inevitable repetitions inherent in the cyclic nature of time that seem to rob the individual will of all potency. Yet it is not just repetition that is involved here, it is recollection as well—that awareness of repetition that, like the Medusa's gaze, paralyzes the will, that awareness that the memory of what has occurred in the past is at the same time the foreknowledge of what will be repeated in the future, the debilitating sense that time is a circular street and that recollection is prophecy. We should note that in temporal doubling a curious reversal occurs. Since it is almost always the person later in time who is aware of the repetition (often the person earlier in time is dead before the second person is even born), we identify with the person later in time as if he were the first self, and as if the person earlier in time were the second self or double, even though it is the person later in time who is the second self and who repeats the earlier actions. This reversal points up the retrospective character of repetition, for in one sense repetition is wholly a function of memory, either on the part of the person who performs the repetition (a repetition that he can become aware of either before or after he performs the repeated act) or on the part of some other person who observes a repetition of which the person performing the act may not himself be aware. Indeed, if there were no memory, either on the part of the person performing the repeated act or on the part of some observer, there would be no repetition.

In this regard, we must distinguish between two different things that look alike—between performing an action *one time* and performing an action *for the first time.* One can perform an action that is never repeated or an action of which no memory remains. That action is performed one time. But if an action that has been performed once is repeated and the previous occurrence is remembered, then the second performance of that action reconstitutes the previous performance as the first time—reconstitutes it as the first time not just by the act of repeating it but by a third action, an act of recollection, in which the second action and the first action are seen as related. In repetition, then, at the time that an action is performed for the first time it is never the first time; it only becomes the first time later, after its second occurrence, when in a third act it is imaginatively reconstituted by the memory. And that third act, which imaginatively reconstitutes the first act as first (and implicitly reconstitutes the state prior to the first act as zero), simultaneously reconstitutes the second act as the repetition. But it does so, paradoxically, by treating the second act as primary and the first act as secondary—that is, by understanding the first act in light of the second act. Thus, though the first and second acts occur in one order, they are understood as first and second only by the mind's moving through them in a reverse order.

Obviously, in talking about repetition, we are dealing with the ordinal numbers (first, second, third, etc.) —numbers considered as an expression of order or succession within a series—as opposed to the cardinal numbers, which express quantity, and we should keep in mind two things about ordinal numbers that bear on repetition. First, the idea of succession is not necessarily the same thing as the succession of ideas, for though the mind may move or appear to move successively through the numbers in a series, yet the series, because the very stuff of its composition is the interrelationship of its members, is implicitly treated as a simultaneous given mutually constituted by all of its members at once. Second, when the idea of generation is annexed to the idea of succession—that is, when linear causality is attached to the numbers in a successive series so that, for example, any given number is understood as being produced by adding one to the previous number—then we find that as the series moves forward, the linear causality moves backward. Certainly, there is a very real sense in which we can say that we live our lives by moving forward, but that we understand our lives, that we introduce causality into our lives, by moving backward.

As one would expect, there is an analogy between the reverse movement inherent in repetition and the fantasy of the reversal of generations. Consider the series grandfather-father-son, let them be represented by the letters A, B, and C respectively, and then imagine that the grandfather is the absolute starting point, that is, that he has no antecedents, or what amounts to the same thing in this case, that his antecedents are not remembered. A has a son B, but B is not the repetition of A, for A is a father and B is a son. A dies. At some later time, B has a son C, and with this third generation, B is constituted as the repetition of A, for B, in relation to C, is now a father like A. But since C, in the reversal fantasy, is the reincorporation of A, then B's relationship to C is not just that of a father to a son, it is as well the relationship of a son to a father. The third generation, C, like the third step in the repetitive series, the act of recollection, constitutes A as the first generation by making B a father like A and thus the repetition of A, and at the same time C, by being the reincorporation of A, is, in relation to B, both a father and a son, and thus simultaneously makes B, in relation to C, both a son and a father. The third generation, like the act of recollection in the repetitive series, constitutes the link of relationship, for it unites two roles (father and son) in one person, and relationship is nothing but that ability to hold two in one. Yet that one which relates the two must itself be some third thing, for at the same moment that it holds the two together as related, it also holds them apart, so that the two grasped as one are not destroyed by that grasp and merged into an indistinguishable unit but remain distinctly two. The link of relationship simultaneously maintains both the sameness and the difference of the two that it relates. The analogy between repetition and the reversal fantasy allows us, then, to see the third step in the repetitive series, the act of recollection, as a reincorporation or reliving of the first event, while it allows us at the same time to view the third generation in the reversal fantasy as a kind of recollection, an imaginative re-creation of the first generation by the memory.

Consider, now, Quentin's narration of the story of the Sutpens in light of what we have observed about repetition and the reversal fantasy. The events involving Judith, Henry, and Bon take place in the 1850s and 60s. Quentin is born long after Judith and Bon are dead and Henry has vanished. The events involving Candace, Quentin, and Dalton Ames take place in the summer of 1909. In September 1909 Quentin becomes involved in the story of the Sutpens when he accompanies Rosa Coldfield to the Sutpen place and they discover Henry hiding in the mansion. In conjunction with Rosa Coldfield and then with his father and then with his roommate Shreve, Quentin, in the fall and winter of 1909–10, narrates the story of the Sutpens in what is at once an act of recollection and of imaginative re-creation. If we consider the occurrences of the 1850s and 60s as group A, those of the summer of 1909 as group B, and those events comprising Quentin's narration in 1909–10 as group C, then it is clear that though the events of group A precede those of group B in time, yet for Quentin in the narrative/recollective act of group C the order is reversed, for he experienced the events of group B before he became involved in narrating the events of group A, and thus though A precedes B in time and B is seen as the repetition of A, yet in the recollective act, B is treated as primary and A as secondary, that is, A is recollected or reconstructed in light of B. Theoretically, the reader acts

73

out this same reversal, because the events of the summer of 1909 are presented in *The Sound and the Fury* seven years before the story of the Sutpens is told in *Absalom.*

Surely, there can be no question that Quentin reconstructs the story of Bon, Henry, and Judith in light of his own experiences with Candace and Dalton Ames—that, for example, the long conversations reported in *Absalom* between Quentin and his father in September 1909, concerning Henry Sutpen's efforts to protect his sister's virginity and ranging over the whole subject of virginity both male and female, are simply the continuation of those lengthy discussions reported in *The Sound and the Fury* between Quentin and his father in the summer of 1909 concerning Candace's loss of virginity and Quentin's inability to lose his virginity. As we would expect from the connection between repetition and the reversal fantasy, Quentin's recollection or reconstruction of the events in the story of the Sutpens turns out to be a reincorporation or reliving of those events. For example, Quentin identifies with Dalton Ames as the lover of his sister Candace—indeed, he says that he identifies with all his sister's lovers (p. 167)—and when Quentin and his father discuss Rosa Coldfield, we are told that Rosa identified with her niece Judith as the lover of Charles Bon, "projecting upon Judith all the abortive dreams and delusions of her own doomed and frustrated youth" (p. 71), and later in the narrative Henry Sutpen is portrayed as identifying with his friend Charles Bon as the lover of his sister Judith. But of course, Quentin never becomes his sister's lover, he never commits incest with Candace. His conscience prevents him, which is to say that the castration fear prevents him by rendering him psychologically impotent. As Freud notes, "the punishment threatened by the superego must be an extension of the punishment of castration. Just as the father has become depersonalized in the shape of the superego . . ." (S.E.,

90:128). And in the act of narration Quentin is forced to relive this frustration of desire again and again, for Rosa never becomes Bon's lover, not even by identifying herself vicariously with Judith, since Judith never becomes Bon's wife. Bon, the son who tries to commit incest, is struck down by the father-surrogate, and that one act prevents both the brother seducer from becoming the real lover of his sister and the brother avenger from becoming her vicarious lover.

Early in the narrative, Mr. Compson speculates about why Rosa chose Quentin to accompany her to the Sutpen place and he suggests that since Quentin's grandfather was Sutpen's best friend, Rosa must have thought that whatever she and Quentin discovered at the mansion would somehow still be kept in the family because of that old friendship. Yet certainly there is another, more obvious reason for Rosa's choice—the resemblance, and thus the natural affinity, between Rosa and Quentin. They are both virgins who have refused incest, Quentin with his sister, Rosa with her brother-in-law. They are both obsessed by their frustrated desire, and that frustration has turned desire to hatred. In *The Sound and the Fury* Quentin is portrayed as psychologically impotent, while at the very start of *Absalom* Rosa is described sitting in her parlor with an "air of impotent and static rage" directed against Sutpen, "the long-dead object of her impotent yet indomitable frustration" (p. 7). Quentin's father, with his failure and defeatism, his blend of cynicism and nihilism, has psychologically castrated his son by telling him that his actions are meaningless, worthless, that no masculine act is possible. Mr. Compson is Quentin's most subtle enemy in *The Sound and the Fury,* and there is present in Quentin's section of the book a thinly veiled hatred of his father. At the start of the Civil War, Rosa's father withdrew into the attic of his home, nailed the door shut, and starved himself to death, and for that withdrawal in time of need, she never forgave him, thinking "she had been instinctively right even as a child in hating her father, and so these forty-three years of impotent and unbearable outrage were the revenge on her of some sophisticated and ironic sterile nature for having hated that which gave her life" (p. 170). In looking at Rosa's past, Quentin sees his own future— forty years of frustration, impotent rage, and despair.

We have already noted how Quentin relives his encounters with his father concerning Candace in imagining the confrontations between Sutpen and Henry about Judith. But certainly the most striking example of the way in which Quentin's narrative act becomes a reincorporation of the lives of the people in that narrative is to be found in Quentin and Shreve's identification with Henry and Bon. Indeed, that identification becomes so complete that Quentin and Shreve supply the missing information in the story with the authority of participants and not simply narrators. The interchangeability of roles in this identification is instructive. In imagining the departure of Bon and Henry after Henry's confrontation with his father in the library, Quentin and Shreve identify with the two brothers separately: ". . . now it was not two but four of them riding the two horses through the dark over the frozen December ruts of that Christmas Eve: four of them and then just two—Charles-Shreve and Quentin-Henry . . ." (p. 334). But at other points in the narration Quentin and Shreve both identify with each of the brothers: "They were both in Carolina and the time was forty-six years ago, and it was not even four now but compounded still further, since now both of them were Henry Sutpen and both of them were Bon, compounded each of both yet either neither . . ." (p. 351). This interchangeability of the persons with whom they identify springs from the interchangeability of the roles of brother seducer and brother avenger, for in Quentin's case they are, of course, simply two aspects of a single personality. Since the relationship between the brother avenger and the brother seducer is a substitute for the father-son relationship in the Oedipal triangle, it is not surprising that when Quentin and Shreve identify with Henry and Bon, the narration turns into a father-son dialogue. When Shreve makes a cynical response to Quentin's narration, Quentin thinks, "Yes, too much, too long. I didn't need to listen then but I had to hear it and now I am having to hear it all over again because he sounds just like father . . ." (p. 211). Yet in this father-son dialogue there is also an interchangeability of roles, for in the conversations between Quentin and his father about Candace, it was Quentin who assumed the fatherly role like Sutpen and demanded that they avenge Candace's honor, while his father assumed Henry's role of the reluctant son. Thus, at one point in the narration, Shreve says to Quentin, "Don't say it's just me that sounds like your old man," and Quentin thinks, "*Yes. Maybe we are both Father. Maybe nothing ever happens once and is finished. . . . Or maybe Father and I are both Shreve, maybe it took Father and me both to make Shreve or Shreve and me both to make Father or maybe Thomas Sutpen to make all of us*" (pp. 261–62). This basic interchangeability of the roles of father and son is present in both the reversal fantasy and the incest complex, and it is internalized in the father-son relationship of the roles of the superego and the ego within the self.

We should note that the relationship between Bon and Henry, as it is imagined in the narrative, possesses homoerotic overtones, so that, for example, Bon's intended marriage to Judith is portrayed as a vicarious consummation of the love between Bon and Henry, a love that is in fact consummated in a *liebestod* when Henry kills Bon. The same latent homoeroticism is present in the relationship of the two narrators Quentin and Shreve, as is evidenced in Quentin's obsessive sensitivity in *The Sound and the Fury* when his classmates at Harvard refer to Shreve as Quentin's husband: "Calling Shreve my husband. Ah let him alone, Shreve said, if he's got better sense than to chase after the little dirty sluts, whose business. In the South you are ashamed of being a virgin. Boys. Men. They lie about it" (p. 97). Indeed, the latent homoerotic content in the story of Bon and Henry may well be simply a projection of Quentin's own state made in the act of narration.

The act of recollection, of imaginatively reconstructing the events of the 1850s and 60s, becomes for Quentin a reliving of the events of 1909 (Freud points out that the return of the repressed is a remembering that takes the form of a reliving, S.E., 18:18), and though in the mechanism of this imaginative reconstruction, the events of 1909 are primary and those of the 1850s and 60s are secondary, yet it is the whole point of that reconstruction to portray the events of the 1850s and 60s as primary and those of 1909 as secondary, so that the events of 1909 are seen as an unwilled repetition of the earlier occurrences. This imaginative mechanism which, in the recollective act, shapes a previous event so that one's own actions appear to be a repetition of that event has the effect in Quentin's case of making the individual seem helpless and passive in the face of events, of making Quentin feel that he is fated to repeat the roles of brother seducer and brother avenger for the rest of his life without his willing it or even against his willing it. Thus, on the day of his death Quentin repeats both roles within the space of an afternoon. During his walk in the country, he stops at a village bakery where a little Italian girl, whom he addresses as "sister," is waiting to be served. Quentin buys her a roll and she follows him out of the store. When she won't stop following him,

Quentin decides to take the little girl to her home. They are walking around the village looking for her house when the little girl's brother Julio comes running up and tries to kill Quentin because he thinks that Quentin is a child molester trying to seduce his sister. Julio is restrained by the town marshal, and Quentin is taken into custody, from which he is rescued by the arrival of a party that includes Shreve, Spoade, Gerald Bland, and Gerald's mother, who vouch for Quentin and help him explain what happened. Quentin then joins the party on their outing, even though he instinctively dislikes Gerald, an archetypal seducer whose image in Quentin's mind merges with that of Dalton Ames. Later, at a roadside inn, Quentin suddenly, and without apparent provocation, tries to hit Gerald, and Gerald knocks him unconscious. As Spoade and Shreve recount it,

> "The first I knew was when you jumped up all of a sudden and said, 'Did you ever have a sister? did you?' and when he said No, you hit him. I noticed you kept on looking at him, but you didnt seem to be paying any attention to what anybody was saying until you jumped up and asked him if he had any sisters."
>
> "Ah, he was blowing off as usual," Shreve said, "about his women. You know: like he does, before girls, so they dont know exactly what he's saying. All his damn innuendo and lying and a lot of stuff that dont make sense even. . . . Talking about the body's beauty and the sorry ends thereof and how tough women have it, without anything else they can do except lie on their backs. Leda lurking in the bushes, whimpering and moaning for the swan, see. The son of a bitch. I'd hit him myself. Only I'd grabbed up her damn hamper of wine and done it if it had been me."   (p. 185)

Quentin confronts Gerald using the same words with which he confronted Dalton Ames: "Did you ever have a sister?" But Quentin is no avenger and he is certainly no seducer, and what he unintentionally relives in his encounters with Gerald and the little girl is his failure in both those roles. Indeed, in the sequence of Quentin's stream-of-consciousness narrative, the encounter with the Italian girl immediately precedes Quentin's recollection of his abortive attempt to play the role of brother seducer with Candace at the stream, while the memory of his failure in the role of brother avenger when he confronts Dalton Ames at the bridge leads into the account of his one-sided fist fight with Gerald Bland.

What Quentin must face in this situation and in his narration of the story of the Sutpens is that in terms of the content of an event no actual repetition in time is possible. Indeed, the very nature of time precludes a real repetition, for in the repeated event or act there is always something different, if nothing more than the fact that it occurs at a different time. If Quentin were really able to repeat the events of the summer of 1909, then it would *be* the summer of 1909 again. Time would not have irrevocably passed, but, as in the Christian image of eternity, would be totally spatialized so that the past would continue to exist at the present moment as if it were a place to which we could go. In his book on repetition Kierkegaard argues that the only true repetition is eternity, where the flux of time has been transcended.[13] But if in the course of time no true repetition is possible in terms of the content of an event, what then have we been referring to in speaking of that repetition which, like fate, occurs without an individual's consciously willing it, or even against his willing it, and in the grip of which the individual will seems helpless and passive? It can only be the internal compulsion to repeat, that compulsion to repeat which is rooted in the unconscious and thus operates without or in spite of the conscious will, that compulsion to repeat which, in terms of the content of the repeated event within time, is always frustrated, a frustration that is experienced by the conscious mind, paradoxically, as a failure of will. Yet if the repetition compulsion is always frustrated in terms of the content of the repeated event within time, if the repeated event within time is always different, then it is true that in terms of the abstract form of the repeated event viewed as repetition, that difference is something that is always the same, is always repeated. Thus it is that the repetition compulsion in its very inability to achieve a true repetition in the content of a repeated event because the repeated event is always different does achieve through the eternal recurrence of that difference a sameness which constitutes a true repetition. This simultaneous sameness and difference is, obviously, the very essence of time. As Stevens says of the being of time (perhaps alluding to Augustine's "et est et non est"), "It is and it is not and therefore is."[14] Or as he remarks in "The Monocle of Mon Oncle," contrasting the mythic Christian eternity with the real nature of time, "The honey of heaven may or may not come, / But that of earth both comes and goes at once." The essence of time is that it has its being by always becoming, it *is* by always ceasing to be, it is the same by always being different. We are, of course, dealing with Nietzsche's concept of the eternal recurrence of the same—with the paradox that the endless recurrence of difference constitutes sameness, that the ceaselessness of becoming constitutes being, that the continuance of mutability constitutes the immutable, that the endless flux of time constitutes eternity. Not a Christian eternity, not eternity in Kierkegaard's sense, not a becoming that has wholly become, that is totally spatialized into being, but becoming as being; not eternity as the end of time but eternity as the endlessness of time, meaningless and without a goal. To will that repetition, to will the eternal, meaningless recurrence of the same is the highest act that Nietzsche knows, for while man cannot change the nature of time, within whose grip he is essentially passive and helpless, he can change his

81

relationship to time by actively willing repetition, by actively willing his own passivity. But to will actively one's own passivity in the grip of time is to will that event to which time leads, it is to will one's death, or at the very least, to concur in one's death.

What has all this to do, then, with Quentin's dilemma? First of all, there is a clear connection between the repetition compulsion and doubling, a connection which Freud discusses at length in his essay on the uncanny. He points out that doubling is one of those structures that commonly evoke the feeling of the uncanny, structures which represent, he says, "a harking-back to particular phases in the evolution of the self-regarding feeling, a regression to a time when the ego had not yet marked itself off sharply from the external world and from other people" (S.E., 17:236). He connects the uncanny aspect of doubling with those repetitions of the same thing that "arouse an uncanny feeling" because they recall "the sense of helplessness experienced in some dream-states" (S.E., 17:236–37). And he adds that "it is only this factor of involuntary repetition which surrounds what would otherwise be innocent enough with an uncanny atmosphere, and forces upon us the idea of something fateful and inescapable when otherwise we should have spoken only of 'chance' " (S.E., 17:237). This accords with Freud's observation that the idea of the double, of the other self, includes "all the unfulfilled but possible futures to which we still like to cling in phantasy, all the strivings of the ego which adverse external circumstances have crushed, and all our suppressed acts of volition which nourish in us the illusion of Free Will" (S.E., 17:236).

To explain the nature of that feeling of involuntary repetition that is experienced as the uncanny, Freud invokes "the dominance in the unconscious mind of a 'compulsion to repeat' proceeding from the instinctual impulses and probably inherent in the very nature of the instincts—a compulsion powerful enough to overrule the pleasure principle, lending to certain aspects of the mind their daemonic character, and still very clearly expressed in the impulses of small children; a compulsion, too, which is responsible for a part of the course taken by the analyses of neurotic patients" (S.E., 17:238). And he concludes, "whatever reminds us of this inner 'compulsion to repeat' is perceived as uncanny" (S.E., 17:238). Yet it is not every repetition that evokes the feeling of the uncanny, it is only certain events whose repetition reminds us of that inner compulsion to repeat, and the specific character of those events, according to Freud, is that they all represent the recurrence of something that has been repressed. Freud points out that every emotional affect, whatever its quality, is transformed by repression into morbid anxiety, and that that class of morbid anxiety that is associated with the return of the repressed is what we refer to as the feeling of the uncanny, irrespective of whether the original event aroused dread or some other affect: "this uncanny is in reality nothing new or alien, but something which is familiar and old-established in the mind and which has become alienated from it only through the process of repression" (S.E., 17:241). Freud observes that—besides doubling and involuntary repetition—magic and animism, the castration complex, man's attitude to death, and the omnipotence of thoughts are all capable of evoking the uncanny, so that "an uncanny experience occurs either when infantile complexes which have been repressed are once more revived by some impression, or when primitive beliefs which have been surmounted seem once more to be confirmed" (S.E., 17:249).

Three points should be reemphasized here that bear directly on Quentin's situation: that it is the return of the repressed that reminds us of the repetition compulsion, that the feeling of the uncanny evoked by involuntary repetition is a morbid anxiety, and that involuntary repetition recalls that sense of helplessness sometimes experienced in dreams. First of all, as I have pointed out, much of the story of Bon, Henry, and Judith, as Quentin imagines it, may simply be the return of Quentin's own repressed experiences with Candace and Ames. But even beyond that, the story of Thomas Sutpen and Charles Bon is *about* the return of the repressed. Throughout *Absalom,* Sutpen is presented as a type of the rational ego—a man with a conscious plan for the conduct of his life—a design to acquire land, build a mansion, found a family—a design that he pursues with a radical innocence indistinguishable from ruthlessness, using those people who accord with his design and discarding those who do not. Indeed, Sutpen is portrayed as a kind of Faust, whose grand design represents the rational ego's will to power in its attempt to do away with the undesigned and the irrational: "he struggled to hold clear and free above a maelstrom of unpredictable and unreasoning human beings, not his head for breath and not so much his fifty years of effort and striving to establish a posterity, but his code of logic and morality, his formula and recipe of fact and deduction . . ." (p. 275). But Sutpen's grand design was endangered once by his marriage to a woman who had tricked him, whose instinctual cunning had almost confounded his logical plan, and so, as Sutpen told General Compson, "I merely explained how this new fact rendered it impossible that this woman and child be incorporated in my design" (p. 264), and he put them behind him like the bright ego repressing its connection with the dark, feminine unconscious. But thirty years later, the repressed returns in the person of the dark, feminine Bon—the product of that union. And this time Sutpen's act of repression, his attempt to deny Bon's existence, destroys his design and himself.

The second point that bears directly on Quentin's situation is that the feeling of the uncanny evoked by involuntary repetition is a morbid anxiety. At the same period that Freud was writing his essay on the uncanny he was also writing *Beyond the Pleasure Principle,* in which the repetition compulsion, this principle "powerful enough to overrule the pleasure principle," is discussed at length. Freud points out that in addition to compulsive neurotics, there are many normal people who give the impression "of being pursued by a malignant fate or possessed by some 'daemonic' power," but that analysis reveals that "their fate is for the most part arranged by themselves and determined by early infantile influences" (S.E., 18:21). The form that their fate takes is the periodic recurrence of the same events and actions in their lives: "Thus we have come across people all of whose human relationships have the same outcome. . . . This 'perpetual recurrence of the same thing' causes us no astonishment when it relates to *active* behaviour on the part of the person concerned and when we can discern in him an essential character-trait which always remains the same and which is compelled to find expression in a repetition of the same experiences. We are much more impressed by cases where the subject appears to have a *passive* experience, over which he has no influence, but in which he meets with a repetition of the same fatality" (S.E., 18:22). Freud notes that the manifestations of the repetition compulsion show "an instinctual character and, when they act in opposition to the pleasure-principle, give the appearance of some 'daemonic' force at work" (S.E., 18:35).

But what does it mean to say that the compulsion to repeat is "instinctual," thus locating it on the level of the primary process of the unconscious and its unbound energy? Freud's answer turns the question around, for he suggests that the repetition compulsion is a "universal attribute of instincts" (S.E., 18:36). Thus, it is not so much that the compulsion to repeat is instinctual as that the very essence of the instincts is the compulsion to repeat. He asserts that *"an instinct is an urge inherent in organic life to restore an earlier state of things* which the living entity has been obliged to abandon under the pressure of external disturbing forces; that is, it is a kind of organic elasticity, or, to put it another way, the expression of the inertia inherent in organic life" (S.E., 18:36). Instincts are "an expression of the *conservative* nature of living substance" (S.E., 18:36). From this he concludes that the final goal of all organic striving, the ultimate earlier state which the instincts attempt to restore, is that inanimate condition from which animate life sprang: "If we are to take it as a truth that knows no exception that everything living dies for *internal* reasons—becomes inorganic once again—then we shall be compelled to say that *'the aim of all life is death'* . . ." (S.E., 18:38). When "the attributes of life were at some time evoked in inanimate matter," the "tension which then arose in what had hitherto been an inanimate substance endeavoured to cancel itself out. In this way the first instinct came into being: the instinct to return to the inanimate state" (S.E., 18:38). Freud speculates that the process by which inanimate matter first acquired the attributes of life "may perhaps have been a process similar in type to that which later caused the development of consciousness in a particular stratum of living matter" (S.E., 18:38). The fact that Freud draws an analogy between the development of life from inanimate matter and the development of consciousness from unconscious life would seem to sponsor a further analogy—if the first instinct of animate matter is the instinct to return to the inanimate state, then one could assert that in terms of psychic life the first instinct is that of consciousness to return to the unconscious state.

In discussing what he calls the "death instinct," Freud points out that the instincts of self-preservation, self-assertion, and mastery appear to contradict what he has said about the goal of all life being death, but he maintains that these instincts are in fact in the service of the death instinct: "They are component instincts whose function it is to assure that the organism shall follow its own path to death, and to ward off any possible ways of returning to inorganic existence other than those which are immanent in the organism itself. . . . What we are left with is the fact that the organism wishes to die only in its own fashion. Thus these guardians of life, too, were originally the myrmidons of death. Hence arises the paradoxical situation that the living organism struggles most energetically against events (dangers, in fact) which might help it to attain its life's aim rapidly—by a kind of short-circuit. Such behaviour is, however, precisely what characterizes purely instinctual as contrasted with intelligent efforts" (S.E., 18: 39).

Freud observes, however, that there is a group of instincts that do not show the death drive. The sexual instincts work against the death of the living substance: "They are conservative in the same sense as the other instincts in that they bring back earlier states of living substance; but they are conservative to a higher degree in that they are peculiarly resistant to external influences; and they are conservative too in another sense in that they preserve life itself for a comparatively long period. They are the true life instincts. They operate against the purpose of the other instincts, which leads, by reason of their function, to death. . . . It is as though the life of the organism moved with a vacillating rhythm. One group of instincts rushes forward so as to reach the final aim of life as swiftly as possible; but when a particular stage in the advance has been reached, the other group jerks back to a certain point to make a fresh start and so prolong the journey" (S.E., 18:40–41). What characterizes the life instincts and the death instincts in terms of the compulsion to repeat is that they both seek through repetition to restore an earlier state which has been lost—in the case of the death instincts, to return animate matter to an inanimate condition, and in the case of the sexual instincts, to return living matter to a state prior to the division into sexes. Indeed, Freud refers to the myth, contained in Plato's *Symposium,* of Zeus's division of a primal androgyne to form the sexes, and of the subsequent attempt of the divided halves to become one again, as an example of a poet-philosopher's intuition that the goal of the sexual instincts is to return to a condition prior to that division (S.E., 18:57). Freud asserts that in light of the repetition compulsion, all instincts, both those of life and of death, are regressive (S.E., 18:59). And I think that we are justified in adding that the form that this regression takes is the urge to do away with the category of difference—the difference between animate and inanimate and the difference between masculine and feminine.

Now, what is the relationship between the repetition compulsion, the regressive character of the instincts, and the fact that the feeling of the uncanny evoked by involuntary repetition is a morbid anxiety? And what has this relationship to do with Quentin's situation? One can, I believe, construct a model showing the structural links between the repetition compulsion, the regressive character of the instincts, and the morbid anxiety evoked by the return of the repressed through the involuntary repetition involved in doubling, and this model will serve as an imaginative analogue to Faulkner's texts, shedding light on the structure of Quentin's personal history and the story he narrates.

Our model takes as its starting point the Oedipus complex and the son's sexual desire for his mother, a sexual instinct that inevitably leads to the threat of death in the castration complex. The son must choose between renouncing the object of his desire (the mother) and being castrated, but this choice is further complicated by the son's ambivalence toward his father: his fear of losing the father's love versus his hatred of the father as a rival for the mother. In any case, the son in the first stage of the Oedipus complex must, because of physical inadequacy, renounce the possession of the object of his desire. This renunciation of the first external object of the sexual instinct under the threats of castration and death is the primal act of repression. And in the psychic life of the son this act of repression amounts to an implicit renunciation of another object—the phallus—the possession of which by the son evokes the threat of death. As we noted earlier, Freud maintains that the fear of death is an analogue of the fear of castration, pointing out that the situation to which the ego reacts in both cases is the state of being forsaken by the protecting superego. We should add that the son's renunciation of the phallus amounts to a kind of amputation in which a part is given up to save the whole; but that amputation, whereby the life of the body is temporarily preserved through sacrificing a part of the body, shatters once and for all the sense of bodily and psychic integrity, and as such is a partial foreshadowing of that ultimate dissolution of bodily and psychic integrity that is death. It is as if one kept oneself from being devoured by an animal by feeding the animal a finger, only to realize in that very act that the body *can* come apart and thus that it ultimately *will* come apart.

Freud explains the morbid anxiety, caused by the involuntary return of the repressed and experienced as the uncanny, by pointing out that the very nature of the repressive act is that it transforms the repressed emotional affect, whatever its original quality, into the fear of death. In terms of the castration complex, we can now see why repression endows all repressed material with a death anxiety, for the archetypal form of repression is the son's renunciation of that primal sexual instinct for the mother that evokes the threat of death, so that the son, to avoid the danger of physical castration, performs a psychic self-castration by denying the use of the phallus with which both the sexual instinct and the danger of death are associated. For what is repression but a psychological castration in which a dangerous part of the self is cut off and rejected? The primal act of repression, then, occurs when the son, rather than passively submit to being feminized by the castrating father, actively feminizes himself, and what the return of the repressed always evokes, no matter what the content of the repressed material, is the return of the archetype of the repressing act—i.e., castration.

In the development of the son, the debilitating effect of the castration complex is generally overcome by the substitution of another woman for the mother as the object of sexual desire. But if that debilitating effect is not overcome, if the fear of castration or the fear of losing the father's love is so great that all women, and not just the mother, are prohibited as objects of sexual desire—i.e., become synonymous with death—then there results, as indicated earlier, that fixation in secondary narcissism in which the son's own ego is recathected as the sole object of love. The subject as the sole object of love is unconsciously projected in the figure of the double. The ego loves the double as a copy of itself, but it simultaneously hates and fears the double because it is a copy with a difference—the double is the ego shadowed by the unconscious, the ego tinged with its own death. Thus, in doubling, the ego takes the embodiment of its own death as its object of sexual desire, and the murder of the double becomes a suicidal *liebestod,* an annihilating union in which the sexual instinct and the death instinct (both of which seek to restore an earlier state) fuse in the ultimate regressive act—the suicidal return to the womb, the sexual reentry into Mother Death, an act that obliterates the differences between male and female, subject and object, conscious and unconscious, animate and inanimate. Faulkner says that Quentin loved neither his sister's body nor the idea of incest but "loved only death, loved and lived in a deliberate and almost perverted anticipation of death as a lover loves and deliberately refrains from the waiting willing friendly tender incredible body of his beloved, until he can no longer bear not the refraining but the restraint and so flings, hurls himself, relinquishing, drowning" (pp. 9–10).

In light of the archetypal repressive act, the mechanism by which the figure of the double evokes the death of the ego becomes clear. The son, in the primal act of repression, psychologically castrates himself rather than be physically castrated by the father; he *actively* renders himself *passive* rather than *passively* submit to being rendered *passive* by another. This primal threat of castration seen as an external overruling of the conscious will that renders the son permanently passive amounts to the death of the son's ego, and this threat is evoked by the figure of the double in two ways. First, the double as the *involuntary* return of the repressed recalls the archetypal *form* of the repressing act—castration. Second, in terms of *content,* the figure of the double as a feminized male (a male figure that is the sole object of the son's love—the dark, feminine Bon) evokes that state of physical feminization which the son attempts to avoid through a psychological feminization. And it evokes it in a precise manner. The essence of the physical feminization of the son is that it is permanent and involuntary; it comes from an external force (the father), it overrules the son's will, and it renders him permanently passive. The essence of psychological feminization, on the other hand, is that it originates from within, is voluntary, and is intended to be temporary; the son actively renounces the use of the phallus until the immediate physical danger is past. But since the figure of the double is an unconscious projection of the ego in its fixated state, since the double, as the repressed, returns from an area that lies outside the control of the conscious will, an area that periodically overrules the conscious will, then the double in its character of an involuntary repetition evokes that very danger of the overruling of the son's will by an alien force (the castrating father) that repression had tried to avoid. It is as if one fled a danger by running down a path that suddenly became a circle leading back to the very danger from which one fled. And that is, of course, precisely the danger involved in repression—not just that the repressed will inevitably return, but that repression, as a temporary psychological self-castration to avoid the danger of permanent physical castration, can itself become permanent if the castration fear is strong enough to result in a fixation in secondary narcissism.

In doubling, when the bright self (the ego under the influence of the superego—the impersonalized father) confronts the dark self (the ego influenced by the unconscious), the ego's conscious will seems suddenly in danger of being overruled from two different directions at once. The dark self is an involuntary repetition, an unconscious projection that has returned by means beyond the control of the conscious will. And when the repressed returns, when the unconscious projection rises to the level of consciousness, the conscious will immediately finds itself confronted by another force that attempts to overrule it—the superego's demand that that which has returned be re-repressed. Thus, as a child, the dark, feminine Bon is rejected by his father, and when Bon returns thirty years later as a man, he is again rejected by his father. And that rejection has all the force of repression, for Sutpen does not say, "Yes, you are my son; now go away." If Sutpen had, Bon would have left. But Sutpen tries to repress Bon, to deny Bon's existence as his son and thus deny his existence as a man. Because Bon's mother is part Negro, Bon is not his father's son, he is his mother's son. In miscegenation it was the black parent that determined the race of the child. Bon is not white like his father, he is black like his mother. If a child was as little as one sixty-fourth part black, he was legally black, even if, like Bon, he could pass for white. In Sutpen's world, Bon is legally not his father's son, he can enjoy none of the privileges of sonship, he cannot inherit Sutpen's property— the mansion and the land—and thus he cannot fulfill Sutpen's design to get land, build a house, and found a dynasty. If it had been known in Jefferson that Bon was black, his whole status, his whole existence, would have been determined not by who his father was but by what his mother was. Bon is, then, literally his mother's son, and that dark, feminine quality of Bon's referred to in the narrative assumes a deeper significance. Bon is his mother's son in another sense as well, for she has raised him to be the instrument of her will in taking revenge on his father. Upholding the values of his world, Sutpen must deny Bon's existence not only as his son but as a man, for since Bon is black, he is in his father's eyes not a man but an object, not a son but a slave. We can see why Bon in the role of the dark double would be an especially disturbing figure for Quentin—as the double, he represents the involuntary return of the repressed and the feminized male, both of which evoke the primal threat of the overruling of the son's will by the castrating father. But even beyond

93

that, Bon, as a black in the antebellum South, represents the figure of the son as the slave of the father, the son reduced to total passivity, the son whose will is completely subject to the will of his master-father.

We have now begun to deal more directly with that conflict between the father and the son over the mother that stands behind the conflict between the brother avenger and the brother seducer, for in doubling, when the bright self, the ego as related to the superego, confronts the dark self, the ego as related to the unconscious, we are faced with the internal equivalent of the confrontation between the son as influenced by his father and the son as influenced by his mother. Further, we can see the necessary link between the repetition compulsion and repression. Freud points out that whatever is repressed will inevitably return. It is as if the act of repression endowed the repressed material with the repetition compulsion. But the repressed can return only through a displacement; only by being different can it slip past the conscious defenses to reveal itself as the same. But once it reveals itself as the same, the ego under the influence of the superego attempts to re-repress it. Thus, in the very mechanism of repression, the return of the repressed, re-repression, and re-return, we find an explanation for what Freud, quoting Nietzsche, called in *Beyond the Pleasure Principle* "this 'perpetual recurrence of the same thing' "—the way in which the repressed by continually being different continually reconstitutes itself as the same.

At this point let me add to the model that I am constructing the third feature that I emphasized earlier—the fact that the involuntary repetition which evokes the feeling of the uncanny recalls that sense of helplessness sometimes experienced in dreams. Obviously, a polar opposition that structures much of my analysis of doubling and incest in Faulkner's work is the one between activity and passivity as masculine and feminine determinants, as the poles of man's relationship to repetition and the flux of time, and as the oscillating modes of narrating and listening (as we shall see presently). In this polar opposition, activity and passivity are not two separate states but, rather, the two ends of a continuous spectrum along which the self moves back and forth. In Nietzsche's doctrine of the eternal recurrence and in Freud's discussions of repression and repetition, we have, as well, distinguished two types of passivity: a passivity involuntarily imposed, as when the individual feels himself in the grip of a fate that periodically repeats itself without his willing it or against his willing it, or as when a son feels his will overruled and virtually annulled by the will of his father; and a passivity actively initiated, as when the individual wills the eternal recurrence of the same, or when the son actively wills his own temporary feminization in repression. We should add, of course, that there are important differences between the concepts of actively willing passivity in the works of Nietzsche and Freud: most obviously, Freud denied the existence of free will, calling it a powerful illusion. For Freud, the difference between a passivity involuntarily imposed and a passivity actively willed is an illusory difference—both are involuntarily imposed; they differ only in the modes of imposition. One mode allows the ego the illusion that it (the ego) initiates the passivity or at least concurs in it; the other does not. Nietzsche, with his taste for paradox, would assert that it is by affirming illusion (the play of illusion in the tragic sense, or in this case the illusion of free will) through the conscious willing of repetition that one demonstrates the freedom of will. One might laugh at that statement. Certainly Zarathustra would, pointing out that that laughter, that "lightness," in the Nietzschean sense of the word, was a proof of freedom. For in Nietzsche's thought, the very essence of the will is that it is a "lightness" that opposes itself to the "heaviness" of the world and of events. Surely, it is not without significance that one of the principal areas in which Freud attacked the illusion of free will was precisely that of the apparent freedom of jokes and wit.

Now, what have these various senses of passivity to do with the fact that the involuntary repetition experienced in an uncanny situation, such as doubling, recalls that sense of helplessness sometimes experienced in dreams? Clearly, the passivity that we have been discussing is a kind of helplessness—helplessness in the grip of fate, in the flux of time, helplessness in the face of death, helplessness at the hands of the all-powerful father. It is impossible to say what the first feeling is that an infant experiences, but certainly one of the first and one of, if not *the,* most terrifying is the feeling of being helpless, of being totally passive. Discussing the doubling scenario in which thanatophobia leads to suicide, Rank says that the ego does not so much fear death as find unbearable "the *expectation* of the unavoidable destiny of death." Indeed, the very fact that the person involved in the scenario commits suicide shows that the principal fear is not that of death but of something more terrifying than death—it is the fear of an "unavoidable destiny," the fear of living in a helpless state, in a state where one is passive in the grip of time and change and what they inevitably bring. It is the ego's fear of living in a state where the will's sense of mastery and activity is an illusion. We are familiar enough with the cases of people who, faced with the certainty of being rendered helpless by illness or old age, take their own lives, or with the stories of those who, under a sentence of death, kill themselves rather than passively submit to being executed by another. We should distinguish, however, between those who kill themselves out of despair at this helplessness and those who kill themselves as a last attempt to assert their mastery over their own fate. If the involuntary repetition experienced in doubling recalls the helplessness sometimes experienced in dreams, it is because the double as the return of the repressed evokes by both its form and its content that primal threat of the son's being rendered permanently helpless by the castrating father—an overruling of the will from outside that has as its analogue the internal overruling of the will by the unconscious through the return of the repressed, the same overruling by the unconscious that we meet in dreams.

This sense of helplessness, of impotence, is, of course, the very core of Quentin's dilemma, for when Quentin tries to play an active, masculine role, his will is always frustrated and overruled and he is shifted into a passive, feminine role. Attempting to be the brother avenger, he faints like a girl in the arms of Dalton Ames; trying to be the brother seducer in a *liebestod* with his sister, he is unmanned by her courage and drops his knife. Yet it is not just *within* the scenarios of brother avenger and brother seducer that Quentin's will is frustrated and Quentin rendered helpless, it is also by the very unwilled recurrence of those scenarios within the story that he narrates and in the events with the Italian girl and Gerald Bland that he is again rendered passive in the grip of fate. In telling the story of the Sutpens, Quentin imaginatively enacts a fated repetition of his own situation with Candace and Dalton Ames, yet it is a story whose very point is that its priority to his own situation renders that situation already a fated repetition.

In the story of the Sutpens, Quentin also finds a re-enactment of the way that the fate of a father is passed on to a son. When Sutpen was a child, he received an affront from the black servant of a rich plantation owner. He was told that he could not come to the front door of the planter's house, he had to go around to the back because he was white trash, because he and his family were not as good as the plantation owner. Comparing the plantation owner with his own father, Sutpen rejects his father as a model and adopts the plantation owner as his surrogate father, as his model for what a man should be. And Sutpen feels the same ambivalence toward him that a son would feel for a father. At first, he considers killing him, but then he realizes that he doesn't want to do away with the plantation owner, he wants to become the plantation owner. The ruthless odyssey on which Sutpen embarks is a quest for revenge for the affront that he suffered as a boy—not revenge against a system in which the rich and powerful can affront the poor and powerless but against the luck of birth that made him one of the poor when he should have been one of the rich. Like Gatsby, Sutpen distinguishes between the "Platonic" and the "merely personal." Ideally, he accepts the justice of that mastery which the powerful have over the powerless, which the rich planter has over the poor boy, a father over his son. The fact that circumstance happened to start Sutpen off by casting him in the role of the powerless, poor boy is merely personal. A mere stroke of chance does not invalidate that hierarchy—or rather, patriarchy—of power. Sutpen seeks revenge within the rules of patriarchal power for the affront that he suffered; he does not try to show the injustice of the system, but rather to show that he is as good as any man in the system. If the planter is powerful because he is rich, then Sutpen will have his revenge by becoming richer and more powerful than the planter. And he will pass that wealth and power on to his son, doing for his son what his own father could not do for him. Sutpen comes to terms with the traumatic affront that he suffered as a boy by accepting the impersonal justice of it even though he feels its personal inappropriateness. He incorporates into himself the patriarchal ideal from which that affront sprang in much the same way that a son comes to terms with the image of his father as a figure of mastery and power by impersonalizing and internalizing that image as the superego, accepting the justice of the father's mastery even though that mastery has been exercised against the son. It is a mechanism by which the son tries to overcome the mastery of the personal father while maintaining the mastery of fatherhood—a mechanism in which the personal father dies without the son's having to kill him. Accepting this ideal of patriarchal power, Sutpen determines his fate—to repeat periodically that traumatic affront but in a different role. Henceforth, he will no longer receive the affront, he will deliver it. Thus, he rejects his first wife and son because they are not good enough to share the position to which he aspires. And he passes that fated repetition on to his sons—to Charles Bon, who returns thirty years later seeking admittance to the rich plantation owner's "house" (and thereby represents the return of that repressed traumatic affront of Sutpen's boyhood) and to Henry, who, acting as his father's surrogate, delivers the final affront to Bon, killing him at the gates of the house to prevent his entering.

In his interviews at the University of Virginia, Faulkner repeatedly pointed out that *Absalom* is a revenge story—indeed, a double revenge story: Sutpen's revenge for the affront that he suffered as a boy and Bon's revenge for the affront that he and his mother suffered at Sutpen's hands during Sutpen's quest for revenge. Faulkner said of Sutpen: "He wanted revenge as he saw it, but also he wanted to establish the fact that man is immortal, that man, if he is man, cannot be inferior to another man through artificial standards or circumstances. What he was trying to do—when he was a boy, he had gone to the front door of a big house and somebody, a servant, said, Go around to the back door. He said, I'm going to be the one that lives in the big house, I'm going to establish a dynasty, I don't care how, and he violated all the rules of decency and honor and pity and compassion, and the fates took revenge on him" (p. 35). Sutpen wants revenge not against the injustice of that mastery which the powerful have over the powerless, but against those "artificial standards or circumstances" that determine who are the powerful and who the powerless, against the artificial standard of inherited wealth and the circumstances of one's birth. Faulkner says that Sutpen in his quest for revenge violated all the rules of decency and honor and pity and compassion. But there is one rule that Sutpen does not violate, and that is the rule of power. For the rule that Sutpen follows is that real power springs not from the external, artificial advantages of birth and inherited wealth but from something internal: for Sutpen the source of real power is the force of the individual will. In any group of men, power belongs to the man whose will is strong enough to seize that power and hold it against his fellow men. But that brings us face to face with the central paradox of Sutpen's quest—that he seeks revenge on the artificial standards of birth and inherited wealth as the determinants of power by setting out to establish a dynasty—that is, by trying to confer those very same artificial advantages on his son. Faulkner gives us the key to this paradox when he says that Sutpen "wanted revenge as he saw it, but also he wanted to establish the fact that man is immortal, that man, if he is man, cannot be inferior to another man through artificial standards or circumstances." It is a puzzling statement. First of all, what does it mean to equate Sutpen's attempt to establish that man is immortal with his effort to prove that one man cannot be inferior to another through artificial standards or circumstances? And then, what does it mean to link these two with the quest for revenge?

The idea that lies behind Faulkner's statement is what Nietzsche called "the revenge against time."[15] To understand what this idea involves, let us compare for a moment the careers of Jay Gatsby and Thomas Sutpen. Clearly, what Gatsby and Sutpen both seek in their quests is to alter the past—to repeat the past and correct it. As Sutpen in the role of the poor boy suffered an affront from the rich plantation owner, so Gatsby as the poor boy was rejected by the rich girl Daisy Buchanan, and as the former affront initiated Sutpen's grand design to get land, build a mansion, and establish a dynasty, that is, to repeat the past situation but with Sutpen now in the role of the affronter rather than the affronted and to pass on to his son the rich man's power to affront the poor and powerless, so Daisy's rejection of Gatsby initiates Gatsby's dream of acquiring a fortune, owning a great house, and winning Daisy back, his dream of repeating the past by marrying Daisy this time and obliterating everything that occurred between that rejection and his winning her back. When Nick Carraway realizes the enormity of Gatsby's dream, he tells him, "You can't repeat the past," and Gatsby with his Sutpen-like innocence replies, "Why of course you can." As Sutpen rejected his powerless, real father as a model in favor of the powerful plantation owner, so Gatsby rejected his father who was a failure, changed his name from Gatz to Gatsby, and adopted the self-made man Dan Cody as his surrogate father. But now the question arises, Why does the attempt to repeat the past and correct it turn into the revenge against time? Nietzsche's answer is worth quoting at length:

"To redeem those who lived in the past and to recreate all 'it was' into a 'thus I willed it'—that alone should I call redemption. Will—that is the name of the liberator and joy-bringer; thus I taught you, my friends. But now learn this too: the will itself is still a prisoner. Willing liberates; but what is it that puts even the liberator himself in fetters? 'It was'—that is the name of the will's gnashing of teeth and most secret melancholy. Powerless against what has been done, he is an angry spectator of all that is past. The will cannot will backwards; and that he cannot break time and time's covetousness, that is the will's loneliest melancholy.

"Willing liberates; what means does the will devise for himself to get rid of his melancholy and to mock his dungeon? Alas, every prisoner becomes a fool; and the imprisoned will redeems himself foolishly. That time does not run backwards, that is his wrath; 'that which was' is the name of the stone he cannot move. And so he moves stones out of wrath and displeasure, and he wreaks revenge on whatever does not feel wrath and displeasure as he does. Thus the will, the liberator, took to hurting; and on all who can suffer he wreaks revenge for his inability to go backwards. This, indeed this alone, is what *revenge* is: the will's ill will against time and its 'it was.' "

(pp. 251–52)

Since the will operates in the temporal world and since time moves only in one direction, the will can never really get at the past. The will's titanic, foredoomed struggle to repeat the past and alter it is simply the revenge that the will seeks for its own impotence in the face of what Nietzsche calls the "it was" of time. Nietzsche connects this revenge against time with the envy that a son feels for his father. In a passage on the equality of men, Zarathustra says,

"What justice means to us is precisely that the world be filled with the storms of our revenge"—thus they speak to each other. "We shall wreak vengeance and abuse on all whose equals we are not"—thus do the tarantula-hearts vow. "And 'will to equality' shall henceforth be the name of virtue; and against all that has power we want to raise our clamor!"

You preachers of equality, the tyrannomania of impotence clamors thus out of you for equality: your most secret ambitions to be tyrants thus shroud themselves in words of virtue. Aggrieved conceit, repressed envy—perhaps the conceit and envy of your fathers—erupt from you as a flame and as the frenzy of revenge.

What was silent in the father speaks in the son; and often I found the son the unveiled secret of the father.

They are like enthusiasts, yet it is not the heart that fires them—but revenge.   (p. 212)

Clearly, the doctrine of the equality of men is at odds with the patriarchal principle that fathers are inherently superior to sons, for obviously the doctrine of equality is the doctrine of a son. The son, finding himself powerless in relation to the father, yet desiring power, admits that mastery inheres in the role of the father but disputes the criteria that determine who occupies that role. The doctrine of the son is simply the doctrine of the son's equality of opportunity to assume the role of the father through a combat with the father that will show who is the better man. But that doctrine of equality the father must reject, for from the father's point of view the authority which he holds as the father is not open to dispute; it is not subject to trial by combat because that authority is not something that the father could ever lose, it is not accidental to fatherhood, it inheres in its very nature. That authority is something which has been irrevocably conferred on the father by the very nature of time, for the essence of the authority, the mastery, that a father has over his son is simply priority in time—the fact that in time the father always comes first. And against that patriarchal authority whose basis is priority in time, the son's will is impotent, for the will cannot move backwards in time, it cannot alter the past. In his rivalry with the father for the love of the mother, the son realizes that no matter how much the mother loves him, she loved the father *first*. Indeed, the son carries with him in the very fact of his own existence inescapable proof that she loved the father first and that the son comes second. Any power that the son has, he has not in his own right, but by inheritance from the father, by being a copy of the father, who has supreme authority because he comes first, who has power because of the very nature of time. No wonder, then, that the envy of the son for the father takes the form of the revenge against time.

When Nietzsche speaks of the "envy of your fathers,"

the phrase is intentionally ambiguous, for it is not just the envy that a son feels for his father, it is as well the envy that the son inherits from his father, who was himself a son once. The targets of Sutpen's revenge for the affront that he suffered as a boy are the artificial advantages of high birth and inherited wealth (or the artificial disadvantages of low birth and inherited poverty), that is, generation and patrimony—those modes of the son's dependence on his father, those expressions of the fact that whatever the son is or has, he has received from his father and holds at the sufferance of the father. But again we confront the paradox of Sutpen's solution—that he seeks revenge on the artificial standards that make one man inferior to another, not by trying to do away with those standards, but rather by founding a dynasty, by establishing that same artificial standard of superiority for his family and bequeathing it to his son. Put in that way, the paradox seems clearer: it is the paradox that sons turn into fathers by trying to forget (albeit unsuccessfully) that they were once sons. When Sutpen began his quest for revenge, his quest to supplant the father, his attitude was that of a son: that the authority and power of the father obey the rule of power, that they are subject to a trial by combat, and if the son's will proves the stronger, belong to the son not as a gift or inheritance (which would entail his dependence on the father) but as a right, a mark of his independence. Yet (and here is the paradoxical shift) the proof of the son's success in his attempt to become the father will be the son's denial of the attitude of the son (the rule of power) in favor of the attitude of the father. The proof that Sutpen has achieved his revenge, that he has become the father, will be his affirmation that the authority and power of the father obey not the rule of power but the rule of authority, that is, that they are not subject to dispute or trial by combat since they belong irrevocably to the father through priority in time, that to oppose the father is to oppose time, that authority and power cannot be taken from the father by the son but can only be given as a gift or inheritance by the father to the son. We see why Sutpen's revenge requires that he found a dynasty, for the proof that he has succeeded in becoming the father will finally be achieved only when he bequeaths his authority and power to his son as an inheritance (a gift, not a right), thereby establishing the son's dependence on his father and thus the father's mastery. That proof, of course, Sutpen never achieves, though he dies trying. His is the paradoxical fate of one who tries to seize authority and power by one rule and then hold them by another, the fate of a man who wants to be God. Or we could say, shifting the focus slightly, that Sutpen sets out to vindicate the right of every poor white boy to an equal opportunity to become the rich planter, but that once he has vindicated that right by becoming the rich planter, he immediately denies that same right to black boys, specifically, to his black son Charles Bon. We can also see why Faulkner equated Sutpen's attempt to establish that one man cannot be inferior to another through artificial standards or circumstances with his attempt to prove that man is immortal, for if the former attempt aims at toppling that traditional power of the father over the son's life that is implicit in the inherited advantages of position and wealth (or the inherited disadvantages of poverty and lack of position), and if that aim involves the son's challenging that authority of the father whose basis is priority in time so that the son's will directly opposes itself to the nature of time, then that aim can be successful only if the son is able to free himself from the grip of time, only if man can free himself from time's final sanction—death, that inevitable castration of the son by Father Time—only if man can become immortal.

When Sutpen returns from the Civil War to find one son dead and the other gone, he starts over a third time in his design to found a dynasty, to get the son who will inherit his land and thereby prove, through his dependence, that Sutpen has succeeded in his quest to be the son who seized the power of the father and then, as the father, kept that power from being seized by his own son in turn. For Sutpen can only prove that he is a better man than his father if he proves that he is a better man than his son, since Sutpen's father would have been defeated by his son in that very act. In Sutpen's final attempt to achieve his design, the battle against time receives its most explicit statement: "He was home again where his problem now was haste, passing time, the need to hurry. *He was not concerned,* Mr. Compson said, *about the courage and the will, nor even about the shrewdness now. He was not for one moment concerned about his ability to start the third time. All that he was concerned about was the possibility that he might not have time sufficient to do it in, regain his lost ground in*" (p. 278). But then, "*he realized that there was more in his problem than just lack of time, that the problem contained some super-distillation of this lack: that he was now past sixty and that possibly he could get but one more son, had at best but one more son in his loins, as the old cannon might know when it had just one more shot in its corporeality*" (p. 279). The problem is not just too little time; it is also the physical impotence that time brings, a physical impotence symbolic of Sutpen's "old impotent logic" (p. 279), of the impotence of the son's will in the face of the "it was" of time. Rosa says that when Sutpen gave her her dead sister's wedding ring as a sign of their engagement it was "as though in the restoration of that ring to a living finger he had turned all time back twenty years and stopped it, froze it" (p. 165).

Sutpen's concern that he might be able to get only one

more son leads him to suggest to Rosa that they try it first, and if the child is a male, that they marry. That suggestion drives Rosa from Sutpen's home and leads Sutpen to choose for his partner in the last effort to accomplish his design the only other available woman on his land, Milly Jones, the granddaughter of the poor-white Wash Jones, and that choice brings Sutpen to the final repetition of the traumatic affront. In fact, Sutpen had reenacted that affront from the very start of his relationship with Wash Jones, never allowing Jones to approach the front of the mansion. When Sutpen seduces Milly and when her child is a daughter rather than the required son, Sutpen rejects mother and child as he had rejected his first wife and child. He tells Milly that if she were a mare he could give her a decent stall in his stable—a remark that Wash Jones overhears and that makes Jones realize for the first time Sutpen's attitude toward him and his family. Jones confronts the seducer of his granddaughter and kills him with a scythe. The irony of Sutpen's final repetition of the affront is that, though he delivers the affront in the role of a father rejecting his child, in order to get that child he had to assume the role of the son, he had to become the seducer; and Wash Jones, the poor white who had been the object of Sutpen's paternalism, now assumes the role of outraged father in relation to Sutpen. It is emblematic of the fate of the son in his battle against time that Sutpen, struggling in his old age to achieve his revenge, must again become the son and in that role be struck down by an old man with a scythe.

Certainly, the manner of Sutpen's death suggests the iconography of Father Time—that figure of an old man armed with a scythe or sickle for whom all flesh is grass. And it is more than likely that Faulkner intends that this allusion to the figure of Father Time should remind us of the genesis of that figure in mythology, for Father Time is an ancient conflation, based in part on a similarity of names, of two figures—Kronos, Zeus's father, and Chronos, the personification of Time. As we know, that conflation ultimately led to the attachment of at least two of the major legends of Kronos to Father Time—first, that Kronos is a son who castrated his father, Ouranos, and was in turn castrated by his own son Zeus, and second, that Kronos is a father who devours his children. Discussing the evolution of the iconography of Father Time, the art historian Erwin Panofsky notes that the learned writers of the fourth and fifth centuries A. D. began to provide the old figure of Kronos/Saturn with new attributes and "reinterpreted the original features of his image as symbols of time. His sickle, traditionally explained either as an agricultural symbol or as the instrument of castration, came to be interpreted as a symbol of *tempora quae sicut falx in se recurrent;* and the mythical tale that he had devoured his children was said to signify that Time, who had already been termed 'sharp-toothed' by Simonides and *edax rerum* by Ovid, devours whatever he has created."[16]

In discussing the nature of time, Nietzsche alludes to both the legends of Kronos that became associated with Father Time. In the passage from *Zarathustra* in which he talks about the revenge against time, he mentions "this law of time that it must devour its children" (p. 252), and in *Philosophy in the Tragic Age of the Greeks* he says, "As Heraclitus sees time, so does Schopenhauer. He repeatedly said of it that every moment in it exists only insofar as it has just consumed the preceding one, its father, and then is immediately consumed likewise."[17] One might say that the struggle between the father and the son inevitably turns into a dispute about the nature of time, not just because the authority of the father is based on priority in time, but because the essence of time is that in the discontinuous, passing moment it is experienced as a problem of the endless displacement of the generator by the generated, while in the continuity of the memory trace it is experienced as a problem of the endless destruction of the generated by the generator. In this last sense, we refer not just to the experience that what is generated in and by time is as well consumed in and by time, but also to the experience that the price which the generative moment exacts for its displacement into the past is a castration of the present through memory. In tropes such as "the golden age," "the lost world," "the good old days," the past convicts the present of inadequacy through lack of priority, lack of originality, since to be a copy is to be a diminution, because the running on of time is a running down, because to come after is to be fated to repeat the life of another rather than to live one's own.

The struggle between Quentin and his father that runs through the stream-of-consciousness narrative of Quentin's last day is primarily a dispute about time. The narrative begins with Quentin's waking in the morning ("I was in time again," p. 95) to the ticking of his grandfather's watch, the watch that his father had presented to him, saying, "I give it to you not that you may remember time, but that you may forget it now and then for a moment and not spend all your breath trying to conquer it" (p. 95). Quentin twists the hands off his grandfather's watch on the morning of the day when he forever frees himself and his posterity from the cycles of time and generation. When Quentin is out walking that morning, he passes the shopwindow of a watch store and turns away so as not to see what time it is, but there is a clock on a building and Quentin sees the time in spite of himself: he says, "I thought about how, when you dont want to do a thing, your body will try to trick you into doing it, sort of unawares" (p. 102). And that, of course, is precisely Quentin's sense of time—that it is a compulsion, a fate. For his father has told him that a man is the sum of his misfortunes and that time is his misfortune like "a gull on an invisible wire attached through space dragged" (p. 123). In his struggle against his father and thus against time, Quentin must confront the same problem that he faces in the story of Sutpen and his sons—whether a man's father is his fate. In *Absalom* when Shreve begins to sound like Quentin's father, Quentin thinks, *"Am I going to have to have to hear it all again. . . . I am going to have to hear it all over again I am already hearing it all over again I am listening to it all over again I shall have to never listen to anything else but this again forever so apparently not only a man never outlives his father but not even his friends and acquaintances do"* (p. 277).

When Quentin demands that his father act against the seducer Dalton Ames, Quentin, by taking this initiative, is in effect trying to supplant his father, to seize his authority. But Quentin's father refuses to act, and the sense of Mr. Compson's refusal is that Quentin cannot seize his father's authority because there is no authority to seize. Quentin's alcoholic, nihilistic father presents himself as an emasculated son, ruined by General Compson's failure. Mr. Compson psychologically castrates Quentin by confronting him with a father figure, a model for manhood, who is himself a castrated son. Mr. Compson possesses no authority that Quentin could seize because what Mr. Compson inherited from the General was not power but impotence. If Quentin is a son struggling in the grip of Father Time, so is his father. And it is exactly that argument that Mr. Compson uses against Quentin. When Quentin demands that they act against the seducer, Mr. Compson answers in essence, "Do you realize how many times this has happened before and how many times it will happen again? You are seeking a once-and-for-all solution to this problem, but there are no once-and-for-all solutions. One has no force, no authority to act in this matter because one has no originality. The very repetitive nature of time precludes the existence of originality within its cycles. You cannot be the father because I am not the father—only Time is the father." When Quentin demands that they avenge Candace's virginity, his father replies, "Women are never virgins. Purity is a negative state and therefore contrary to nature. It's nature is hurting you not Caddy and I said That's just words and he said So is virginity and I said you dont know. You cant know and he said Yes. On the instant when we come to realise that tragedy is second-hand" (p. 135). In essence Quentin's father says, "We cannot act because there exists no virginity to avenge and because there exists no authority by which we could avenge since we have no originality. We are second-hand. You are a copy of a copy. To you, a son who has only been a son, it might seem that a father has authority because he comes first, but to one who has been both a father and a son, it is clear that to come before is not necessarily to come first, that priority is not necessarily originality. My fate was determined by my father as your fate is determined by yours." Quentin's attempt to avenge his sister's lost virginity (proving thereby that it had once existed) and maintain the family honor is an attempt to maintain the possibility of "virginity" in a larger sense, the possibility of the existence of a virgin space within which one can still be first, within which one can have authority through originality, a virgin space like that Mississippi wilderness into which the first Compson (Jason Lycurgus I) rode in 1811 to seize the land later known as the Compson Domain, the land "fit to breed princes, states-men and generals and bishops, to avenge the dispossessed Compsons from Culloden and Carolina and Kentucky" (p. 7), just as Sutpen came to Mississippi to get land and found a dynasty that would avenge the dispossessed Sutpens of West Virginia. In a letter to Malcolm Cowley, Faulkner said that Quentin regarded Sutpen as "origin-less."[18] Which is to say, that being without origin, Sutpen tries to become his own origin, his own father, an attempt implicit in the very act of choosing a father figure to replace his real father. When Quentin tells the story of the Sutpens in *Absalom*, he is not just telling his own personal story, he is telling the story of the Compson family as well.

The event that destroyed Sutpen's attempt to found a dynasty is the same event that began the decline of the Compson family—the Civil War closed off the virgin space and the time of origins, so that the antebellum South became in the minds of postwar Southerners that debili-tating "golden age and lost world" in comparison with which the present is inadequate. The decline of the Comp-sons began with General Compson "who failed at Shiloh in '62 and failed again though not so badly at Resaca in '64, who put the first mortgage on the still intact square mile to a New England carpetbagger in '66, after the old town had been burned by the Federal General Smith and the new little town, in time to be populated mainly by the descendants not of Compsons but of Snopeses, had begun to encroach and then nibble at and into it as the failed brigadier spent the next forty years selling fragments of it off to keep up the mortgage on the remainder" (p. 7). The last of the Compson Domain is sold by Quentin's father to send Quentin to Harvard.

Mr. Compson's denial of the existence of an authority by which he could act necessarily entails his denial of virginity, for there is no possibility of that originality from which authority springs if there is no virgin space within which one can be first. And for the same reason Quentin's obsession with Candace's loss of virginity is necessarily an obsession with his own impotence, since the absence of the virgin space renders him powerless. When Mr. Compson refuses to act against Dalton Ames, Quentin tries to force him to take some action by claiming that he and Candace have committed incest—that primal affront to the authority of the father. But where there is no authority there can be no affront, and where the father feels his own inherited impotence, he cannot believe that his son has power. Mr. Compson tells Quentin that he doesn't believe that he and Candace committed incest, and Quentin says, "If we could have just done something so dreadful and Father said That's sad too, people cannot do anything that dreadful they cannot do anything very dreadful at all they cannot even remember tomorrow what seemed dreadful today and I said, You can shirk all things and he said, Ah can you" (p. 99). Since Mr. Compson believes that man is helpless in the grip of time, that everything is fated, there is no question of shirking or not shirking, for there is no question of willing. In discussing the revenge against time, Nietzsche speaks of those preachers of despair who say, "Alas, the stone *It was* cannot be moved" (p. 252), and Mr. Compson's last words in Quentin's narrative are "was the saddest word of all there is nothing else in the world its not despair until time its not even time until it was" (p. 197).

Is there no virgin space in which one can be first, in which one can have authority through originality? This is the question that Quentin must face in trying to decide whether his father is right, whether he is doomed to be an impotent failure like his father and grandfather. And it is in light of this question that we can gain an insight into Quentin's act of narration in *Absalom,* for what is at work in Quentin's struggle to bring the story of the Sutpens under control is the question of whether narration itself constitutes a space in which one can be original, whether an "author" possesses "authority," whether that repetition which in life Quentin has experienced as a compulsive fate

113

can be transformed in narration, through an act of the will, into a power, a mastery of time. Indeed, Rosa Coldfield suggests to Quentin when she first involves him in the story of the Sutpens that becoming an author represents an alternative to repeating his father's life in the decayed world of the postwar South: " 'Because you are going away to attend the college at Harvard they tell me,' Miss Coldfield said. 'So I dont imagine you will ever come back here and settle down as a country lawyer in a little town like Jefferson, since Northern people have already seen to it that there is little left in the South for a young man. So maybe you will enter the literary profession as so many Southern gentlemen and gentlewomen too are doing now and maybe some day you will remember this and write about it' " (pp. 9–10). We noted earlier that the dialogue between Quentin and his father about virginity that runs through the first part of *Absalom* appears to be a continuation of their discussions of Candace's loss of virginity and Quentin's inability to lose his virginity contained in Quentin's section of *The Sound and the Fury*. Thus, the struggle between father and son that marked their dialogue in *The Sound and the Fury* is continued in their narration of *Absalom*. For Quentin, the act of narrating Sutpen's story, of bringing that story under authorial control, becomes a struggle in which he tries to best his father, a struggle to seize "authority" by achieving temporal priority to his father in the narrative act. At the beginning of the novel, Quentin is a passive narrator. The story seems to choose him. Rosa involves him in the narrative against his will, and he spends the first half of the book listening to Rosa and his father tell what they know or surmise. But in the second half, when he and Shreve begin their imaginative reconstruction of the story, Quentin seems to move from a passive role to an active role in the narrative repetition of the past.

So far I have mainly discussed the experience of repetition as a compulsion, as a fate, using Freud's analysis of the mechanism of the repetition compulsion in *Beyond the Pleasure Principle* as the basis for my remarks. But in that same text, Freud also examines the experience of repetition as a power—repetition as a means of achieving mastery. He points out that in children's play an event that the child originally experienced as something unpleasant will be repeated and now experienced as a source of pleasure, as a game. He describes the game of *fort/da* that he had observed being played by a little boy of one and a half. The infant would throw away a toy and as he did, utter a sound that Freud took to be the German word *fort*— "gone." The child would then recover the toy and say the word *da*—"there." Freud surmised that the child had created a game by which he had mastered the traumatic event of seeing his mother leave him and into which he had incorporated the joyful event of her return. Freud points out that the mechanism of this game in which one actively repeats an unpleasant occurrence as a source of pleasure can be interpreted in various ways. First of all, he remarks that at the outset the child "was in a *passive* situation—he was overpowered by the experience; but, by repeating it, unpleasurable though it was, as a game, he took on an *active* part. These efforts might be put down to an instinct for mastery that was acting independently of whether the memory was in itself pleasurable or not. But still another interpretation may be attempted. Throwing away the object so that it was 'gone' might satisfy an impulse of the child's, which was suppressed in his actual life, to revenge himself on his mother for going away from him. In that case it would have a defiant meaning: 'All right, then, go away! I don't need you. I'm sending you away myself'" (S.E., 18:16).

Freud makes a further point about the nature of children's games that has a direct bearing on our interest in the son's effort to become his father: ". . . it is obvious that all their play is influenced by a wish that dominates them the whole time—the wish to be grown-up and to be able to do what grown-up people do. It can also be observed that the unpleasurable nature of an experience does not always unsuit it for play. If the doctor looks down a child's throat or carries out some small operation on him, we may be quite sure that these frightening experiences will be the subject of the next game; but we must not in that connection overlook the fact that there is a yield of pleasure from another source. As the child passes over from the passivity of the experience to the activity of the game, he hands on the disagreeable experience to one of his playmates and in this way revenges himself on a substitute" (S.E., 18:17). Significantly, Freud refers to this mastery through repetition as "revenge," and his remarks suggest that this revenge has two major elements—repetition and reversal. In the game of *fort/da* the child repeats the traumatic situation but reverses the roles. Instead of passively suffering rejection when his mother leaves, he actively rejects her by symbolically sending her away. And in the other case, the child repeats the unpleasant incident that he experienced but now inflicts on a playmate, on a substitute, what was formerly inflicted on him.

In this mechanism of a repetition in which the active and passive roles are reversed, we have the very essence of revenge. But we must distinguish between two different situations: in the ideal situation, the revenge is inflicted on the same person who originally delivered the affront—the person who was originally active is now forced to assume the passive role in the same scenario; in the other situation, the revenge is inflicted on a substitute. This second situation sheds light on Sutpen's attempt to master the traumatic affront that he suffered as a boy from the man who became his surrogate father, to master it by repeating that affront in reverse, inflicting it on his own son Charles Bon. This scenario of revenge on a substitute sheds light as well on the connection between repetition and the fantasy of the reversal of generations and on the psychological mechanism of generation itself. The primal affront that the son suffers at the hands of the father and for which the son seeks revenge throughout his life is the very fact of being a son—of being the generated in relation to the generator, the passive in relation to the active, the effect in relation to the cause. He seeks revenge on his father for the generation of an existence which the son, in relation to the father, must always experience as a dependency. But if revenge involves a repetition in which the active and passive roles are reversed, then the very nature of time precludes the son's taking revenge on his father, for since time is irreversible, the son can never really effect that reversal by which he would become his father's father. The son's only alternative is to take revenge on a substitute—that is, to become a father himself and thus repeat the generative situation as a reversal in which he now inflicts on his own son, who is a substitute for the grandfather, the affront of being a son, that affront that the father had previously suffered from his own father. We can see now why Nietzsche, in connecting the revenge against time with the "envy of your fathers" (that envy which the son feels for his father and which the son has inherited from his father, who was himself a son), says, "What was silent in the father speaks in the son; and often I found the son the unveiled secret of the father."

When Sutpen takes revenge on a substitute for the affront that he received as a boy, he takes revenge not just on Charles Bon but on Henry as well. For if the primal affront is the very fact of being a son, then acknowledgment and rejection, inheritance and disinheritance are simply the positive and negative modes of delivering the affront of the son's dependency on the father. Further, we can see the centrality of the notion of revenge on a substitute to the figure of the double. The brother avenger and the brother seducer are, as I have pointed out, substitutes for the father and the son in the Oedipal triangle, but if the revenge which the father inflicts on the son is a substitute for the revenge that the father wishes to inflict on his own father, then the brother avenger's killing of the brother seducer becomes a double action: the avenger's murder of the seducer (son) is a symbolic substitute for the seducer's murder of the avenger (father). This adds another dimension to Henry's murder of Bon: Henry is the younger brother and Bon the older, and the killing of the older brother by the younger is a common substitute for the murder of the father by the son. Thus, when Henry kills Bon, he is the father-surrogate killing the son, but since Henry, like Bon, is also in love with their sister Judith, he is as well the younger brother (son) killing the older brother who symbolizes the father, the father who is the rival for the mother and who punishes incest between brother and sister, son and mother. The multiple, reversible character of these relationships is only what we would expect in a closed system like the Oedipal triangle, and it is precisely this multiple, reversible character that gives the Oedipal triangle a charge of emotional energy that becomes overpowering as it cycles and builds. The very mechanism of doubling is an embodiment of that revenge on a substitute which we find in generation, for it is the threat from the father in the castration fear that fixes the son in that secondary narcissism from which the figure of the double as ambivalent Other springs. When the bright self (the ego influenced by the superego) kills the dark self (the ego influenced by the unconscious), we have in this murder of the son as related to his mother by the son as related to his father the reversed repetition of that repressed desire which the son felt when he first desired his mother and was faced with the threat of castration—the desire of the son to murder his father. For the psychologically impotent son who cannot have a child, the act of generating a double is his equivalent of that revenge on the father through a substitute which the potent son seeks by the act of generating a son.

Keeping in mind this notion of revenge on a substitute, we can now understand how Quentin's act of narration in *Absalom* is an attempt to seize his father's authority by gaining temporal priority. In the struggle with his father, Quentin will prove that he is a better man by being a better narrator—he will assume the authority of an author because his father does not know the whole story, does not know the true reason for Bon's murder, while Quentin does. Instead of listening passively while his father talks, Quentin will assume the active role, and his father will listen while Quentin talks. And the basis of Quentin's authority to tell the story to his father is that Quentin, by a journey into the dark, womblike Sutpen mansion, a journey back into the past, has learned more about events that occurred before he was born than either his father or grandfather knew:

> "Your father," Shreve said. "He seems to have got an awful lot of delayed information awful quick, after having waited forty-five years. If he knew all this, what was his reason for telling you that the trouble between Henry and Bon was the octoroon woman?"
> "He didn't know it then. Grandfather didn't tell him all of it either, like Sutpen never told Grandfather quite all of it."
> "Then who did tell him?"
> "I did." Quentin did not move, did not look up while Shreve watched him. "The day after we—after that night when we—"
> "Oh," Shreve said. "After you and the old aunt. I see. Go on. . . ." (p. 266)

In terms of the narrative act, Quentin achieves temporal priority over his father, and within the narrative Quentin takes revenge against his father, against time, through a substitute—his roommate Shreve. As Quentin had to listen to his father tell the story in the first half of the novel, so in the second half Shreve must listen while Quentin tells the story. But what begins as Shreve listening to Quentin talk soon turns into a struggle between them for control of the narration with Shreve frequently interrupting Quentin to say, "Let me tell it now." That struggle, which is a repetition in reverse of the struggle between Mr. Compson and Quentin, makes Quentin realize the truth of his father's argument in *The Sound and the Fury*—that priority is not necessarily originality, that to come before is not necessarily to come first. For Quentin realizes that by taking revenge against his father through a substitute, by assuming the role of active teller (father) and making Shreve be the passive listener (son), he thereby passes on to Shreve the affront of sonship, the affront of dependency, and thus ensures that Shreve will try to take revenge on him by seizing "authority," by taking control of the narrative. What Quentin realizes is that generation as revenge on a substitute is an endless cycle of reversibility in which revenge only means passing on the affront to another who, seeking revenge in turn, passes on the affront, so that the affront and the revenge are self-perpetuating. Indeed, the word "revenge," as opposed to the word "vengeance," suggests this self-perpetuating quality—*re-*, again + *venger*, to take vengeance—to take vengeance again and again and again, because the very taking of revenge is the passing on of an affront that must be revenged. We might note in this regard that the repetition compulsion is itself a form of revenge through a substitute. If, as Freud says, the act of repression always results in the return of the repressed, that is, if repression endows the repressed material with the repetition compulsion, and if the repressed can return only by a displacement, can slip through the ego's defenses only by a substitution in which the same is reconstituted as different, then the repetition compulsion is a revenge through substitution, wherein the repressed takes revenge on the ego for that act of will by which the repressed material was rejected, takes revenge by a repetition in reverse, by a return of the repressed that is experienced as a compulsive overruling of the will, a rendering passive of the will by the unwilled return of that very material which the will had previously tried to render passive by repressing it. As revenge on a substitute is a self-perpetuating cycle of affront and revenge, so too repression, return of the repressed, re-repression, and re-return are self-perpetuating. In his work on compulsion neurosis, the psychoanalyst Wilhelm Stekel discusses the case of a patient who reenacted the Oedipal struggle with his father through the scenario of an incestuous attachment to his sister and a struggle with his brother. Stekel notes that the patient's compulsive-repetitive acts were a "correction of the past," and he links this impulse to correct the past to that "unquenchable thirst for revenge so characteristic of compulsion neurotics."[19] At one point in the analysis, the patient describes his illness as an "originality neurosis" (p. 449).

In his narrative struggle with Shreve, Quentin directly experiences the cyclic reversibility involved in revenge on a substitute—he experiences the maddening paradox of generation in time. At the beginning of their narrative, Quentin talks and Shreve listens, and in their imaginative reenactment of the story of the Sutpens, Quentin identifies with Henry, the father-surrogate, and Shreve identifies with Charles Bon, the son, the outsider. But as the roles of brother avenger and brother seducer are reversible (precisely because the roles for which they are substitutes—

father and son—are reversible through substitution), so Quentin and Shreve begin to alternate in their identifications with Henry and Bon, and Quentin finds that Shreve is narrating and that he (Quentin) is listening and that Shreve sounds like Quentin's father. Quentin not only learns that *"a man never outlives his father"* and that he is going to have to listen to this same story over and over again for the rest of his life, but he realizes as well that in their narration he and Shreve *"are both Father"*—*"Maybe nothing ever happens once and is finished. . . . Yes, we are both Father. Or maybe Father and I are both Shreve, maybe it took Father and me both to make Shreve or Shreve and me both to make Father or maybe Thomas Sutpen to make all of us."* In terms of a generative sequence of narrators, Mr. Compson, Quentin, and Shreve are father, son, and grandson (reincarnation of the father). Confronting that cyclic reversibility, Quentin realizes that if sons seek revenge on their fathers for the affront of sonship by a repetition in reverse, if they seek to supplant their fathers, then the very fathers whom the sons wish to become are themselves nothing but sons who had sons in order to take that same revenge on their own fathers. Generation as revenge against the father, as revenge against time, is a circular labyrinth; it only establishes time's mastery all the more, for generation establishes the rule that a man never outlives his father, simply because a man's son will be the reincarnation of that father. And if for Quentin the act of narration is an analogue of this revenge on a substitute, then narration does not achieve mastery over time; rather, it traps the narrator more surely within the coils of time. What Quentin realizes is that the solution he seeks must be one that frees him alike from time and generation, from fate and revenge: he must die childless, he must free himself from time without having passed on the self-perpetuating affront of sonship. What

Quentin seeks is a once-and-for-all solution, a non-temporal, an eternal solution. When Mr. Compson refuses to believe that Quentin and Candace have committed incest and simply says, "we must just stay awake and see evil done for a little while its not always," Quentin replies, "it doesnt have to be even that long for a man of courage":

> and he do you consider that courage and i yes sir dont you and he every man is the arbiter of his own virtues whether or not you consider it courageous is of more importance than the act itself than any act otherwise you could not be in earnest. . . . but you are still blind to what is in yourself to that part of general truth the sequence of natural events and their causes which shadows every mans brow even benjys you are not thinking of finitude you are contemplating an apotheosis in which a temporary state of mind will become symmetrical above the flesh and aware both of itself and of the flesh it will not quite discard you will not even be dead and i temporary . . . (p. 196)

Of Quentin's search for an eternal solution Faulkner says, in the appendix to *The Sound and the Fury,* that as Quentin "loved not his sister's body but some concept of Compson honor precariously and (he knew well) only temporarily supported by the minute fragile membrane of her maidenhead," so he "loved not the idea of incest which he would not commit, but some presbyterian concept of its eternal punishment: he, not God, could by that means cast himself and his sister both into hell, where he could guard her forever and keep her forevermore intact amid the eternal fires" (p. 9).

From Mr. Compson's statement and from Faulkner's, we can abstract the elements of the solution that Quentin seeks. First, it will be an action that transforms the temporal into the eternal: "a temporary state of mind will become symmetrical above the flesh"; a temporary virginity will, by an eternal punishment, be rendered "forevermore intact." Second, the action, a death, will be a punishment in which the one who punishes and the one punished will be the same, it will be self-inflicted—a suicide. Quentin, not God, will cast himself and his sister into the eternal fires, cast not just himself but Candace as well, so that Quentin's suicide will also be a symbolic incest (a return to the waters of birth, to the womb) that maintains not just Candace's virginity but Quentin's too. Third, this action, this death, will be an "apotheosis," a deification. And finally, in this death whereby "a temporary state of mind will become symmetrical above the flesh and aware both of itself and of the flesh it will not quite discard," Quentin "will not even be dead." Considering these elements, we can see who the model is for Quentin's solution and why Faulkner places Quentin's suicide in the context of Christ's passion—that self-sacrifice of the son to satisfy the justice of the father, that active willing of passivity as a self-inflicted revenge. When Quentin tries to clean the blood off his clothes from the fight with Gerald Bland, he thinks, "Maybe a pattern of blood he could call that the one Christ was wearing" (p. 190).

As the central enigmatic event in *Absalom* is Henry's murder of Bon, so its equivalent in *The Sound and the Fury* is Quentin's suicide, and the structures of both books, with their multiple perspectives in narration, point up the fact that the significance of these events is irreducibly ambiguous. Thus, Henry's murder of Bon can be seen as the killing of the son by the father, but it can also be seen as the killing of the father by the son. And what of Quentin's suicide—is it finally an act of nihilistic despair, or a last desperate effort of the will to assert its mastery over time, or is it an active willing of passivity that, as a distorted image of Christ's death, is meant to be "redemptive" of Quentin's unborn, and now never to be born, progeny, who have been freed once and for all from mortality and from the spirit of revenge that is generation?

Certainly, by putting Quentin's suicide in the context of Christ's death, Faulkner makes the significance of Quentin's act more ambiguous, but this strategy works in two directions, for it also points up the irreducible ambiguities in the significance of Christ's death itself. With characters like Quentin and Joe Christmas, Faulkner uses the context of Christ's death to raise questions about the actions of these characters, and he uses their actions to question the meaning of the Christ role. His most explicit questioning of the ambiguous significance of Christ's redemptive act occurs in *A Fable* (1954), where Christ's passion and death are reenacted during the First World War in that struggle between the old general and the corporal, between the father who has supreme authority and the illegitimate son who is under a sentence of death.

Viewing Quentin's suicide in the context of Christ's willing sacrifice of his own life, we find in the very concept of sacrifice a link that joins those two triadic structures whose interplay shapes *The Sound and the Fury* and *Absalom, Absalom!*—the Oedipal triangle (father, mother, son) and the three generations of patrilinearity (grandfather, father, son, or father, son, grandson). The psychoanalyst Guy Rosolato has discussed the way in which the fantasy of the murder of the father sustains the movement from the closed Oedipal triangle to the indefinite linearity of generation (three generations of men) within the religious structure of sacrifice. Rosolato argues that all sacrifice is a putting to death of the father through the victim, and he discusses the sacrifices of Isaac and Jesus as structures in which the lethal confrontation between the father and the son in the Oedipal triangle is transformed into an alliance between the father and the son by the substitution of another male figure for the female figure in the triad. This transformation involves a mutation in the image of the father. What Rosolato calls the Idealized Father (the father of prehistoric times, "ferocious, jealous, all-powerful, whose control over others and over his sons is unlimited, a protector in exchange for total submission, an absolute master of the laws of which he is the sole origin"[20]) is a figure whose relationship with the son follows the rule of two, that is, there exist only two alternatives in the son's relationship with his father—all or nothing, victory or defeat. The relationship of the son to the Idealized Father is a fight to the death in which, from the son's point of view, the Idealized Father must become the Murdered Father. Sacrifice transforms this situation by means of the rule of three, the rule of mediation. Through the use of a substitute, the murder of the father can be accomplished in an indirect, in a symbolic manner, so that the figure of the Dead Father takes the place of the figure of the Murdered Father. Through the symbolic substitution inherent in the mediating sacrifice, the Oedipal situation is surmounted, and one passes into the patrilineal situation.

Discussing the sacrifice of Isaac, Rosolato points out that in that covenant between God and Abraham which is to become the covenant between the father and the son, there exist two different times. First, a time of preparation (Gen. 17), in which the marks of that covenant are established, so that it is as if the Law were imposed in anteriority without the knowledge of either Abraham or Isaac. Thus, the father, Abraham, is not the origin of the law but must submit to it just like his son Isaac. There are three marks of the covenant between God and Abraham: in the name, in the flesh, and in the future promise. First, God changes Abram's name to Abraham as a sign of his nomination; second, God establishes circumcision as a visible sign of the agreement between God, Abraham, and his posterity; and finally, God promises Abraham and Sara a son in their old age. With the birth of Isaac, who bears the name designated by God and who is circumcised eight days after his birth according to God's command, the third masculine person is now present and the alliance between the father and the son can now supplant their conflict in the Oedipal triangle, an alliance between God and Abraham that the sacrifice of Isaac will "definitively confirm" (p. 65). In that sacrifice, God, Abraham, and Isaac are related as grandfather, father, and son, so that when Abraham raises the knife over Isaac it is the father threatening the son, but since the son is the reincorporation of the grandfather, it is also the son threatening the father, and at that moment Abraham realizes the principle on which the alliance is based—that the death wish against one's father means the death of one's son. When God suspends the sacrifice of Isaac, God, the Idealized Father, is transformed into the Dead Father, for God takes upon himself the death that would have been meted out to the son. The angel that stops Abraham from killing Isaac shows him the ram that will take the place of the son in the sacrifice—a substitution indicative of the fact that Isaac is himself a substitute. The ram will now take the place of God in the sacrifice, and by accepting this death, God, the Idealized Father (the sole origin of the law, the one to whom the law is responsible and who can abrogate it at will), is transformed into the Dead Father (one who is responsible *to* the law, one who is bound by a covenant).

When Abraham suspends the threat against his son, "he opts for a law: precisely that of an order, of a succession of generations in death" (p. 68). The law that Abraham accepts is that in time fathers die before their sons—as opposed to the law of the Idealized Father in the Oedipal triangle whereby sons die before their fathers. Abraham "accepts this succession, and refuses, what was possible for him, to destroy Isaac; he admits this new generation which he could have destroyed, repulsed or denied. He recognizes

Isaac" (p. 68). And the mark of that recognition is circumcision, the mark that the father has accepted his own death, has accepted his displacement, his succession by his son—the mark on the son's phallus that is a sign of the surmounting of the Oedipal castration threat. Isaac carries this mark of recognition as an "assurance that he (Isaac) will have in turn to experience a similar mutation and recognition" (p. 68). Abraham "accepts the fact that Isaac could harbor toward him the same death wish; he assumes that danger: circumcision is still there to testify to the surmounting; it is an assurance of his confidence in the identical progression by Isaac" (p. 68). Rosolato points out that the ram, Isaac's substitute in the sacrifice, is an animal with seminal connotations, and that in the sacrifice the ram represents a "partial object"—the penis. The destruction of the ram represents the father's renunciation of the phallic power in favor of his successor, his son, a renunciation that has its reward in the son's progeny. Thus, when Abraham returns from the sacrifice, he learns that children have been born in his absence, one of whom, Rebecca, will be Isaac's future wife.

Circumcision as a mark of recognition that the father confers on the son points up the fact that, in the alliance, paternity involves two acts: generation and acknowledgment. The very nature of birth makes it clear who the son's mother is, but the establishment of who the son's father is requires an act of acknowledgment—the father must "recognize" the child as his son. The substitutive, sacrificial ram considered as a partial object, as the penis, emphasizes the fact that the whole basis of the sacrificial structure is the intermediary third term, the substitute, the link. Like God's recognition of Abraham, Abraham's recognition of Isaac involves three marks of identification: circumcision (the visible marking of the penis), the conferring of a name, and the promise that Isaac will now have sons in turn. Thus, there is an equivalence established between the grandson, the penis, and the name as intermediary third terms linking the grandfather and the father (i.e., the father and the son), for the law of succession that Abraham accepts is also a law of transmission. The father's acceptance of his own death, of his succession by his son, his renunciation of the phallic power, is a transmission of that phallic power to his son, a transmission that requires identifying marks precisely because what is transmitted is not just the power to generate, but the power to generate *in a line descending from the father.* And that is why the religion that is established by God's covenant with Abraham (a covenant confirmed by Isaac's sacrifice) is a religion of patriarchs, a religion of genealogy. Rosolato points out that in the one, two, three order of succession of grandfather, father, son, the zero point is the death of the father, and he notes that the succession, the transmission in which the father dies while the name identified with the generative power is passed on and the phallic, linking power is reborn "corresponds to the act of symbolization where the thing 'dies' in order to be reborn with renewed vigor in the network of the laws of language" (p. 70).

Comparing the sacrifice of Isaac with that of Jesus, Rosolato notes that in the latter case the two triadic structures linked by the death of the father are apparent: the Oedipal triangle (the Holy Family) and the three masculine persons (the Trinity). Rosolato contends that though the elements of the Oedipal triangle are present in the Holy Family, the corresponding desires do not appear. Yet one must point out that the fecundation of Mary by God is a supplanting of Joseph in that triangle, and since Jesus, the son, is himself that God, then it is, in a sense, the son who has impregnated his own mother, and Jesus' birth, as befits the birth of a god, is incestuous. By an incestuous birth that somehow preserves the virginity of his mother, Jesus is born in order to sacrifice himself, thereby redeeming man from time and mortality by giving him eternal life. One thinks of Quentin's distorted solution in which a suicide, a putting to death of oneself, as a symbolic incest (the return to the womb) is meant to preserve eternally intact the temporary virginity of his sister and himself as well as free his descendants from time and death by freeing them from generation.

The numerous differences that exist between the sacrifices of Isaac and Jesus pertain to a shift in the concept of genealogy. The first and most notable difference is that in the sacrifice of Isaac the son is spared, while in the sacrifice of Jesus the son dies. With Isaac, the ram is substituted for the son, but with Jesus, the son is substituted for the paschal lamb (the male lamb that was killed so that the first-born would be spared). In the sacrifice of Jesus, the son offers himself up (Jesus is both the priest and the victim) as an atonement for man's offense against God. Thus, the son is put to death to satisfy the guilt that man feels for the Oedipal death wish against the father, but since the Son is the Father ("I and the Father are one," John 10:30), then "this sacrifice allows beneath the cover of the Son the representation of the Oedipal wishes (the death of the Father, or of God)" (p. 78). In the sacrifice of Jesus, the sovereignty of a single God is put to death: the death of the supreme authority of the Idealized Father. As in the sacrifice of Isaac where the Idealized Father, who is the origin of the law and who can abrogate the law at will, is transformed, by God's taking death upon himself, into the Dead Father, who is responsible to the law (the covenant between God and Abraham—the Old Law), so in the sacrifice of Jesus, the unlimited authority of the Idealized Father is slain by God's taking death upon himself, and the Dead Father is now responsible to the New Law. The Old Law is a law of genealogical succession and transmission:

the father accepts the law that fathers die before their sons. Thus, Isaac is spared, and the covenant is transmitted to and by his progeny. But in the sacrifice of Jesus, the only son dies, and here we find that shift in the concept of genealogy that is the principal difference between the sacrifices of Isaac and Jesus, for the sacrifice of the childless only son marks an "interruption of genealogy" (p. 82). Judaism is a religion of progeniture, a religion of continuity according to the blood, of physical descent from the fathers. Christianity, on the other hand, is a religion not of physical genealogy but of conversion. That interruption of genealogy represented by the sacrifice of Jesus is, in fact, a substitution of a spiritual genealogy for a physical genealogy. In the sacrifice of Isaac, the promise of the phallic power to generate new physical life in the face of death is transmitted by a line of physical descent from father to son, but with the sacrifice of Jesus, the promise is no longer one of a new physical life but of a new spiritual life. No longer is it a question of that physical immortality which one achieves through one's children; it is, rather, a question of personal immortality in an afterlife. And that future promise is transmitted not according to a physical genealogy but according to a spiritual one, and thus it is open through conversion to any man who accepts the sacrifice of Jesus. The priests who renew that sacrifice in the Mass are, like Jesus, celibate, partly as a sign that they have to do not with the generation of new physical life, a physical life that must always be in bondage to death, but with the generation of a new spiritual life—they are ghostly fathers.

This shift in the concept of genealogy between the sacrifices of Isaac and Jesus takes the form of a shift within the triadic structures pertaining to each sacrifice. In the triad of God, Abraham, and Isaac, the person who is to be sacrificed is the third member, Isaac, while in the triad

131

of the Father, the Son, and the Holy Spirit it is the second member, Jesus, who is sacrificed. By the substitution of the sacrificial ram for Isaac, the father can renounce the phallic power by the *physical* destruction of the ram and then have that power restored to *physical* life in Isaac and his progeny. But with the sacrifice of Jesus, we have the destruction of *physical* life in the Crucifixion and the restoration of *spiritual* life in the Resurrection. When Jesus, the second member of the triad, offers himself up, it is as if, in the earlier triad, Abraham had turned the sacrificial knife on himself, as if Abraham had become the sacrificial ram. And indeed, one of the titles of Jesus is the Lamb of God. In the Christian triad, that phallic, intermediary term whereby the power to generate spiritual life is transmitted is not the Son, who after his sacrifice returns to the Father, but the Holy Spirit, whom the Son asks the Father to send into the world: "And I will ask the Father, and he shall give you another Paraclete, that he may abide with you forever" (John 14:16). The very name "Paraclete"—advocate, pleader, intercessor, comforter—indicates the mediatory role of the third person, and his phallic power is shown in the spiritual fecundation that takes place at Pentecost, and in the phallic representation of the third person as a dove (Rosolato, pp. 79–80).

The procession of the persons within the Trinity sheds further light on the shift that takes place between the sacrifices of Isaac and Jesus. In terms of Christian dogma, the relationship between the Father and the Son is called *generation:* active on the part of the Father as *paternity;* passive on the part of the Son as *filiation.* The Father is without antecedents; he is his own origin. The procession of the Son is a procession of knowledge. The Father comprehends himself, that is, he knows himself insofar as he is knowable; he puts himself so wholly into that idea of himself that that idea constitutes a separate person—the

Son. We noted earlier that fatherhood involved not just generation but acknowledgment as well—the father's recognition of himself in the son. In the Trinity, the Father's act of self-knowledge, of self-recognition, *is* the generation of the Son—the Logos, the knowledge of the Father. The procession of the Holy Spirit differs from that of the Son, for the Holy Spirit proceeds from both the Father *and* the Son by an act known as *spiration:* "active on the part of the Father and the Son, and passive on the part of the Holy Spirit" (p. 79). As the procession of the second person was an act of knowledge, so that of the third person is an act of will, an act of love between the Father and the Son. The Father and the Son look at each other and seeing that each is perfect, they love each other completely, putting themselves so wholly into that love that that love constitutes a separate person—the Holy Spirit. We should note that the processions of the Son and the Holy Spirit represent a kind of narcissistic doubling in which God makes himself, first, the sole object of his own knowledge, and then the sole object of his own love. Further, the generative relationship of the Son to the Father—filiation—is a passive relationship, and the climax of that sacrifice, whose denouement is the Crucifixion, is Jesus' active willing of his own passivity in the hands of the Father: "My Father, if it be possible, let this chalice pass from me. Nevertheless, not as I will, but as thou wilt" (Matt. 26:39). The climax of the sacrifice is the total submission of the Son's will to the Father's will, so that the Son's will becomes one with, is wed to, that of the Father. In this connection, we should also note that in some heterodox Christian traditions a feminine element is reintroduced into the masculine triad, thus reproducing the Oedipal triangle. Sometimes it is the Son who is feminized, as with the medieval mystic Julian of Norwich, who, discussing the "motherhood of God" in *The Revela-*

tions of Divine Love, speaks of "Mother Jesus."[21] Sometimes it is the Holy Spirit, as with certain early Christian
sects for whom the Paraclete was a feminine principle
(Rosolato, p. 87). Yeats refers to these traditions of a
feminine element in the Trinity in his series of poems
called "Supernatural Songs." One need only add that there
is an obvious movement from the Son's passivity in relation to the Father and their generation of a third person
between them to a concept of the second person as feminine. Indeed, the imagery of the climactic moment when
Jesus accepts his Father's will suggests the feminization of
the Son. Referring to his approaching death, Jesus does
not say, "Let this sword pass from me," but "Let this
chalice pass from me." The image of the cup, with its
feminine connotations, accords with that death in which,
by an active willing of his own passivity, Jesus will have his
hands and feet pierced by nails and his side pierced by a
lance. Indeed, one could view that death as a *liebestod,* a
sexual act that, because Jesus is both the priest and the
victim, is incestuous.

Rosolato points out that there exists, on the margins of
Christianity, the aim of "a sort of revenge against God" by
means of the sacrifice itself (p. 82). Since Jesus' sacrifice is
an atonement for an offense of man against God, justice
requires that the sacrificial victim be both man and God.
In that sacrifice, man puts God to death in an action
symbolic of man's attempt to supplant God (the son to
supplant the father, i.e., the doctrine of equality) within
the context of religion as evolving humanism. In Christianity, not only does God become man, and man put God
to death, but as a result of that death, man now enjoys a
privilege that formerly belonged only to the gods—
immortality. The structure of atonement by means of a
sacrificial victim is, of course, that of revenge on a substitute. The collective guilt that the sons feel for the death

wish against the father is discharged by putting that guilt on a scapegoat who will represent the son in relation to the communal priest (the father), but that sacrifice of a substitute allows a further unconscious substitution in which the victim represents the father, and the community (the band of brothers) is able to act out the death wish against him.

With Rosolato's speculations on the sacrifices of Isaac and Jesus in mind, let us examine Faulkner's allegorical retelling of Christ's passion in *A Fable,* and then apply what we learn from that reading to *Absalom* and *The Sound and the Fury.* During the First World War, the corporal, who is Christ, along with his squad of twelve, leads a mutiny in which his regiment refuses to participate in an attack against the Germans. For that act, the corporal is executed. Faulkner makes it clear that that refusal, which leads to the corporal's execution, is an active willing of passivity in the face of death. Realizing the significance of the corporal's refusal, the English runner thinks, "even ruthless and all-powerful and unchallengeable Authority would be impotent before that massed unresisting undemanding passivity. He thought: *They could execute only so many of us before they will have worn out the last rifle and pistol and expended the last live shell.* . . ."[22] The corporal's refusal is a challenge to military authority, that is, to the authority of the father. The group commander says to the division commander,

> "A moment ago you said that we must enforce our rules, or die. It's no abrogation of a rule that will destroy us. It's less. The simple effacement from man's memory of a single word will be enough. But we are safe. Do you know what that word is?"
>
> The division commander looked at him for a moment. He said: "Yes?"
>
> "Fatherland," the group commander said. . . ."   (p. 54)

If the rule of war is *dulce et decorum est pro patria mori,* and if, as the proverb says, in peace fathers die before their sons, but in war sons die before their fathers, then war seems to be the abrogation of the rule of succession, of the alliance, and the return of the Oedipal struggle between father and son, for in war the rule of three, the rule of mediation, has given way to the rule of two—all or nothing, victory or defeat. The old general's version of the rule of two presents war as a narcissistic love-death: "the phenomenon of war is its hermaphroditism: the principles of victory and defeat inhabit the same body and the necessary opponent, enemy, is merely the bed they self-exhaust each other on: a vice only the more terrible and fatal because there is no intervening breast or division between to frustrate them into health by simple normal distance and lack of opportunity for the copulation from which even orgasm cannot free them . . ." (p. 305). In *A Fable* the Oedipal struggle is played out between the old general, who has supreme authority and who addresses everyone as "My child," and the corporal, the general's illegitimate son, whose life is in the general's hands.

As part of Faulkner's reworking of Christ's passion, characters like the old general are made to play more than one role, so that the significance of those roles in the original story is called into question. Thus, the old general is clearly God the Father, yet some of the incidents in his youth are reminiscent of the life of Jesus, while at the end, in his confrontation with the corporal, he assumes the role of Satan, who takes Jesus up to the mountaintop and tempts him with the promise of worldly power (Matt. 4:8–11). That confrontation between the general and the corporal forms the climax of the book, a lengthy debate whose central themes are the concept of sacrifice and the ambiguous relationship between the father and the son. When the general takes the corporal up to the Roman citadel overlooking the city and offers him his freedom, the corporal says that he will not desert his followers. The general replies,

> "One of them, your own countryman, blood brother, kinsman probably since you were all blood kin at some time there—one Zsettlani who has denied you, and the other, whether Zsettlani or not or blood kin or not, at least was—or anyway had been accepted into—the brotherhood of your faith and hope—Polchek, who had already betrayed you by midnight Sunday. Do you see? You even have a substitute to your need as on that afternoon God produced the lamb which saved Isaac—if you could call Polchek a lamb. I will take Polchek tomorrow, execute him with rote and fanfare; you will not only have your revenge and discharge the vengeance of the rest of those three thousand whom he betrayed, you will repossess the opprobrium from all that voice down there which cannot even go to bed because of the frantic need to anathemise you. Give me Polchek, and take freedom."
>
> "There are still ten," the corporal said.   (p. 346)

As an alternative to the corporal's sacrifice of his own life, the general proposes the sacrifice of Isaac in which another will be substituted for the son, and with diabolical economy, he suggests that that other be the betrayer Polchek, so that the son will have not only his own life but revenge as well. That revenge will, of course, involve a repetition in reverse, a reversal of roles between betrayer and betrayed: if the corporal accepts the gift of life from his father, then he will betray Polchek to that very death to which Polchek had previously betrayed him. It is worth noting that the general says Polchek will be like "the lamb which saved Isaac" rather than the ram of the Old Testament version.

The notion of substituting Polchek for the corporal amounts to the substitution of Judas for Jesus, that is, the substitution of a suicide for the self-sacrificed victim. This evokes not only that parallelism between the deaths of Jesus and Judas that is suggested in the Gospels, as if Judas were the dark double of Jesus, it also prepares us for the

137

suicide of the priest whom the old general sends to argue the corporal into accepting his offer. The priest pleads the rules of an established religion against the dictates of an individual conscience. He tells the corporal, "It wasn't He with His humility and pity and sacrifice that converted the world; it was pagan and bloody Rome which did it with His martyrdom. . . . It was Paul, who was a Roman first and then a man and only then a dreamer and so of all of them was able to read the dream correctly and then realise that, to endure, it could not be a nebulous and airy faith but instead it must be a *church*, an *establishment*, a morality of behavior inside which man could exercise his right and duty for free will and decision, not for a reward resembling the bedtime tale which soothes the child into darkness, but the reward of being able to cope peacefully, hold his own, with the hard durable world in which . . . he found himself" (pp. 363–64). The priest, a chaplain, is a surrogate of Christ in the service of the powers of the world, and thus a betrayer of the Christ role he fills, a Judas. The priest even tells the corporal, who has not read the Bible, the story of Christ's temptation by Satan, trying to show the unreasonableness of Christ's position. But the corporal refuses to be swayed, and the priest, realizing that in doing the old general's bidding he has betrayed Christ's teachings, kneels at the corporal's feet: " 'Save me,' he said. 'Get up, Father,' the corporal said" (p. 366). The priest leaves and later pierces his own side with a bayonet.

The interview between the priest and the corporal is a repetition of the earlier interview between the old general and the corporal, but with a characteristic reversal. The priest is a spiritual father precisely because he is a surrogate of the Son. In the interview the priest speaks for the father, and the corporal, the son, resists, but at the end when the priest tries to recant and regain the role of Christ the Son, when he asks the corporal to save him as Christ asked his Father to save him in the Garden of Gethsemane, the corporal, assuming the role of the father, simply says, "Get up, Father," and sends the priest off to take his own life, to kill himself in a manner that evokes the piercing of Christ's side with the lance. It is a reversal that points up not just how much of the father is in the son, but how the father and the son, through their very opposition, mutually constitute one another, define one another, indeed, *exist* in and by one another through that opposition—that opposition between a real world of social order achieved by authority at the expense of any given individual and an ideal world of individual worth, of the uniqueness and sacredness of every person, a world whose highest expression is the hope of personal immortality guaranteed by Christ's death. The general says to his son, "we are two articulations, self-elected possibly, anyway elected, anyway postulated, not so much to defend as to test two inimical conditions which, through no fault of ours but through the simple paucity and restrictions of the arena where they meet, must contend and—one of them—perish: I champion of this mundane earth which, whether I like it or not, is, and to which I did not ask to come, yet since I am here, not only must stop but intend to stop during my allotted while; you champion of an esoteric realm of man's baseless hopes and his infinite capacity—no: passion—for unfact. No, they are not inimical really, there is no contest actually; they can even exist side by side together in one restricted arena, and could and would, had yours not interfered with mine" (pp. 347—48). That reversibility implicit in the roles of father and son is evoked by the very names "general" and "corporal," for it is the "general" who speaks for the particular, concrete world, while it is the "corporal" who speaks for the ideal world. Indeed, it is precisely because the general is pleading the case of the real, physical world that he proposes, as an alternative to

139

the corporal's sacrifice, the sacrifice of Isaac in which the son is spared and new physical life continues to be generated.

Since the two opposing principles exist by means of the very opposition between them, like left and right, high and low, father and son, they are always and everywhere implicated in one another. The old general himself points out that he must cooperate in his son's sacrifice. When the quartermaster general tries to resign in protest over the threatened execution of the corporal, the old general tells him,

> "A man is to die what the world will call the basest and most ignominious of deaths: execution for cowardice while defending his native—anyway adopted—land. That's what the ignorant world will call it, who will not know that he was murdered for that principle which, by your own bitter self-flagellation, you were incapable of risking death and honor for. Yet you don't demand that life. You demand instead merely to be relieved of a commission. A gesture. A martyrdom. Does it match his?"
>
> "He won't accept that life!" the other cried. "If he does—" and stopped, amazed, aghast, foreknowing and despaired while the gentle voice went on:
>
> "If he does, if he accepts his life, keeps his life, he will have abrogated his own gesture and martyrdom. If I gave him his life tonight, I myself could render null and void what you call the hope and the dream of his sacrifice. By destroying his life tomorrow morning, I will establish forever that he didn't even live in vain, let alone die so. Now tell me who's afraid?"
>
> (pp. 331–32)

The very nature of the corporal's sacrifice requires not just the cooperation of the general, but the cooperation of Polchek as well, for in this death, father and son, betrayer and betrayed, executioner and executed all have a part to play. This sense of the oscillation between polar opposites, of that reversibility whereby the opposites hold each other in existence, the sense of a mutual complicity, calls into question the whole concept of a morality based upon free will. If, for example, the son's sacrifice requires that he be betrayed, then the betrayer's action is somehow fore-ordained, and how can the betrayer be morally culpable? The mystery of the opposition between providence and free will, between the father and the son, which Faulkner treats within the context of the corporal's sacrifice is the same problem that he treated in the opposition between Mr. Compson and Quentin—does the son have free will, or does a man's father determine a man's fate?

Certainly, one has the sense in *A Fable* that the old general is manipulating the corporal, that by playing the role of Satan the tempter in offering the corporal his life, he is relying on that opposition between father and son to make the corporal refuse that offer and sacrifice his life. The old general realizes that, because of the mutually constitutive nature of opposites, it is only by maintaining the existence of the ideal world that he is able to maintain the existence of the real world, it is only by fostering the illusion of free choice that he can maintain the possibility of authority, for if the ideal world of individual free will is an illusion, it is an illusion with a uniquely privileged status, since it is that illusion which constitutes, by means of an opposition, the real world of determinism.

The sense that the old general is manipulating the corporal into "freely" choosing death is supported by an earlier incident in the general's career when, as a young officer, he tricked an enlisted man into sacrificing his life to save the lives of others. It had happened in a small garrison in the African desert. The soldier had raped and murdered a Riff girl, and the Riff chieftain sent an ultimatum to the general, who was then a sublieutenant in command of the post, to turn over the soldier ("there were three involved but the chief would be content with the principal one," p. 266) before dawn of the next day or the chief would invest the garrison and obliterate it. The old general's solution was to ask "for a volunteer to slip away that night, before the ultimatum went into effect at dawn and the place was surrounded, and go to the next post and bring back a relieving force" (pp. 266–67). He knew full well that the guilty man would volunteer because "this was the man's one chance" (p. 267). By this act, the soldier "was not even escaping, he was not even entering mere amnesty but absolution; from now on, the whole edifice of France would be his sponsor and his purification, even though he got back with the relief too late, because he not only had the commandant's word, but a signed paper also to avouch his deed and command all men by these presents to make good its reward" (p. 267). But when the soldier slipped out of the garrison that night, the Riffs were waiting in ambush, and they tortured him to death. And the implication is that the general had betrayed the soldier to the Riffs. Thus, the general's solution maintained the illusion of free will by allowing the soldier to volunteer for a mission that would save the lives of his fellow men, a mission that would be an "absolution," though not the kind of absolution that the soldier expected, since the general had tricked him into sacrificing his life to save his comrades and also into atoning for his offense by his death. The general's solution transformed the death of a miscreant into the death of a hero while at the same time maintaining the general's authority, for the general did not give in to the Riffs' ultimatum, nor was his garrison over-run. He did not hand over the man, he simply lost a soldier on a dangerous mission in the line of duty. The corporal's death is a repetition in reverse of that earlier situation where the death of a miscreant became that of a hero, for with the corporal a heroic death becomes, to all appearances, the death of a coward. Another reversal occurs later when the body of the corporal, who was executed for refusing to defend his country, is enshrined in the tomb of the unknown soldier, the representative of all those heroes who sacrificed their lives defending their fatherland. It is a reversal indicative of the way in which Christ's death as an opposition to a worldly establishment became, after Paul's revisionism, the cornerstone of a worldly establishment.

The maintenance of the general's authority requires that he force the corporal to resist that authority by "freely choosing" to sacrifice his own life, for in that senseless slaughter of war where men die en masse like cattle, the possibility of an individual's dying a meaningful death, of a man's taking his life into his own hands and sacrificing it for a purpose, seems to have been lost, and if it is lost, then what is lost with it is the chief sanction by which military authority holds sway—the distinction between a good death and a bad death, that distinction which makes men choose a patriot's death at the hands of the enemy rather than a coward's death before a firing squad. The general requires that the corporal sacrifice his own life, for that act, though it appears to be a coward's death, will be in fact that heroic spending of one's life for a belief, the principle of which is the basis for a soldier's death in battle. The paradox, which the general understands only too well, is that the distinction between a good death and a bad death, between a meaningful death and a meaningless death in the real world, is an ideal distinction. In terms of the real world, all deaths are alike; no such distinction exists. It is in the very loss of the sense that a meaningful death is possible that we find the explanation for the other suicide in A Fable—that of the English aviator. Unknowingly, the aviator has taken part in a mock air battle in which the guns on both sides were firing blanks, a mock battle to cover the visit of the German general to the British aerodrome. When the aviator returns to his field, he sees the German general execute his own pilot with a pistol for following orders to land his plane at an enemy field, orders that a patriotic soldier should not have followed. The English aviator realizes that the war is like a play, like a game in which men do not die meaningful deaths, but rather die whimsical, accidental, arbitrary deaths. In despair at this realization, the aviator shoots himself, and the imagery of the scene recalls Quentin Compson's suicide, for the aviator, like Quentin, treads "his long shadow" into the ground (p. 323).

When, in his confrontation with the corporal, the general fails to tempt his son with the offer of freedom, he makes another offer—the offer of acknowledgment and inheritance: " 'Then take the world,' the old general said. 'I will acknowledge you as my son; together we will close the window on this aberration and lock it forever' " (p. 348). And the general offers as an inheritance "that Paris which only my son can inherit from me—that Paris which I did not at all reject at seventeen but simply held in abeyance for compounding against the day when I should be a father to bequeath it to an heir worthy of that vast and that terrible heritage. A fate, a destiny in it: mine and yours, one and inextricable. Power, matchless and immeasurable; oh no, I have not misread you—I, already born heir to that power as it stood then, holding that inheritance in escrow to become unchallenged and unchallengeable chief of that confederation which would defeat and subjugate and so destroy the only factor on earth which threatened it . . ." (pp. 348–49). And he adds, "What can you not—will you not—do with all the world to work on and the heritage I can give you to work with? . . . You will be God, holding him [man] forever through a far, far stronger ingredient than his simple lusts and appetites: by his triumphant and ineradicable folly, his deathless passion for being led, mystified, and deceived" (p. 349). But the corporal rejects both the acknowledgment and the inheritance, for as the old general points out, to accept the inheritance is to accept "a fate, a destiny" from his father. And the acknowledgment must be refused simply because the role of the son in its very opposition to the "legitimate" and legitimizing authority of the father must in a sense always be a role of illegitimacy. One thinks of *Absalom*, where the son, seeking acknowledgment from his father, is refused and killed, while in *A Fable* the father offers both acknowledgment and inheritance which the son refuses by choosing to sacrifice his life.

In view of the ambiguous relationship between the general and the corporal, what are we to understand as the significance of the corporal's sacrifice? Is it a successful act of free will on the part of the son in opposition to the father, or is it the acting out of a fate subtly imposed by the father, who relies on the workings of that very opposition in order to manipulate the actions of his son? Is the act redemptive, is the death of the childless, only son a redemption from the spirit of revenge whereby one passes on the affront of sonship? And if it is not revenge, is it an act of vengeance? In their interview, the corporal's half sister Marthe tells the old general that when the corporal refused both the girls that she and her husband had proposed as possible wives for him, she thought that by avoiding marriage he was "demanding not even revenge on you but vengeance" (p. 298). But when the corporal then married a whore, Marthe says that she thought that he was seeking "revenge and vengeance": "a whore, a Marseille whore to mother the grandchildren of your high and exalted blood . . ." and "this whore's children would bear not his father's name but my father's" (p. 300). The corporal's having children by the whore would be revenge in that it would perpetuate the affront of sonship, but it would also be vengeance because it would interrupt the line of descent, for the children would bear not the old general's name but the name of that man who had been dispossessed of his rights when the general adulterously sired an illegitimate son on his wife and whose rights would now be symbolically vindicated with the transmission of his name. Indeed, Marthe's comments about the way in which the general displaced her father make it clear that that displacement is to be understood as the son's attempt to supplant the father and alter the past: "all four of us, not just yourself and the one you had begot but the other two whose origin you had had no part in, all branded forever more into one irremediable kinship by that one same passion which had created three of our lives and altered forever the course or anyway the pattern of your own; the four of us together even obliterating that passion's irremediable past in which you had not participated: in your own get you dispossessed your predecessor; in Marya and me you effaced even his seniority; and in Marya, her first child, you even affirmed to yourself the trophy of its virginity" (p. 296). They are the three classic steps of the son's dream of possessing his mother: first, to supplant the father; second, to establish his priority to the father, to efface the father's seniority, so that as the mother's lover the son would come before the father; and third, to establish the son's originality by affirming the mother's virginity so that the son does not merely come *before*, he comes *first*. The attempt to escape "from the long rigid mosaic of seniority" (p. 251) is a recurring motif in the quartermaster general's description of the old general's youth, a description in which the old general appears as a son striving to become his own origin. The general was "a millionaire and an aristocrat from birth, an orphan and an only child, not merely heir in his own right to more francs than anyone knew . . ." but heir as well "to the incalculable weight and influence of the uncle who was the nation's first Cabinet member even though another did bear the title and the precedence, and of that godfather whose name opened doors which (a *Comité de Ferrovie* chairman's) because of their implications and commitments, or (a bachelor's) of their sex, gender, even that of a Cabinet Minister could not ..." (p. 247). The advantages of wealth and birth, the influence of the uncle and the godfather, the dependency of being an heir—all these the old general sets out to circumvent by joining the army, using "the power and the influence to escape the power and the influence" (p. 258). The quartermaster general says to him, "to free yourself of flesh without having to die, without having to lose the awareness that you were free of the flesh: not to escape from it and you could not be immune to it nor did you want to be: only to be free of it, to be conscious always that you were merely at armistice with it at the price of constant and unflagging vigilance, because without that consciousness, flesh would not exist for you to be free of it and so there would be nothing anywhere for you to be free of ... —the supreme golden youth who encompassed all flesh by putting, still virgin to it, all flesh away" (pp. 258–59). One is struck by how much this description of the old general's renunciation of the flesh resembles Mr. Compson's description of Quentin's intention to renounce life: "you are contemplating an apotheosis in which a temporary state of mind will become symmetrical above the flesh and aware both of itself and of the flesh it will not quite discard you will not even be dead." The similarity of the descriptions is due at least in part to the fact that both renunciations are distorted images of Christ's sacrifice.

We noted in the confrontation between the general and the corporal how much of the father is in the son, and the description of the old general's youth shows how much the general is himself simply a son who has tried to resist a paternal influence only to discover that resisting an influence is just an influence in reverse, that to resist an inheritance is to inherit the role of resistance. As the general says to his son, "Remember whose blood it is that you defy me with" (p. 356). When Marthe asks the general if it is too late for the corporal to receive the locket that the general had given the corporal's mother, he says,

> "It's not too late. . . . He will receive it."
> "So he must die." They looked at each other. "Your own son."
> "Then will he not merely inherit from me at thirty-three what I had already bequeathed to him at birth?" (p. 301)

Let us now look again at *Absalom* and at the Biblical context that its title evokes. When David learns that Amnon has raped his own sister Tamar, David refuses to take any action against his son. In the Douay-Rheims translation (2 Kings 13:21), the reason given for David's refusal is that "he would not afflict the spirit of his son Amnon, for he loved him, because he was his firstborn," an explanation that does not appear in the King James translation. Absalom kills his brother Amnon because David will not kill him, and this usurpation by Absalom of the father's authority to punish incest is as well the murder of the eldest son by a younger son, the acting out on a substitute of Absalom's death wish against his father. Absalom subsequently tries to supplant David and succeeds in driving his father by force from Jerusalem. To show that he has assumed his father's place, Absalom openly takes over David's concubines (2 Sam. 16:21–22). When David's army engages Absalom's forces, David gives orders that Absalom is not to be harmed, but the orders are disobeyed. Escaping from the battle on a mule, Absalom becomes stuck in an oak tree, and while he is hanging from the tree, Absalom is pierced with a lance. The Biblical account notes that "Absalom in his lifetime had taken and reared up for himself a pillar, which *is* in the king's dale: for he said, I have no son to keep my name in remembrance: and he called the pillar after his own name: and it is called unto this day, Absalom's place." (2 Sam. 18:18) When the news of Absalom's death is brought to his father, David cries out, "O my son Absalom, my son, my son Absalom! would God I had died for thee, O Absalom, my son, my son!" (2 Sam. 18:33).

As an allusive background to the story of the Sutpens, the Biblical account of the struggle between Absalom and David heightens, with its own ambiguous significance, the ambiguities of the novel. Like Absalom's murder of Amnon, Henry's murder of Bon is the killing of the eldest son by a younger son, and since Absalom does subsequently drive out his father and take over David's wives, the Biblical context would seem to support the double significance of Henry's act as a killing of the son by the father and of the father by the son. Faulkner's juxtaposition of the Biblical story and the novel serves to call into question David's role, for like Sutpen's sons, David's sons are destroyed, and the implication is that their fate is the result of David's successful supplanting of his father-in-law Saul. By refusing to act against Amnon and by giving instructions that Absalom is not to be harmed, David is apparently trying to preserve the alliance established by Isaac's sacrifice. Indeed, David's own words when he learns of Absalom's death ("would God I had died for thee, O Absalom, my son") appear to be a statement of that rule of succession whereby the father accepts the principle that fathers die before their sons. But David's sons die before their father, for since David successfully supplanted his father-in-law, he is fated to meet with that same attempt from his own sons, so that he must either kill or be killed. Though David tries to affirm that rule of physical succession that was ratified by the sacrifice of Isaac, the death of Absalom, who is pierced with a lance while hanging on a tree, evokes a distorted image of Jesus' sacrifice in which that physical succession is interrupted, a distorted image that finds its resonance in the death of the narrator of *Absalom*. It is worth noting that the imagery surrounding Absalom's death suggests the interrupted transmission of the phallic power, for while Jesus, dying on the Cosmic Tree, the dead tree of the cross, transforms physical succession into spiritual succession through the transmission, in the person of the Holy Spirit, of the phallic power to generate new spiritual life, Absalom dies on the living phallic tree whose image subsequently metamorphoses into that of the dead phallic pillar that Absalom erected to bear his name (the sign of phallic transmission) because he had no son. One thinks of how much Quentin and his father make of the tombstone that Sutpen carried with him during the war and that is the only monument that remains to his name after his dream of founding a dynasty has failed.

If the breakdown of the alliance between father and son transforms a state of peace into a state of war, turns the rule of mediation into the rule of victory or defeat, the law of culture into the law of nature, then it is significant that the struggle between Sutpen and Bon and between Henry and Bon merges with the Civil War, a war between brothers, significant that the struggle between David and Absalom turns into a civil war that divides the kingdom, and that the struggle between the old general and the corporal takes place as part of the First World War.

As Faulkner places Quentin's suicide in the context of Christ's sacrifice partly to call the meaning of that sacrifice into question, so he puts the story of the Sutpens in the context of the Biblical account of David and Absalom in order to question the moral significance of that account, for what is at issue is nothing less than a questioning of that Judaeo-Christian morality, based on the Bible, that in Sutpen's world not only tolerated the enslavement of blacks but even justified it on the authority of the Bible. In *Absalom* there is a direct reference to this Biblical justification for slavery: ". . . niggers, that the Bible said had been created and cursed by God to be brute and vassal to all men of white skin . . ." (p. 282). It is a reference to the incident in Genesis (9:20–27) where Noah gets drunk and his son Ham looks upon his father's nakedness. As a punishment for Ham's offense, Noah curses Ham's son Canaan. In light of what we have said about the way that the death wish against one's father is punished by the death of one's son, it is significant that the punishment for Ham's offense of looking at his father's phallus is imposed not on Ham but on Ham's son, and that the punishment is that Canaan will be "a servant of servants . . . unto his brethren." Ham is, of course, the traditional ancestor of the African peoples. The sense that blackness is the mark of a father's curse on the progeny of an offending son, a curse that makes that progeny the servants of their brothers, adds a further dimension to the relationship between Sutpen, Bon, and Henry and to the fact that Bon's name, by the time that it is passed on to the third generation, has become "Bond."

As Absalom's murder of Amnon and Henry's murder of Bon are both actions with a double significance, so Quentin's suicide is a double action as well. As the murder of the brother seducer by the brother avenger (the drowning of the shadow self), Quentin's suicide is obviously the killing of the son by the father, but as the merging of the shadow with the mirror image in the water, the image of his sister Candace, it is the son's reentry into his mother's womb, a supplanting of the father that amounts to a "killing" of the father. Yet the very essence of the narcissistic love-death, the key feature that makes the act of love an act of death, is that the son's entry into his mother's womb is not made by means of the son's phallus as a *part* of the son's self but, rather, by means of the phallus as the *whole* of the son's self—by means of a total identification of the son's self with the phallus as *detached object* (the common regressive identification of penis and child), so that the entry of the phallus into the mother's womb becomes a total reabsorption or reincorporation of the son into his mother as if he were an infant in the womb. At one point Quentin thinks, "When I was little there was a picture in one of our books, a dark place into which a single weak ray of light came slanting upon two faces lifted out of the shadow. *You know what I'd do if I were King?* she never was a queen or a fairy she was always a king or a giant or a general *I'd break that place open and drag them out and I'd whip them good.* It was torn out, jagged out. I was glad. I'd have to turn back to it until the dungeon was Mother herself she and Father upward into weak light holding hands and us lost somewhere below even them without even a ray of light" (p. 191).

We can see how, in the narcissistic *liebestod,* castration is transformed into death, for when the son, out of the fear of castration, performs a psychological self-castration, he identifies himself not with what remains, with what is saved (the living, castrated son) but with what is lost (the dead, detached phallus). In this mechanism, the living subject sees itself as the dead object. And yet by a paradoxical reversal, the son's identification with the detached phallus becomes in a new way an identification with the castrated son, for the son without a phallus is a woman, and when, in the narcissistic *liebestod,* the son, who is wholly identified with the detached phallus, enters the mother's womb, that total *reincorporation* of the son into the mother becomes an *identification* of the son with the mother—the son becomes a woman. In the narcissistic love-death, the son plays not just the two masculine roles in the Oedipal triangle, he plays the feminine role as well, and it is precisely this narcissistic solution of one self playing all three roles at once that is self-destructive, for the three roles, by collapsing into one, collapse into none. All differentiation is effaced—castration merges with death; the love instinct and the death instinct fuse; in a total consummation masculine and feminine consume one another; conscious and unconscious, animate and inanimate by merging destroy that opposition by means of which each exists. Quentin's reply to Mr. Compson's nihilism, to his feeling that nothing makes any difference, is an act that does away with all difference, an act that denies that difference makes any difference.

Quentin's love of death incorporates his incestuous love for his sister precisely because his sister, as a substitute for Quentin's mother, is synonymous with death. On the morning of the day he dies, Quentin thinks, "I dont suppose anybody ever deliberately listens to a watch or a clock. You dont have to. You can be oblivious to the sound for a long while, then in a second of ticking it can create in the mind unbroken the long diminishing parade of time you didn't hear. Like Father said down the long and lonely lightrays you might see Jesus walking, like. And the good Saint Francis that said Little Sister Death, that never had a sister. . . . That Christ was not crucified: he was worn away by a minute clicking of little wheels. That had no sister" (pp. 95–96). Christ had no sister, but he had a mother with whom he becomes progressively identified, so that, for example, when he is taken down from sacrificing his life on the phallic tree, he is laid in his mother's lap, and the iconography of the Pietà becomes that of the Madonna and Child. As a further link between Quentin's suicide and Christ's sacrifice, we should note that the principle of sacrifice is the same as that of self-castration— the giving up of a part to save the whole, and in both sacrifice and self-castration the part is given up to save the whole from the wrath of the father. But in Christ's sacrifice and Quentin's suicide, the *son* is the part that is given up, and self-castration is death. In his discussion of the sacrifices of Isaac and Jesus, Rosolato points out that for the psychotic the notion of sacrifice becomes the fantasy of murder or suicide. The psychotic concept of sacrifice is located in the realm of an Idealized Father whose image blends the images of the Father and the Mother: "in reality, one can intervene for the other; they are interchangeable in a single ambivalence" (p. 92). In this situation, sacrifice "is a manner of extricating oneself from all genealogy and merging oneself with that megalomaniac and punctiform image" (p. 92). Rosolato adds that "to this situation central for psychosis, always in quest of an impossible sacrifice in which the subject would be himself the agent or the victim, corresponds, in myth, the connecting point of the Passion and the Sacrifice" (p. 93). The essence of Christ's sacrifice and Quentin's suicide is that in each the subject is both the agent and the victim, at once active and passive, a conjunction of masculine and feminine.

If the Biblical context of Candace's name suggests that Quentin is his sister's eunuch, then it is worth noting that in the Gospels Christ recommends that his disciples make themselves eunuchs for the kingdom of heaven: "For there are some eunuchs, which were so born from *their* mother's womb: and there are some eunuchs, which were made eunuchs of men: and there be eunuchs, which have made themselves eunuchs for the kingdom of heaven's sake. He that is able to receive *it,* let him receive *it*" (Matt. 19:12). In Quentin's distorted version of Christ's sacrifice, what is transmitted beyond death is not the phallic power but the interruption of that power. A few months after Quentin's suicide, Candace's daughter is born, and she is named Quentin after her dead uncle. The female Quentin is an embodiment of that interruption of genealogy effected by her uncle's death, for as Faulkner says, she is "fatherless nine months before her birth, nameless at birth and already doomed to be unwed from the instant the dividing egg determined its sex" (p. 19). There is as well in this transmission of interrupted genealogy an element of revenge, a reversal inflicted on a substitute, for as the male Quentin's death is put in the context of Christ's death and resurrection, so the female Quentin, on the day before Easter in 1928, escapes from the womb of the Compson home, stealing in the process the money that her Uncle Jason had withheld from her allowance—a theft that is presented as a symbolic castration of Jason (who is his father's namesake and who had his younger brother Benjy gelded) by the dead Quentin's namesake. Faulkner says of Jason, "Of his niece he did not think at all, nor the arbitrary valuation of the money. Neither of them had had entity or individuality for him for ten years; together they merely symbolized the job in the bank of which he had been deprived before he ever got it. . . . 'I'll think of something else,' he said, so he thought about Lorraine. He imagined himself in bed with her, only he was just lying beside her, pleading with her to help him, then he thought of the money again, and that he had been outwitted by a woman, a girl. If he could just believe it was the man who had robbed him. But to have been robbed of that which was to have compensated him for the lost job, which he had acquired through so much effort and risk, by the very symbol of the lost job itself, and worst of all, by a bitch of a girl" (pp. 321, 323). Since Jason's friend Lorraine is a prostitute, the theft of Jason's money is a castration of his power to buy sex, and since the money that was stolen was in part money that Jason had stolen from his niece, Jason is rendered impotent, he is powerless to gain any legal redress. Jason dies a childless bachelor.

In *A Fable* the figure who represents the deformed transmission of the phallic power is the English runner. Clearly, the runner, with his missing arm and leg, is an embodiment of that interruption of physical genealogy that was accomplished by the corporal's act of sacrificial self-castration. (Significantly, when the corporal is shot, the wooden post to which he is tied, unlike those of the two men executed with him, breaks off and falls flat with the corporal's body.) If the runner's maimed condition embodies the interruption of physical generation, it is because a physical power has presumably been transformed into a spiritual power by the corporal's sacrifice. When the old general dies, he is laid in state at the tomb of the unknown soldier—his son—and the runner, who has received the corporal's *Medaille Militaire* from Marthe, steps forward and hurls the medal at the general's coffin. The runner is mobbed, and as he lies bleeding in the gutter, the quartermaster general, who was in the crowd, tries to help him. The runner, in reply to a member of the mob who shouts, "Maybe he will die this time," says, "That's right. . . . Tremble. I'm not going to die. Never" (p. 437). As a counterpoint to the transmission of interrupted physical genealogy that we find in the English runner and the female Quentin, the two youngest male descendants of the Sutpen and Compson families, the black Jim Bond and the white Benjy Compson, are both congenital idiots whose physical condition, in this final instance of black-white doubling, evokes the traditional biological punishment of that incest from which all doubling springs. But of course, no real physical incest occurs in the Sutpen or Compson families as far as we know, so that the condition of Jim Bond and Benjy Compson is a symbol of that psychological incest that pervades both families and that makes the families in turn symbolic of a place and a time.

One could continue indefinitely multiplying examples

of doubling between the stories of the Sutpen and Compson families and finding in other Faulkner novels incidents in which these doublings are doubled again, but by now we have established the outlines and the importance of a structure that is central to Faulkner's work. In this structure, the struggle between the father and the son in the incest complex is played out again and again in a series of spatial and temporal repetitions, a series of substitutive doublings and reversals in which generation in time becomes a self-perpetuating cycle of revenge on a substitute, the passing on from father to son of a fated repetition as a positive or a negative inheritance. Religion as "the longing for the father," to use Freud's phrase, attempts, successfully or not, to release man from this spirit of revenge through the mechanism of sacrifice and the alliance of the father and the son. In sacrifice, the impulses of the father against the son and those of the son against the father are simultaneously acted out on a symbolic, mediatory third term, so that the contrary impulses momentarily cancel each other out in a single act with a double psychological significance. Yet obviously, religious sacrifice as an institutionalized substitute for those impulses is also a conscious, communal preserver and transmitter of those impulses, capable at any moment of reconverting the symbolic death struggle between father and son into the real death struggle.

This structure, as I have tried to present it in all its complexity, exists in no single Faulkner novel nor in the sum total of those novels; it exists, rather, in that imaginative space that the novels create *in between* themselves by their interaction. The analysis of one novel will not reveal it, nor will it be revealed by an analysis of all the novels in a process of simple addition, for since the structure is created by means of an interplay between texts, it must be approached through a critical process that, like the solving of a simultaneous equation, oscillates between two or more texts at once. The key to the critical oscillation that I have attempted between *Absalom, Absalom!* and *The Sound and the Fury* is, of course, the figure of Quentin Compson—Quentin, whose own oscillation constantly transforms action into narration and narration into action.

It is tempting to see in Quentin a surrogate of Faulkner, a double who is fated to retell and reenact the same story throughout his life just as Faulkner seemed fated to retell in different ways the same story again and again and, insofar as narration is action, to reenact that story as well. And just as Quentin's retellings and reenactments are experienced as failures that compel him to further repetitions that will correct those failures but that are themselves experienced as failures in turn, so Faulkner's comments on his own writing express his sense of the failures of his narratives, failures that compel him to retell the story again and again. In one of his conferences at the University of Virginia, Faulkner said of the composition of *The Sound and the Fury:* "It was, I thought, a short story, something that could be done in about two pages, a thousand words, I found out it couldn't. I finished it the first time, and it wasn't right, so I wrote it again, and that was Quentin, that wasn't right. I wrote it again, that was Jason, that wasn't right, then I tried to let Faulkner do it, that still was wrong" (p. 32).

It is as if, in the character of Quentin, Faulkner embodied, and perhaps tried to exorcise, certain elements present in himself and in his need to be a writer. Certainly, Quentin evokes that father-son struggle that a man inevitably has with his own literary progenitors when he attempts to become an "author." He evokes as well Faulkner's apparent sense of the act of writing as a progressive dismemberment of the self in which parts of the living subject are cut off to become objectified in language, to become (from the writer's point of view) detached and deadened, drained, in that specific embodiment, of their obsessive emotional content. In this process of piecemeal self-destruction, the author, the living subject, is gradually transformed into the detached object—his books. And this process of literary self-dismemberment is the author's response to the threat of death; it is a using up, a consuming of the self in the act of writing in order to escape from that annihilation of the self that is the inevitable outcome of physical generation, to escape by means of an ablative process of artistic creation in which the self is worn away to leave only a disembodied voice on the page to survive the writer's death, a voice that represents the interruption of a physical generative power and the transmission, through the author's books, of the phallic generative power of the creative imagination. This act of writing is sacrificial and mediatory, a gradual sacrificing of the self in an attempt to attain immortality through the mediation of language. It is as well an active willing of the author's passivity in the grip of time, for since time inevitably wears away the self to nothing, that actively willed wearing away of the self in the ablative process of creation is an attempt to transform necessity into a virtue, *ananke* into *virtù*, a fate into a power. Clearly, for Faulkner, writing is a kind of doubling in which the author's self is reconstituted within the realm of language as the Other, a narcissistic mirroring of the self to which the author's reaction is at once a fascinated self-love and an equally fascinated self-hatred. In one of the conferences at Virginia, Faulkner said that *Absalom* was in part "the story of Quentin Compson's hatred of the bad qualities in the country he loves." There is a sense in which that ambivalence, that "hatred of the bad qualities in the country he loves," defines as well Faulkner's novelistic effort, his relationship to a geographic and an artistic, an outer and an inner, "fatherland." The structure that we have found in the interplay between *Absalom, Absalom!* and *The Sound and the Fury* is central to Faulkner's novels precisely because it is, for Faulkner, central to the art of writing novels.

What is remarkable is that Faulkner's conscious under-standing of this structure as a metaphor for his art seems to have been complete almost from the beginning. In his second novel, *Mosquitoes* (1927), Faulkner's most exten-sive examination of the interaction between the artist and his creation, the influence of the structure is immediately recognizable. There are the brother and sister, Josh and Pat Robyn, whose relationship not only has incestuous over-tones but also explicit elements of twinning and masculine-feminine reversal: "He raised his face, suspending his knife blade. They were twins: just as there was something mas-culine about her jaw, so there was something feminine about his."[23] As an emblem of this reversibility, both brother and sister call each other by the same nickname, Gus. The sculptor Gordon, one of Faulkner's surrogates in the novel, is in love with Pat, obsessed by "her flat breast and belly, her boy's body which the poise of it and the thinness of her arms belied. Sexless, yet somehow vaguely troubling" (p. 24). But Gordon realizes that his love for Patricia is hopeless—that the artist's fated substitute for the real sexual possession of the virgin must be the posses-sion of her in the virgin purity of the work of art. He has sculpted the headless, armless, legless torso of a girl, and when he tells Pat about Cyrano, who had tried to capture a girl and hold her forever in a book, she says,

"Was he in love with her?"

"I think so. . . . Yes, he was in love with her. She couldn't leave him, either. Couldn't go away from him at all. . . . He didn't take any chances. He had her locked up. In a book."

"In a book?" she repeated. Then she comprehended. "Oh . . . That's what you've done, isn't it? With that marble girl without any arms and legs you made? Hadn't you rather have a live one? Say, you haven't got any sweetheart or anything, have you?"

"No," he answered.   (pp. 269–70)

But what Gordon tells the girl is only part of the truth. The whole truth is that the artist's love for his work of art is not so much a substitute for his love for a real woman as that his love for a real woman is a substitute for, a symbol of his love for, the work of art, the work of art that is simply the embodiment of the feminine aspect of the artist's masculine self. At one point the novelist Dawson Fairchild says that a man is always writing "for some woman, that he fondly believes he's stealing a march on some brute bigger or richer or handsomer than he is; I believe that every word a writing man writes is put down with the ultimate intention of impressing some woman that probably don't care anything at all for literature, as is the nature of women. Well, maybe she ain't always a flesh and blood creature. She may be only the symbol of a desire. But she is feminine" (p. 250).

Since the work of art is dual—the feminine aspect of the masculine self—the artist's relation to the work is also dual, involving a kind of emotional bisexuality. The masculine self as related to the feminine-masculine work of art immediately suggests the man-woman-man interaction of the Oedipal triangle. No wonder, then, that Fairchild's friend Julius Wiseman says that the artist who writes a book in order to possess by means of his art the woman that he cannot win in real life is simply taking revenge: " 'Lucky he who believes that his heart is broken: he can immediately write a book and so take revenge (what is more terrible than the knowledge that the man you just knocked down discovered a coin in the gutter while getting up?) on him or her who damaged his or her ventricles. Besides cleaning up in the movies and magazines. No, no,' he repeated, 'you don't commit suicide when you are disappointed in love. You write a book'" (p. 228). In his biography of Faulkner, Joseph Blotner points out that *Mosquitoes* is based in part on Faulkner's relationship with Helen Baird and her brother Josh during the years 1925–26, and the implication is that, because of Helen Baird's indifference to Faulkner's love, Faulkner set out in *Mosquitoes* to take just the kind of revenge through art that Julius Wiseman describes. Blotner also points out that during the summer of 1926 Faulkner wrote for Helen Baird "a forty-eight-page allegorical novelette" called "Mayday," details from which were to be used later in Quentin's section of *The Sound and the Fury:* "The protagonist was another of his wounded-soldier heroes: Sir Galwyn of Arthgyl. Like a quester-knight he had journeyed on, flanked by companions called Hunger and Pain. He conversed with a figure called Time and was vouchsafed a vision of St. Francis of Assisi. He finally freed himself of his troublesome companions as, joining a maiden called Little Sister Death, he drowned himself in a river at the end of his quest."[24]

When Julius Wiseman says ". . . you don't commit suicide when you are disappointed in love. You write a book," he, like Gordon, is telling only part of the truth. For writing a book, creating a work of art, is not so much an alternative to suicide as a kind of alternative suicide: writing as an act of autoerotic self-destruction. In a moment of consummate narcissism, Gordon, standing on a wharf in New Orleans, looks down at his reflection in the water and thinks:

> stars in my hair in my hair and beard i am crowned with stars
> christ by his own hand an autogethsemane carved darkly out
> of pure space but not rigid no no an unmuscled wallowing
> fecund and foul the placid tragic body of a woman who
> conceives without pleasure bears without pain. . . .
> He flung back his head and laughed a huge laugh in the
> loneliness . . . from the other shore a mirthless echo mocked
> him . . .   (pp. 47–48)

The last detail suggests, of course, the myth of Narcissus, whose fate is a punishment meted out by the Goddess of Love because Narcissus scorned the love of a woman, the virgin Echo. In Gordon's thoughts as he looks at his own image in the water, the three major elements of the artist's relation to his work are apparent—incest, autoeroticism, and self-destruction. The artist's reflection of himself conjoined with the work of art is as "a woman who conceives without pleasure bears without pain," yet this psychic incest of the masculine self with the feminine-masculine work is also an autoerotic act, the self making love to the self, a kind of creative onanism in which, through the use of the phallic pen on the "pure space" of the virgin page or the chisel on the virgin marble, the self is continually spent and wasted in an act of progressive self-destruction. Indeed, when Gordon looks at his image and thinks, "christ by his own hand an autogethsemane," the phrase "by his own hand" simultaneously suggests a self-portrait, self-destruction, and self-abuse. At various points in the novel the image of art as a kind of psychic masturbation recurs. Faulkner says of the dilettante-connoisseur Talliaferro that he "often mused with regret on the degree of intimacy he might have established with his artistic acquaintances had he but acquired the habit of masturbation in his youth" (p. 10). And Julius Wiseman tells Fairchild, "You are an artist only when you are telling about people, while Gordon is not an artist only when he is cutting at a piece of wood or stone. And it's very difficult for a man like that to establish workable relations with people. Other artists are too busy playing with their own egos, workaday people will not or cannot bother with him, so his alternatives are misanthropy or an endless gabbling of esthetic foster sisters of both sexes" (pp. 51–52).

In Gordon's thoughts, incest, autoeroticism, and self-destruction all merge in the image of the artist as a Christ-figure who, because of the self's love for the self, sacrifices the personal self to that objectified other self that is the work of art. Describing the essence of the creative act, Fairchild compares it to Christ's suffering and death as an active willing of passivity: "It is that Passion Week of the heart, that instant of timeless beatitude which some never know, which some, I suppose, gain at will, which others gain through an outside agency like alcohol, like to-night— that passive state of the heart with which the mind, the brain, has nothing to do at all, in which the hackneyed accidents which make up this world—love and life and death and sex and sorrow—brought together by chance in perfect proportions, take on a kind of splendid and time-less beauty" (p. 339).

That the author's book is the dark double of the au-thor's self is made explicit by Faulkner in the discussion that Fairchild and Wiseman have about the volume of poems written by Wiseman's sister Eva. Fairchild says,

> "All artists are kind of insane. . . . It's a kind of dark thing. It's kind of like somebody brings you to a dark door. Will you enter that room, or not?"
>
> "But the old fellows got you into the room first," the Semitic man said. "Then they asked you if you wanted to get out or not."
>
> "I don't know. There are rooms, dark rooms, that they didn't know anything about at all. Freud and these other—"
>
> "Discovered them just in time to supply our shelterless literati with free sleeping quarters. . . ." (p. 248)
>
> Fairchild turned a few pages. "It's kind of difficult for me to reconcile her with this book," he said slowly. "Does it strike you that way?"
>
> "Not so much that she wrote this," the other answered, "but that she wrote anything at all. That anybody should. But there's no puzzle about the book itself. Not to me, that is. But you, straying trustfully about this park of dark and rootless trees which Dr. Ellis and your Germans have recently thrown open to the public . . ."
>
> "Emotional bisexuality," Fairchild said.
>
> "Yes. But you are trying to reconcile the book and the author. A book is the writer's secret life, the dark twin of a

man: you can't reconcile them. And with you, when the
inevitable clash comes, the author's actual self is the one that
goes down, for you are of those for whom fact and fallacy gain
verisimilitude by being in cold print."   (p. 251)

In reply, Fairchild reads aloud one of Eva Wiseman's
poems, a poem of overpowering narcissism:

> " 'Lips that of thy weary all seem weariest,
> Seem wearier for the curled and pallid sly
> Still riddle of thy secret face, and thy
> Sick despair of its own ill obsessed;
> Lay not to heart thy boy's hand, to protest
> That smiling leaves thy tired mouth reconciled,
> For swearing so keeps thee but ill beguiled
> With secret joy of thine own woman's breast.
>
> " 'Weary thy mouth with smiling; canst thou bride
> Thyself with thee and thine own kissing slake?
> Thy virgin's waking doth itself deride
> With sleep's sharp absence, coming so awake,
> And near thy mouth thy twinned heart's grief doth hide
> For there's no breast between: it cannot break.'

> " 'Hermaphroditus,' " he read. "That's what it's about. It's
> a kind of dark perversion. Like a fire that don't need any fuel,
> that lives on its own heat. . . ."   (p. 252)

Later in the novel, Fairchild takes up this theme again,
portraying art as a simultaneous, double act of self-
creation and self-destruction, a procreative devouring of
the artist's masculine self by the feminine work of art:

> "A woman conceives: does she care afterward whose seed it
> was? Not she . . . But in art, a man can create without any
> assistance at all: what he does is his. A perversion, I grant you,
> but a perversion that builds Chartres and invents Lear is a
> pretty good thing. . . ."
> "Creation, reproduction from within . . . Is the dominating
> impulse in the world feminine, after all, as aboriginal peoples
> believe? . . . There is a kind of spider or something. The female
> is the larger, and when the male goes to her he goes to death:
> she devours him during the act of conception. And that's a
> man: a kind of voraciousness that makes an artist stand beside

165

himself with a notebook in his hand always, putting down all the charming things that ever happen to him, killing them for the sake of some problematical something he might or might not ever use. . . ." (p. 320)

This image of the artist standing beside himself echoes an earlier discussion in which the novelist is depicted as an "emotional eunuch" (p. 131). Fairchild says, "I always did want to be one of those old time eunuchs, for one night. . . . They must have just laughed themselves to death when those sultans and things would come visiting. . . . There'd sure be a decline in population if a man were twins and had to stand around and watch himself making love" (pp. 184–85).

In the discussion between Fairchild and Wiseman about Eva's poems, there are, of course, multiple doublings. There is the image of the double, male-female self in the poem that Fairchild reads. There is the doubling of phrase and imagery from this passage in later Faulkner novels, as when the ending of the poem—" 'And near thy mouth thy twinned heart's grief doth hide / For there's no breast between: it cannot break. . . . Hermaphroditus . . .' "—is echoed more than twenty years later in A Fable when the general tells the corporal that "the phenomenon of war is its hermaphroditism: the principles of victory and of defeat inhabit the same body and the necessary opponent, enemy, is merely the bed they self-exhaust each other on: a vice only the more terrible and fatal because there is no intervening breast or division between to frustrate them into health. . . ." Or when Fairchild's characterization of art as "a kind of dark thing . . . like somebody brings you to a dark door. Will you enter that room, or not?" is echoed in Absalom in the image of Rosa's and Quentin's act of narration as a perpetual lurking outside a dark door that they can never pass (pp. 150, 172). In Faulkner's first novel, Soldiers' Pay (1926), the image of the dark door is directly linked with the mirror of Narcissus. One of the characters, Januarius Jones ("Januarius" from "Janus," the Roman god of doors and portals, the god with a double face), stands in front of a door that has just been locked by a girl that he has been pursuing:

> "Damn your soul," he spoke in a quiet toneless emotion, "open the door."
> The wood was bland and inscrutable: baffling, holding up to him in its polished depths the fat white blur of his own face. Holding his breath he heard nothing beyond it save a clock somewhere.
> "Open the door," he repeated, but there was no sound. Has she gone away, or not? He wondered, straining his ears, bending to the bulky tweeded Narcissus of himself in the polished wood.[25]

(The doubling of phrase and image in the later novels is, from the reader's point of view, retrospective, since it depends on the rereading of an earlier text in light of a later text. Yet this is inevitable because the reader's understanding of Faulkner's work must move backward as the work itself moves forward.) Certainly, the most intriguing instance of doubling in the conversation between Fairchild and Wiseman turns on the relationship of Faulkner to his own writings, for the poem of Eva Wiseman's that Fairchild reads and the other poems that he quotes from are in fact Faulkner's own poems, published in his 1933 collection, *A Green Bough,* but here assigned to a female poet whose relationship to her work is explained by "emotional bisexuality." The analysis of the poem in the novel amounts to a kind of autocriticism, and this same type of role reversal between author and character, between creator and creation, occurs earlier in the novel when we suddenly find one of the characters talking about Faulkner and using the imagery of black/white doubling to describe him. The shopgirl Jenny tells Patricia about a man she met in New Orleans:

"I got to talking to a funny man. A little kind of black man—"

"A nigger?"

"No. He was a white man, except he was awful sunburned and kind of shabby dressed—no necktie and hat. . . . He said he was a liar by profession, and he made good money at it, enough to own a Ford as soon as he got it paid out. I think he was crazy. Not dangerous: just crazy."

". . . What was his name?"

". . . Walker or Foster or something . . ."

". . . You don't remember it, then."

"Yes, I do. Wait. . . . Oh, yes: I remember—Faulkner, that was it."

"Faulkner?" the niece pondered in turn. "Never heard of him," she said at last, with finality. . . .

". . . He got to talking to Pete and Roy while me and Thelma was fixing up downstairs, and he danced with Thelma. He wouldn't dance with me because he said he didn't dance very well, and so he had to keep his mind on the music while he danced. He said he could dance with either Roy or Thelma or Pete, but he couldn't dance with me. I think he was crazy. Don't you?"   (pp. 144–46)

As Josh and Pat Robyn represent a kind of brother-sister doubling and as Gordon's desire for Pat stands for the masculine artist's desire for his feminine-masculine other self embodied in the work of art, so the triangle is completed in the doubling between Gordon and Josh. Gordon has sculpted the torso of a virgin, Josh spends the whole novel carving the wooden bowl of a pipe. In these parallel activities of the two male figures in the triangle, we find the two images that, along with the myth of Narcissus, dominated Faulkner's sense of the artist's relation to his work, for surely Josh's carving of the bowl of a pipe is the embryonic form of that image of the vase or Grecian urn found in *Sartoris* and *Light in August,* just as Gordon's sculpting of an ideal virgin whom he subsequently identifies with Pat is derived from the myth of Pygmalion and Galatea. Obviously, the urn and the sculpture are conjugate, reversible images. In the myth of Pygmalion and Galatea, the statue of an ideal woman becomes a real, live girl because of the sculptor's love for his creation, while in the case of Keats's Grecian urn a real, live girl becomes an immortal, ideal woman painted on the side of a vase, her virgin purity preserved forever intact by art—"Thou still unravished bride of quietness." (One need only recall that in Ovid's *Metamorphoses* [Book Ten], Cinyras, the grandson of Pygmalion and Galatea, commits incest with his daughter Myrrha, thus repeating in a third generation Pygmalion's act of making love to the virgin that he had sculpted, that he had "fathered" by his art. In shame at the incestuous union, Cinyras kills himself.) In *Sartoris* the identification of the womblike vase and the woman is made explicit and linked to the narcissism that lies at the heart of artistic creation. Narcissa Benbow's brother Horace makes glass vases, and after several attempts he finally "produced one almost perfect vase of clear amber, larger, more richly and chastely serene, which he kept always on his night table and called by his sister's name in the intervals of apostrophizing both of them impartially in his moments of rhapsody over the realization of the meaning of peace and the unblemished attainment of it, as 'Thou still unravished bride of quietness.' "[26] But the woman-vase is a dual image: it is the womb of art only because it is also the burial urn of the artist's self. In *Light in August* the opening image of the fecund Lena riding in the wagon, motionless as a figure on an urn, is balanced by Joe Christmas's vision of "a diminishing row of suavely shaped urns in moonlight, blanched. And not one was perfect. Each one was cracked and from each crack there issued something liquid, deathcolored, and foul" (pp. 177–78).

In 1933 Faulkner wrote an introduction for a new edition of *The Sound and the Fury*, an introduction that he decided not to publish and that remained unpublished for almost forty years. In it he describes the genesis of the novel:

> ... one day it suddenly seemed as if a door had clapped silently and forever to between me and all publishers' addresses and booklists and I said to myself, Now I can write. Now I can just write. Whereupon I, who had three brothers and no sisters and was destined to lose my first daughter in infancy, began to write about a little girl.
>
> I did not realise then that I was trying to manufacture the sister which I did not have and the daughter which I was to lose, though the former might have been apparent from the fact that Caddy had three brothers almost before I wrote her name on paper.[27]

Later in the introduction he says that since writing *The Sound and the Fury* he learned that "the emotion definite and physical and yet nebulous to describe which the writing of Benjy's section of *The Sound and the Fury* gave me—that ecstasy, that eager and joyous faith and anticipation of surprise which the yet unmarred sheets beneath my hand held inviolate and unfailing—will not return. The unreluctance to begin, the cold satisfaction in work well and arduously done, is there and will continue to be there as long as I can do it well. But that other will not return. I shall never know it again" (pp. 160–61). What Faulkner describes here is the author's sense of the loss of the original virgin space ("that ecstasy, that eager and joyous faith and anticipation of surprise which the yet unmarred sheets beneath my hand held inviolate and unfailing") and his mature acceptance of repetition ("The unreluctance to begin, the cold satisfaction in work well and arduously done, is there and will continue to be there as long as I can do it well").

The introduction ends:

> There is a story somewhere about an old Roman who kept at his bedside a Tyrrhenian vase which he loved and the rim of which he wore slowly away with kissing it. I had made myself

a vase, but I suppose I knew all the time that I could not live forever inside of it, that perhaps to have it so that I too could lie in bed and look at it would be better; surely so when that day should come when not only the ecstasy of writing would be gone, but the unreluctance and the something worth saying too. It's fine to think that you will leave something behind you when you die, but it's better to have made something you can die with. Much better the muddy bottom of a little doomed girl climbing a blooming pear tree in April to look in the window at the funeral. (p. 161)

Faulkner revised the introduction several times. In its final version, in which Faulkner doubles Quentin's own words in the novel, the ending fuses a series of images that are separated in earlier versions:

One day I seemed to shut a door between me and all publishers' addresses and book lists. I said to myself, Now I can write. Now I can make myself a vase like that which the old Roman kept at his bedside and wore the rim slowly away with kissing it. So I, who had never had a sister and was fated to lose my daughter in infancy, set out to make myself a beautiful and tragic little girl.[28]

Faulkner realized that it is precisely because the novelist stands outside the dark door, wanting to enter the dark room but unable to, that he *is* a novelist, that he must imagine what takes place beyond the door. Indeed, it is just that tension toward the dark room that he cannot enter that makes that room the source of all his imaginings—the womb of art. He understood that a writer's relation to his material and to the work of art is always a loss, a separation, a cutting off, a self-castration that transforms the masculine artist into the feminine-masculine vase of the work. He knew that in this act of progressive self-destruction "the author's actual self is the one that goes down," that the writer ends up identifying himself not with what remains but with what is lost, the detached object that is the work. It is precisely by a loss, by a cutting off or separation that the artist's self and his other

171

self, the work, mutually constitute one another—loss is the very condition of their existence. Discussing the image of Candace in the stream, that "beautiful and tragic little girl" that stands for the artist's lost, other self, Faulkner said,

> I saw that peaceful glinting of that branch was to become the dark, harsh flowing of time sweeping her to where she could not return to comfort him, but that just separation, division, would not be enough, not far enough. It must sweep her into dishonor and shame too. And that Benjy must never grow beyond this moment; that for him all knowing must begin and end with that fierce, panting, paused and stooping wet figure which smelled like trees. That he must never grow up to where the grief of bereavement could be leavened with understanding and hence the alleviation of rage as in the case of Jason, and of oblivion as in the case of Quentin.   (p. 159)

Appendix 1 /
Knight's Gambit: Poe, Faulkner, and the Tradition of the Detective Story

Like the machine gun, the detective story is an American invention. We can assign its origin to a specific author and story. The author is Edgar Allan Poe, and the story the 1841 tale "The Murders in the Rue Morgue." The detective genre has, of course, enjoyed worldwide popularity since Poe's day, but perhaps because of its native roots it has always had a special place in American literature, in both popular and serious fiction. Needless to say, Faulkner is a major inheritor of Poe in this genre, and I would even go so far as to maintain that *Absalom, Absalom!*, with its two young narrators puzzling over the facts of a very old murder trying to understand the motive, represents in some sense the culmination of the gothic detective form.

What I would like to discuss is Faulkner's relationship to the genre's origin (Poe's Dupin stories) in his own practice of detective fiction, that is to say, the way in which Faulkner interprets or inflects various conventions and images associated with the genre, devices that were for the most part invented by Poe. And I would like to center my discussion on Faulkner's 1949 collection *Knight's Gambit*.

Let me begin with a fairly clear cut example of Faulkner's work in the genre, the story called "An Error in Chemistry," first published in *Ellery Queen's Mystery Magazine* in 1946 and awarded a second prize in the magazine's annual contest for the best stories to appear in its pages during the year.[1] (The first prize that year, by the way, went to a writer named Manly Wade Wellman for a story with an American Indian setting called "A Star for a Warrior.") What I would like to discuss is the story's relationship to the first and third of Poe's Dupin tales—"The Murders in the Rue Morgue" and "The Purloined Letter." As you recall, "The Murders in the Rue Morgue" is a "locked-room" mystery. A mother and daughter have been brutally murdered in their apartment, and when the police arrive at the scene they find that all the apartment's windows and doors are locked from the inside and that the killer has escaped without leaving any trace of his "means of egress,[2] a puzzle that Dupin must solve on his way to unraveling the still deeper puzzle of the killer's bizarre identity. In "The Purloined Letter," on the other hand, we are confronted with a "hidden-object" mystery. A compromising letter has been stolen from the Queen by the Minister D—, and the police have rigorously searched the Minister's home and person without turning up the missing object. Dupin is certain that if the letter is to be of any use to the Minister in blackmailing the Queen, it must be ready to hand, which is to say that it must be hidden somewhere in the Minister's residence. And the mystery then turns upon the fact that the missing object is undoubtedly present within a finite physical enclosure (the Minister's house) without, as it were, making a physical appearance during the minute searches conducted by the police. Dupin solves the mystery by realizing that the Minister has hidden the letter under the very noses of the authorities by not seeming to hide it at all, by simply turning the letter inside out, readdressing it to himself in a feminine hand, and then leaving it in plain sight in a card rack hanging from the mantelpiece.

As you might conclude from this brief description of the two stories, "locked-room" and "hidden-object" mysteries are structurally related. In the former, a physical body (that of the murderer) is absent from an internally sealed space without there being any apparent means of egress; while in the latter a physical object is present within what we might call an externally sealed space (externally sealed because all the possible hiding places for the object outside the space have been logically eliminated) without the object's making a physical appearance. In the former instance (the locked room) we are certain that what we seek *is not inside a given space,* in the latter (the hidden object) that what we seek *cannot possibly be outside it.* Indeed, part of the peculiar force of the hidden-object and locked-room types of detective stories is that they seem to present us with a physical embodiment, a concrete spatial-ization, of the very mechanism of logical inclusion/exclusion on which rational analysis is based, present us with this as an apparent confounding of rational analysis.

Now it seems clear that Faulkner had registered the structural resemblance of these two types of mysteries, for in "An Error in Chemistry" he creates his own combination of a locked-room and hidden-object problem. The tale begins with Joel Flint telephoning the sheriff to say that he has killed his wife at the home of his father-in-law, Wesley Pritchel. When the sheriff arrives, he finds the killer Flint and the body of the victim. But Wesley Pritchel has locked himself in his room and won't come out. The sheriff sees Pritchel looking out the window, and the assumption is that Pritchel had witnessed the crime. In the sheriff's account to Gavin Stevens, Faulkner goes out of his way to emphasize the locked-room aspect of the scene by having Stevens ask whether Pritchel's room was locked from the inside or the outside. "On the inside," the sheriff replies.[3] And to compound matters, it seems to the sheriff that Joel Flint, who phones the authorities, waits for them to arrive, and then freely confesses to his wife's murder, is in search of his own locked room. As the sheriff says, "It's like he *wanted* to be locked up in jail. Not like he was submitting to arrest because he had killed his wife, but like he had killed her so he would be locked up" (112). So the sheriff locks Flint up, and the next morning Flint's cell is empty. As the narrator, Chick Mallison, describes it, "He had not broken out. He had walked out, out of the cell, out of the jail, out of town and apparently out of the country—no trace, no sign, no man who had seen him or seen anyone who might have been him" (116). And as he says later, "It was as if Flint had never been here at all—no mark, no scar to show that he had ever been in the jail cell" (120). Concerned about the witness's safety with Joel Flint on the loose, the sheriff sends his deputy out to Wesley Pritchel's place with instructions "not to let that locked door—or old Pritchel himself, if he comes out of it—out of his sight" (117). The deputy reports that Pritchel is still in his locked room and that he doesn't leave it even for his daughter's funeral.

Joel Flint's plan is remarkably simple: The motive is greed. Three Northern businessmen have offered Wesley Pritchel a sizable amount of money for his farm, but Pritchel won't sell. And even if he did, he would never give any of the money to his son-inlaw, whom he despises. So Flint decides to kill Pritchel and then use his talents as a make-up artist (Flint had performed for years in vaudeville billed as "Signor Canova, Master of Illusion, He Disappears While You Watch Him" [129]) to impersonate Pritchel, sell the farm, and pocket the money. The only problem with the plan is that while Flint might be able to fool someone like Gavin Stevens, who has only seen Pritchel twice in his whole life, or Chick Mallison, who has never seen him, Flint would never be able to fool his own wife, who is Pritchel's daughter. Consequently, Flint has to kill his wife, who would be a witness not necessarily to Pritchel's murder but the fact of Flint's impersonation (and thus implicitly to the fact that something had happened to remove from the scene the man he was impersonating). And the brilliance of Flint's plan is that he decides to reverse the usual sequence in the murders of an intended victim and a witness, which is to say, he decides to kill the witness (his wife) first and then kill the real victim (Pritchel) later. And he is able to accomplish this plan precisely because he has duped the authorities into misinterpreting the roles of Pritchel and of Flint's wife in the affair. He has created the illusion that his wife was the intended victim (when the sheriff asks Flint why he killed her, Flint says, "Why do men ever kill their wives? Call it for the insurance") and that his father-in-law was the witness.

All of which casts a somewhat different light on the locked-room aspect of the case. The standard locked-room problem requires that the murderer and victim be together at the moment of the crime in the same internally sealed space. But in Faulkner's version of the problem, the locked room has, so to speak, been split and doubled. There are two locked rooms, the jail cell containing the killer Joel Flint, locked from the outside, and Wesley Pritchel's bedroom containing the victim, locked from the inside. At some point during the night after he has been jailed for the murder of his wife, Joel Flint escapes from his cell. Faulkner doesn't say how this was accomplished, but in telling us that Flint had worked in vaudeville as an illusionist and escape artist, he has in effect finessed the question. For unlike Poe, Faulkner is not really interested in the mechanics of how the killer got out of the locked room without leaving any physical evidence of his means of escape.

Once Flint is on the loose, he goes to his father-in-law's farm, makes his way into the locked bedroom, and kills Pritchel. Flint then disguises himself to look like Pritchel and in turn tries to make the victim's corpse look like Flint. He obliterates Pritchel's face with a blow from a shovel and then buries him in a shallow grave with a scrapbook full of Flint's press clippings from vaudeville. Flint then locks himself in the bedroom, and by the next morning when the sheriff discovers Flint's escape and sends the deputy out to Pritchel's farm with instructions "not to let that locked door . . . out of his sight," it is Flint disguised as Pritchel behind that door. And it is Flint who stays there during the funeral of Pritchel's daughter, since he doesn't want to risk having his impersonation discovered by people who might have known Pritchel well. The way Flint has it figured, if he simply stays in the locked room, acting as if he were afraid that the escaped killer might still come back to eliminate the witness to the crime, then the only people that he may ever have to confront in his disguise are the three Northern businessmen who want to buy Pritchel's farm, and they have only seen Pritchel once before.

Flint's illusionary feat is ingenious, and so is Faulkner's. For in the very act of creating Flint's plan, Faulkner has, right before our eyes, reversed the standard structure of a locked-room mystery. When the law arrives at Pritchel's farm the first time, there hasn't in fact been a locked-room murder. Pritchel's daughter has been killed outside the house, and the person inside the locked room is the witness to the crime, who fears for his life. But when the law arrives at Pritchel's farm the second time in the person of the deputy who, after Flint's escape, has been sent to check on the old man's safety, Pritchel's bedroom has now almost certainly become the scene of a "locked-room" murder. But with this difference: it is now the killer who is present in, and the victim's corpse that is absent from, the internally sealed space. And this reversal in regard to the occupant of the locked room grows out of that earlier reversal in the order of the murders, the killing of the witness prior to the killing of the real victim, a trick that Faulkner, like any master of illusion, can't help calling our attention to when he has the puzzled sheriff remark, "It don't make sense. If he was afraid of a possible witness, he not only destroyed the witness before there was anything to be witnessed but also before there was any witness to be destroyed. He set up a sign saying 'Watch me and mark me'" (115). And that is, of course, just what Flint did, because as an illusionist he knows that the way to pull off a trick is to draw the audience's attention in one direction while doing something in another, that is, to make the audience misinterpret what it is that they are seeing.

Flint in effect tricks the sheriff into misreading the roles of the three people at the scene of the crime. When Hub Hampton arrives at Pritchel's farm the first time, he finds a triad of murderer, victim, and witness. He sees, correctly enough, that Flint is the murderer; but he reverses the other two roles in the triad, even though he senses that there is something amiss in his reading of the roles. He says to Gavin Stevens, "The wrong one is dead" (114)—by which he means that if the motive for the murder was greed, as Flint's remark about his wife's insurance suggests, then the amount of money to be gained from the insurance is trifling compared to the amount to be gained from the sale of Pritchel's farm to the three Northern businessmen. But for Flint to get his hands on that money, his victim would have to be Pritchel.

Faulkner's manipulation of the triad of murderer, victim, and witness in the tale has a familiar ring to it. As I argued in *Doubling and Incest*, Faulkner has a predilection for triangular or triadic structures, most obviously for the Oedipal triangle— a structure that he tends to inflect in a variety of ways by substituting different figures in the three roles. Thus, for example, in *Absalom, Absalom!* he substitutes for the standard triad of father, mother, and son the figures of brother avenger (Henry Sutpen), sister (Judith), and brother seducer (Charles Bon), while keeping intact the same structural relationships, the same sexual tensions, associated with the standard triad of the family romance. And as I further argued, the structural principle that governs the dynamics of this triangular relationship is the narcissistic principle of doubling, whereby one figure in the triangle tries to play more than one role within it, as when the son desires to usurp the father's role and thus enjoy a dual relationship to the mother—that of both son and husband.

The ultimate goal of the structural principle of doubling, as it operates within the Oedipal triangle, is the collapsing of all three roles into one. And something very like this is what happens in the triangular structure of murderer, victim, and witness in "An Error in Chemistry." In the sheriff's interpretation of the initial crime scene, Flint's real intended victim Pritchel appears to play the role of the witness, an appearance that deceives the sheriff and that ultimately makes it possible for the murderer also to play the role of the witness when Flint kills Pritchel and assumes his identity. As the narrator says at one point in commenting on the resemblance in physical build of Flint and Pritchel, "he and his father-in-law could easily have cast that same shadow which later for a short time they did" (110), and we know that for Faulkner the image of the shadow almost always evokes the notion of doubling.

Victim as witness, murderer as witness—it is as if the roles of the two people actively involved in the crime (murderer and victim) had been collapsed into that of passive observer (and indeed, the dynamic principle at work here is a kind of death drive that seeks a state of quiescence, of absolute passivity, for the self). Moreover, it is not without significance that the persons who fill these three roles are already linked together in a triangular family relationship as father-in-law, son-in-law, and daughter, the male-male-female structure of the Oedipal triangle. (We might note that in Faulkner's fiction a locked room or a closed door often signifies the site not of a murder but of a primal scene, a fantasized scene of parental intercourse in which the child interprets the sounds of love-making as the sounds of violence perpetrated by the father against the mother.) At one point in the tale, Gavin Stevens gives his own reading of the triangular structure of the crime as a kind of shadow-play, "That triumvirate of murderer, victim, and bereaved—not three flesh-and-blood people but just an illusion, a shadow-play on a sheet—not only neither men nor women nor young nor old but just three labels which cast two shadows for the simple and only reason that it requires a minimum of two in order to postulate the verities of injustice and grief" (121).

But at this point we should pause and ask ourselves if Faulkner hasn't in fact performed another illusion before our very eyes in regard to the "locked-room" character of the story, another disappearing act as startling as the murderer's switching places with the victim in the role of the witness. We suggested a moment ago that when the deputy arrives at Pritchel's home the morning after Flint's escape and stations himself outside the locked bedroom door, he confronts in effect a locked-room mystery, finds an internally sealed space that is the scene of a murder, though in this instance the sealed space contains the living body of the killer rather than the dead body of the victim. Yet isn't it precisely upon that difference in the degree of animation of the room's occupant that the "mystery" in a locked-room problem hinges? Corpses can't lock doors, so to find a corpse alone in a room whose doors and windows have been locked from the inside is mysterious. But where's the mystery in finding the internally sealed space occupied by a living murderer, even if that murderer is disguised as the victim he has done away with in that locked room? The only thing that might resemble a mystery here is how Flint got out of the locked jail cell and then into Pritchel's locked bedroom to kill him, but as we said, Faulkner finesses that problem by making Flint an escape artist. What Faulkner has done in effect is to switch, under the reader's nose, the type of problem that lies on the other side of the locked door. He has set up a situation that bears the obvious marks of a locked-room puzzle, but when we open that locked door we find that it has changed into a hidden-object problem.

Instead of a purloined letter, the object that everyone is seeking in Faulkner's tale is the missing killer. However, like the purloined letter, whose appearance was altered by turning it inside out, readdressing it to the Minister D— in a feminine hand, and then leaving it in plain view in the Minister's drawing room, the killer has also altered his appearance and hidden himself in plain sight. And just as part of altering the purloined letter's appearance was the turning of the letter inside out, so part of altering the murderer's "appearance" in Faulkner's tale is the turning of the locked-room mystery's spatial coding of killer and victim inside out. Which is to say that the person who should be outside the internally sealed space (the killer) is inside it, and the person who should be inside that space (the victim) is outside it (buried under the feed room in the stable).

From what we have said so far it should be clear that

Faulkner was a profound student of the origin and conventions of detective fiction and that he wrote his own detective stories with an eye to situating them within the tradition of that genre that had been originated by a fellow Southerner almost a hundred years before. However, what we must add is that while it may be interesting to discuss a tale like "An Error in Chemistry" in terms of its manipulation of traditional detective story devices and thus Faulkner's inflection of the genre's origin in Poe, that is, interesting to give a reading of it in terms of literary history, it is much less satisfying to read "An Error in Chemistry" simply in terms of the pleasures of a standard detective story. For the tale is marred in two important ways.

First, Faulkner's decision to make the killer a former vaudeville illusionist and escape artist inevitably strikes the reader as being itself a kind of vaudeville trick, an illusion that lets Faulkner escape from the traditional challenge of coming up with a solution to the locked-room problem different from the one which Poe originated. As any student of the genre knows, this is a challenge to which detective story writers have consistently addressed themselves over the years. (Indeed, one might note in passing that if the author of a detective story is going to allow himself the liberty of making the killer an illusionist and escape artist, then he might as well go all the way and make his killer the invisible man or superman. A large part of our interest in murder mysteries depends upon the killer's being someone with ordinary human powers like you and me—not a ghost or a creature from outer space.) Second, the way in which Flint's imposture is revealed and his capture effected is not the result of Gavin Stevens's analytic investigations but of an accident: Flint disguised as Pritchel makes the mistake of mixing a cold toddy in Stevens's and the sheriff's presence by trying to dissolve the sugar in raw whiskey, the kind of mistake that a Southerner like Pritchel would never make, but that the Northerner Flint would. Seeing this,

Stevens and the sheriff leap upon Flint, wrestling him to the floor and wrestling him out of some of his make-up—a climax that leaves the reader with the feeling that he has witnessed, if not a *deus ex machina*, at least an instance of *iustitia ex ampulla*, justice poured out of a bottle.

All of which leads me to suggest that as a writer of detective fiction Faulkner is most successful when he takes the conventions of the genre and shapes them to his own materials, his own obsessive concerns, rather than when he competes with the genre's originator on terms that are almost wholly Poe's. The reason for this is fairly straightforward. Faulkner's strengths as a fiction writer tend to be in the direction of character and setting and in the poetry of the language, while the detective story is a form that essentially favors plot and has a low tolerance for highly developed characterization or highly evocative language. Indeed, in the history of the genre one finds not great characters but rather great caricatures. From Dupin to Holmes to Poirot, we are confronted not with fully-rendered personalities but with monsters of idiosyncrasy, figures conveyed through one or two odd traits as trademarks. Yet to say that the detective story is a form which essentially favors plot is not to imply that Faulkner has a weakness when it comes to plotting; it is simply to say that the specialized kind of plot which forms the core of the genre demands a type of ingenuity that was the great strength of the genre's inventor, but not of Faulkner, as "An Error in Chemistry" and several of the other tales in *Knight's Gambit* make clear. It is only when Faulkner pushes the detective story to the limits of the short story form that he is able to bend it to his own artistic will, as he did with the tale that gives the collection its title. And it is on the story called "Knight's Gambit" that I would like to focus the rest of my discussion.

Faulkner originally wrote "Knight's Gambit" as a short story, completing it by January 1942. He described it as "a love story, in which Stevens prevents a crime (murder) not for justice but to gain (he is now fifty plus) the childhood sweetheart which he lost 20 years ago" (Blotner, 2: 1097). Some four years later in early 1946, Faulkner began revising and expanding the tale, stretching it from short story to almost novella length before it was completed in November 1948. What I would like to concentrate on is the way that Faulkner took two devices that originated with Poe—the imagery of a chess game used to evoke the battle of wits between detective and criminal, and the notion of the detective's having a personal motive for becoming involved in the solution or prevention of the crime—and, by annexing these devices to standard Faulknerian material, made them his own.

The action of "Knight's Gambit" begins on the evening of 4 December 1941, three days before the Japanese attack on Pearl Harbor. Gavin Stevens and his nephew Chick Mallison are playing chess at home when a young man named Max Harriss and his sister burst into the room. The brother and sister are the spoiled children of Melisandre Backus Harriss, a childhood friend of Chick's mother. Max Harriss has come to demand that Stevens, as the county attorney, take action to get Captain Sebastian Gualdres out of their house, to have him deported if need be. Young Harris says that Gualdres, an Argentine fortune hunter whom the Harriss family had met during their foreign travels, was at first engaged to his sister but has since jilted her and intends to marry his mother. Harriss wants Gavin Stevens to intervene, challenging the older man by asking, "You're the Law here, aren't you?"[4] And Harriss implies that if Stevens doesn't act, then he (Harriss) will take matters into his own hands and kill Gualdres.

The situation is a familiar one in Faulkner's fiction. A young man confronts his father or a father-surrogate (an older man who represents authority, who embodies a patriarchal Law) and demands to know what the older man is going to do about the womenfolk, whether he intends to protect the young man's sister or mother from an interloper, which is to say, to protect the womenfolk from themselves. One thinks of Quentin Compson and his father in *The Sound and the Fury* and of Henry and Thomas Sutpen in the story that Quentin helps narrate, *Absalom, Absalom!* And indeed the father-son analogy certainly applies to the confrontation between Gavin Stevens and Max Harriss. For as we learn in the course of the story Stevens had been briefly and secretly engaged to Harriss's mother when she was a girl of sixteen, and the implication is that, had they married, Stevens would have been the father of her son, much as he is to become her present son's stepfather by the story's end. Moreover, young Harriss's real father, a New Orleans bootlegger, was murdered, and just as the role of Max's father has been violently vacated once before, so now Max is threatening to make it violently vacant once again by killing the man who plans to marry his mother—a state of affairs that, given Stevens's feelings about Max's mother, is not lost on the county attorney. Which is simply to say that when young Harriss presents himself to Stevens in a situation that we recognize from other Faulkner fiction as being that of a son confronting a father to demand that the father exercise paternal authority, he is, from Stevens's point of view, in ef- fect challenging Gavin to exhibit his *own* qualifications to fill the role of stepfather, challenging him to exhibit an authority that is not only able to protect the womenfolk by repulsing the intruder but also able to make the son obey the paternal will by not breaking the law, by not killing the prospective stepfather—a matter of no small importance if Stevens him- self ultimately intends to fill that role.

Part of the tale's artistry is that, by having Harriss and his sister interrupt Gavin's and Chick's chess game in order to tell their story, Faulkner is able to assimilate the details of their story to the imagery of chess and thus able to evoke young Harriss's challenge to Stevens in chivalric terms, to present it as a contest, a joust, between a younger and an older knight. As I mentioned earlier, chess is associated with the detective genre from the very beginning. In the first Dupin story, "The Murders in the Rue Morgue," the narrator cites the game as an example, along with draughts and whist, to illustrate the workings of that analytic power which he considers the essence of detection, and in the third Dupin story, "The Purloined Letter," Poe presents us with a scenario that is strongly reminiscent of a chess game—there is a king and queen, and there is a battle of wits between two knights (Dupin is a *Chevalier*, and we must assume that his double the Minister D— is at least of equal rank), a battle for possession of a letter that concerns the queen's honor and that could, in the Minister's hands, reduce the queen to being a pawn. Given the game's presence at the genre's origin, it is not surprising that the image of a chess game is one of the most frequently used figures for the battle of wits between detective and criminal in the form's history, a figure of the detective's attempt to double the thought processes of his opponent so as to end up one move ahead of him. This doubling of an opponent's thoughts, in which one mentally plays out possible moves, countermoves, and responses against an antithetical mirror-image of one's own mind, at once reflects the kind of thinking that goes on in a chess game and is reflected in turn by the physical structure of the game itself in which the opposing pieces at the start face each other in a mirror-image relationship.

Faulkner would have been exposed to an especially interesting example of the association of chess with both the detective genre and the image of chivalry in the project that he worked on in late 1944—the screenplay of Raymond Chandler's *The Big Sleep*, on which he collaborated with Leigh Brackett and Jules Furthman. Chandler's detective Philip Marlowe always keeps a chessboard in his apartment with a problem laid out on it. At one point in the novel, Marlowe returns home to find that there is another kind of problem laid out in his apartment—his client's daughter, the nymphomaniacal Carmen Sternwood, naked in his Murphy bed with monkey business in mind. Predictably enough, Marlowe's chivalrous nature immediately turns to thoughts of chess: "I went . . . across the room . . . to the chessboard on a card table under the lamp. There was a problem laid out on the board, a six-mover. I couldn't solve it, like a lot of my problems. I reached down and moved a knight."[5] Several moments later, he adds, "The move with the knight was wrong. I put it back where I had moved it from. Knights had no meaning in this game. It wasn't a game for knights" (146). Yet for all his tough talk Marlowe doesn't take advantage of his client's mentally unstable daughter.

Indeed, Chandler had always thought of Marlowe as a kind of modern knight-errant: the detective in search of the solution like a knight in quest of the Grail. Chandler had named an earlier version of his detective Mallory, alluding to the author of the *Morte D'Arthur*; and references to Arthurian romance fill the novels. In *The High Window*, for example, Marlowe is described as a "shop-soiled Galahad";[6] while in *Farewell, My Lovely* Velma Valento, the woman that Marlowe has been in quest of throughout the novel, hides her identity behind the name Helen Grayle. And of course one of the Marlowe novels is even named *The Lady in the Lake*. The tone of Marlowe's slightly ironic, somewhat battered chivalry is set at the very beginning of *The Big Sleep*, when he comes to the home of his client General Sternwood and notices above the front door a "stained-glass panel showing a knight in dark armor rescuing a lady who was tied to a tree and didn't have any clothes on . . . he was fiddling with the knots on the ropes that tied the lady to the tree and not getting anywhere. I stood there and thought that if I lived in the house, I would sooner or later have to climb up there and help him" (1).

It is a short step from Chandler's Marlowe (read Malory), a chessplaying detective and modern knight-errant who uses his wits to uphold his personal code of chivalry, to Faulkner's Gavin Stevens, another chessplaying detective whose own chivalrous nature (as evidenced in his encounters with Eula Varner Snopes and her daughter Linda) is evoked by his Christian name's suggestion of King Arthur's nephew and most famous knight, Gawain. (Recall in this regard that the failed knight in Faulkner's 1926 giftbook for Helen Baird, *Mayday*, is named Galwyn.) But the difference is that where Chandler and Faulkner both use the game of chess, with its kings and queens and knights, to evoke the chivalrous character of their detectives, Faulkner, with an eye to the game's presence at the origin of the genre in Poe's Dupin stories, also uses the game to evoke that basic structure of the analytic act which both chess and detection share—that alogical attempt to project an image of the opponent's mind as an antithetical mirror-image of one's own mind so that one can anticipate the opponent's next move and end up one jump ahead of him, a form of mirror doubling that, as we said, is reflected in the physical structure of the game itself. Indeed, at one point Faulkner alludes to this mirror-image aspect of chess when he has Gavin reply to Chick's apparent dismissal of chess as "a game" by remarking, "Nothing by which all human passion and hope and folly can be mirrored and then proved, ever was just a game" (192).

Faulkner evokes the structure of mirror doubling shared by chess and analytic detection at the very start of "Knight's Gambit." When Max Harriss and his sister burst into Gavin's study, interrupting the chess game, Chick remarks almost in passing that the brother and sister look so much alike that "at first glance they might have been twins" (135). Now there is an obvious appropriateness in having a brother and sister who look like twins interrupt a game whose physical structure involves a mirror-image symmetry in the opening alignment of the pieces, an alignment that evokes the opposing black and white chessmen as antithetical twin images of each other. And this appropriateness was to become even greater some eight years after the appearance of "Knight's Gambit" when, with the publication of *The Town* in 1957, we learn that one of the chessplayers in this scene, Gavin Stevens, is himself a twin.[7] Gavin's twin sister Margaret is Chick Mallison's mother, and as Chick implies on several occasions in *The Town* the twin- ship of his mother and uncle seems almost to involve their knowing each other's thoughts—apropos the kind of mental doubling associated with analysis in chess. Thus, when the Harrisses burst in on the chess game between Gavin and Chick, a brother and sister who look like twins confront a man who is playing a game of mirror-image symmetries against the son of his twin sister. And what all this twinning and mirroring is ultimately meant to make the reader notice is that the rela- tionship between Captain Gualdres and Max Harriss is the mirror image, the antithetical double, of the relationship be- tween Gavin Stevens and Chick Mallison.

In each case there is an older man and a younger: in one instance the older man is a father-figure for the younger (Gavin and Chick), while in the other the older man aspires to a role that would involve his becoming a father-figure for the younger (Gualdres and Max). And in both cases the father-figure's task is to bring the young man from adolescense to maturity, to conduct a kind of rite of passage by establishing, through a veiled, and sometimes not so veiled, competition with the young man, the older man's authority to instruct him, a pa- ternal authority able to command the young man's respect and thus allow him to learn from the older man. But while this instructive competition or competitive instruction has been eminently successful in the case of Gavin and Chick (Chick not only respects his uncle, he idolizes him), it has been a disaster in the case of Gualdres and Max.

The competition in the latter case turns upon skills that are quite literally knightly—riding, fencing, and romantic dalli- ance. As Max Harriss's sister describes it to Stevens, her brother is "the rich young earl" and Gualdres "the dark romantic for- eign knight that beat the young earl riding the young earl's own horses and then took the young earl's sword away from him with a hearthbroom. Until at last all he had to do was ride at night up to the young earl's girl friend's window, and whistle" (183). One senses a sexual overtone to the first two of these knightly skills (riding a horse and using a sword) that is made explicit in the third, and one further senses that this competition between the older and younger man for the affection of the same woman (the young Cayley girl) is a displacement of the Oedipal struggle initiated by Gualdres's aspiring to marry Max's mother. But where the instructive competition between Gualdres and Max involves skills that are literally knightly, the competitive instruction between Gavin and Chick involves a sublimation of knightly combat into the mental combat of chess and into the verbal fencing that accompanies Gavin's and Chick's games. Indeed, to emphasize the parallel between these two types of combat, Faulkner has Chick momentarily best his uncle in a discussion of the relative sensitivity of younger men and older men and has Gavin reply, "All right. . . . *Touché* then. Will that do?" (174). But then Gavin beats Chick again at chess and becomes sarcastic, and Chick says that Gavin would probably have a better game by playing against himself, "at least you'd have the novelty of being surprised at your opponent's blunders" (176). To which Gavin replies, "All right, all right. . . . Didn't I say *touché?*" (176).

The fact that Chick every so often scores a hit in his verbal fencing with Gavin suggests why this competitive instruction of the nephew by the uncle works so well, for though Chick may come to the end of these encounters feeling chagrined, he never feels hopeless or humiliated, never feels that he hasn't had some degree of success in making his uncle treat him like a man. But it is precisely a sense of humiliation that Max Harriss continually feels in his encounters with Gualdres, for in just those areas in which Max most prides himself (riding and fencing), Gualdres beats him as if he were a child. Or as

Max's sister says, "It wasn't even because of Mother. It was because Sebastian always beat him. At everything" (181). It is worth noting here, as regards the kinship of Gavin and Chick, that in those cultures with communal rites of passage for young men, the relative usually given the responsibility for the young man's initiation to adulthood is the maternal uncle rather than the father, the communal wisdom apparently being that the Oedipal tensions between father and son are such that a male relative from the mother's side of the family is a more effective initiator of the son, particularly if the initiation ceremony involves, as is usually the case, the son's symbolic death and rebirth.

The artistry involved in Faulkner's assimilation of the knightly combat of Max and Gualdres to the mental jousting of Gavin's and Chick's chess games depends in large part, of course, upon the fact that the game of chess, according to virtually every psychoanalytic reading of its structure and symbolism, is a ritual sublimation of father murder played out as the checkmating of the king. The word "checkmate" is from the Persian "shah mat," the king is dead. As the psychoanalyst and chess master Reuben Fine points out, since "genetically, chess is more often than not taught to the boy by his father, or by a father substitute," it naturally "becomes a means of working out the father-son rivalry."[8] And as another chess critic has noted, "chess is a matter of both father murder and the attempt to prevent it. This mirror function of chess is of extreme importance; obviously the player appears in both a monstrous and a virtuous capacity—planning parricide, at the same time warding it off; recreating Oedipal fantasy, yet trying to disrupt it. Yet the stronger urge is the monstrous one; the player wants to win, to kill the father rather than defend him."[9]

It is because Gavin has done his work so well in sublimating Oedipal tension, in conducting his nephew from adolescence to maturity through a prolonged rite of passage symbolically evoked by their combative encounters across the chessboard, that Gavin is able to outwit Max Harriss, prevent the son from breaking the patriarchal law by killing the prospective stepfather, and establish his own right to fill the role of stepfather by virtue of his having commanded the son's respect and obedience. And the agency by which Gavin establishes his authority over Max Harriss is in some sense his relationship with Chick, establishes this authority not merely in the sense that he has demonstrated his ability to be an enabling father-figure in his shepherding of Chick from boyhood to manhood, but in the sense that he has literally created through his relationship with Chick a bright young adult who is his devoted helper, an assistant bright enough to know when patriarchal commands must be obeyed and when they must be set aside. And this latter knowledge is crucial, for it is Chick, of course, who brings Gavin the piece of information that allows him to foil Max's plan—the information that Rafe McCallum had sold his wild stallion to Max that afternoon—brings it to his uncle even though Gavin is shut up in his study working on his translation of the Old Testament, that labor of twenty years which no one is allowed to interrupt once he has closed his study door, as Chick says, "nor man woman nor child, client well-wisher or friend, to touch even the knob until his uncle turned it from inside" (207). But Chick has come to maturity as a young man so confident of his own judgment, or rather, so confident of his uncle's respect for his judgment, that he bursts into the study and disturbs his uncle in order to deliver the piece of information that he senses is somehow critical (though he himself doesn't quite know how), disturbs this imposing, white-haired father-figure in the task of translating the patriarchal law.

Together with McCallum, Gavin and Chick hurry to the Harriss mansion aiming to thwart Max's plan, and it is part of the wittiness of Faulkner's plot that the method which Harriss has chosen to eliminate his intended victim constitutes a kind of double entendre, evoking that sexual overtone to the chivalric skill of horseback riding that we mentioned earlier. Gualdres owns a blind mare that he keeps in a separate stable at the Harriss place and that he rides every night, but the people of Jefferson have come to feel that the mare is itself a blind to cover Gualdres's nightly romantic adventures, that Gualdres has trained the mare to gallop around the empty paddock at night at varying gaits as if it were being ridden so as to conceal the fact of its rider's absence in search of young women. The humor of Max's plan turns upon his having removed the mare from its stable and substituted McCallum's wild stallion, so that when Gualdres comes for his (k)nightly ride, he'll find an animal that will jump up and down on top of him rather than the reverse—a switch in the gender of the animal to be ridden that smacks faintly of French farce, as if the seducer had gotten by mistake into the husband's bedroom rather than the wife's. No doubt, Max considers this an appropriate demise for the expert rider and swordsman who had galloped his horse up to the Cayley girl's verandah and tried to beat Max's time. (We might note in passing that horseback riding as a sexual metaphor was used more than once by Faulkner during this period. In the film version of *The Big Sleep*, which Faulkner worked on between writing "Knight's Gambit" as a short story and rewriting it as a novella, Philip Marlowe and Vivian Rutledge, played by Humphrey Bogart and Lauren Bacall, engage at one point in a verbal fencing match in which they appraise each other's romantic possibilities as if they were sizing up the physical abilities of racehorses. Having given her estimate of Marlowe, Vivian Rutledge invites Marlowe to reciprocate, and he says, "Well, I can't tell till I've seen you over a distance of ground. You've got a touch of class, but uh . . . I don't know how . . . how far you can go." To which she replies, "A lot depends on who's in the saddle." [One recalls that when Faulkner first met Lauren Bacall during the filming of *To Have and Have Not* he told an

195

acquaintance that "Bogie's . . . new girl friend" was "like a young colt" (Blotner, 2:1156).])

Gavin, of course, saves Gualdres from entering the dark stable and having his brains bucked out, and Faulkner evokes their confrontation as a kind of chivalric combat between the two prospective suitors of the widow Harriss, a duel in which Gualdres's knightly skills are no match for Gavin's prowess in intellectual jousting honed over the chessboard. With a certain *noblesse oblige*, Gavin begins the conversation in the native tongue of his rival, and Faulkner underlines the at once humorous and knightly character of their encounter by having Chick remark that he could understand some of the Spanish because he had read *Don Quixote* and *The Cid*. Gavin structures this verbal exchange as if it were a wager: he bets Gualdres that he doesn't want to enter the darkened stable. And for this life-saving piece of information, Gualdres agrees to marry the young Harriss girl and take her away with him, thus leaving the widow Harriss free for someone else.

And it is with this final ploy of Gavin's that we can see most clearly that other device which Faulkner took from Poe's Dupin stories to use in "Knight's Gambit"—the detective's personal motive for becoming involved in the solution or prevention of the crime. The trajectory of the development of the detective genre within the Dupin stories runs from the pole of physical violence in the first story (the brutal murder of a mother and daughter by a killer ape) to the pole of intellectual violence in the third story (the mental victimization involved in the blackmail of the queen by the Minister D—). And just as the movement from the first to the third Dupin story seems to involve a muting of the form, a sublimation or attentuation of the crime's violence, so this movement also involves a progressive simplification or reduction of what constitutes the mysterious element in the tale. In the first Dupin story, "The Murderers in the Rue Morgue," we are not only confronted with the problem of "who done it," or more precisely "what done it," but also with the problems of "how he done it" (the locked room mystery) and "why he done it" (the senseless savagery of the crime). But by the time of the third Dupin story, "The Purloined Letter," we know at the outset who took the letter, how he took it, why he took it, and what use he intends to make of it. The only mystery is how the Minister D— has concealed the letter in his home so that the police can't find it.

It is as if the inventor of the genre in producing a series of detective stories had to find an ongoing challenge to his ingenuity in order to spur his imagination to new heights, and that that challenge was to see how much he could pare away or reduce the mysterious element in the tale, the element that needed solution, and still have a detective story. But what happens in "The Purloined Letter" is that with the attenuation of the mysterious element in the crime, its reduction to a single, circumscribed problem, a mysterious element from another quarter enters the story toward the end to fill the vacuum—the mystery of the detective's motive for taking the case. For though at first it seems that Dupin becomes involved in the affair of the letter because he is being well-paid or because he is a supporter of the queen's cause (both of which are true), we learn at the end that the real reason for his taking the case is that he has an old score to settle with the Minister D—. The Minister had done Dupin "an evil turn" once in Vienna which Dupin told the Minister "quite good-humoredly" he would remember (3:993). Consequently, Dupin goes to the trouble of retrieving the letter himself from the Minister's residence, so that he can substitute for it a duplicate letter informing the Minister who it was that made the switch and brought about his downfall.

Something very like this scenario of creating a new source of mystery from the detective's motives, as the mysterious element in the crime is being reduced to a bare minimum, occurs in "Knight's Gambit." We know at the start by his own admission who the prospective killer is, we know the intended victim and the reason for the crime, and we know that it will be committed within a few days. The only thing we don't know is how it will be done. But as those standard mysterious aspects of the crime are being pared away in the course of the story to a single problem, another mystery is emerging, the problem of the identity of the man who was secretly engaged to Max's mother when she was a girl of sixteen. The realization that it was Gavin Stevens comes about simultaneously with our realizing that Gavin's involvement in preventing the murder has not been simply in an official capacity, but rather has been a personal involvement in order to win the hand of the woman he was once engaged to. For if he allows Max's plan to succeed, then as county attorney he will have to handle the case, and I think that it is still conventional wisdom in the South, as elsewhere, that the best way to advance one's suit with a wealthy widow is not to prosecute her only son for first-degree murder.

But Gavin's problem is more difficult than that, for there are two other obstacles—the lovestruck daughter and the foreign suitor. And the solution that Gavin works out makes us realize how early in the affair he had begun planning to turn matters to his own ends if the situation permitted, how early he had begun to think of the matter not as a chess game but a chess problem, as Faulkner suggests when he has Gavin, at the end of the evening when first Max Harriss and his sister and then Miss Harriss and the Cayley girl interrupt his chess games, sweep the board clean and set up a chess problem "with the horses and rooks and two pawns" (192). Of course, in Gavin's personal chess problem, the object is not to checkmate the king (indeed, it is precisely that Oedipal content he tries to repress), but rather to capture the queen. And the alignment of pieces in his problem is somewhat different from the one he sets up on the board for Chick: there are two dark knights, one older, one younger (Gualdres and Max), one white knight (the white-haired Gavin, read Gawain), a young dark queen (Max's sister), an older white queen (the widow Harriss), and one white rook (the widow's property). The solution goes like this: in exchange for Gavin's saving his life, the older dark knight settles for the young dark queen and half the white rook, or as Gavin puts it, "a princess and half a castle, against some of his bones and maybe his brains too" (218). And in exchange for Gavin's saving Max's life as well, which is to say, for Gavin's preventing him from committing murder and per-haps being executed, the young dark knight acknowledges Gavin's authority and accepts that penalty which small town prosecutors have for years offered to local boys as an alterna-tive to being charged with a first offense—he joins the army. (Indeed, part of Faulkner's wit in setting the story on the eve of America's entrance into the Second World War is the way that this allows him to bundle up all the Oedipal conflict, adolescent mischief-making, and chivalrous yearning for des-perate glory and ship it off to the front in the persons of Max, Gualdres, and Chick.) With all the obstacles removed from his path, the white-haired knight rides up to the empty castle and captures the white queen.

But we should have expected this conclusion in a story named "Knight's Gambit," for while there is no chess opening called "the knight's gambit," Chick does tell us that his uncle's favorite opening move was pawn to queen four, that is, the first move of the queen's gambit. And Gavin had said to his nephew during one of their chess games, when Chick had forked Gavin's queen and rook, that in that situation you should always take the queen and let the castle go because "a knight can move two squares at once and even in two directions at once," but "he cant move twice" (176). Chick later applies this remark about the knight's being able to move in two di-rections at once to Gualdres's attentions to both the widow Harriss and her daughter, but surely Faulkner means for the reader to apply the remark to another knight who in one move was able to carry out his public duty by preventing a murder and at the same time accomplish the most personal of goals, the winning of a wife.

In his reworking of this device of the detective's personal motive for involving himself in the investigation, as in his annexing of the imagery of chess to the detective story, Faulkner shows his debt to Poe, but he also shows how far he could expand and develop such devices when he joined them to the kind of material that was closest to his imagination, thus revealing himself not only as a worthy successor but a formidable competitor of the genre's originator.

Appendix 2 /
Horace Benbow and the Myth of Narcissa

Sometimes a writer gets an idea for the structure of a character, and one fictional incarnation isn't enough to exhaust the possibilities inherent in it, possibilities in its development that may often be mutually exclusive. Something like that is what happened with Faulkner and the basic structure underlying the figures of Quentin Compson, Horace Benbow, and Gavin Stevens. Clearly, Faulkner set out to imagine a twentieth-century male descendant of an aristocratic Southern family, a descendant more or less weighed down by his sense of the past and more or less unsuited by education and temperament for thriving in the modern world, a descendant who personified, if not the South, then the ruling class in the South at a certain point in this century, determined to live in the past by staying enclosed in its own region, self-absorbed with its own image in a way that inevitably reminded Faulkner of the figure of Narcissus.

At first glance the similarities between these three characters seem clear enough. Noel Polk, for one, has described the structural resemblance between Quentin and Horace: "Both . . . are Prufrockian intellectuals; both are hopelessly idealistic and obsessively narcissistic; both are sexually interested in their sisters, and overly concerned with their sister's virginity; . . . both are dominated by bedridden mothers; . . . and both are incapable of dealing with the real world on its own terms. Horace is, in effect, a forty-three-year-old and completely jaded Quentin, surely what Quentin would have become had he lived another quarter-century."[1] And that, of course, is one of the reasons Faulkner needed another fictional incarnation of this character's structure. For one plausible, not to say probable, outcome was that this type of person would succumb in adolescence to melancholy self-absorption and take his own life. So that another embodiment was required to imagine the character's maturity, to imagine his destiny as not the early death of a morbidly romantic youth but the living death of an ineffectual middle-aged failure.

203

One could make an equally persuasive list of the resemblances between Horace Benbow and Gavin Stevens. Both are lawyers; both have a combination of an American and European education (Horace at Sewanee and Oxford; Gavin at Harvard and Heidelberg); both have a special relationship with an only sister; both work for the Y.M.C.A. in France during the First World War, and both take Montgomery Ward Snopes with them; both have aesthetic avocations (Horace's glass-blowing; Gavin's retranslation of the Old Testament into ancient Greek); both marry women who have been married before and who have children by the previous marriage; and though neither man fathers a child, both serve as surrogate fathers (Horace to Little Belle, and Gavin to Chick Mallison); and both are fond of quoting the same line of poetry, "Less oft is peace" (Horace in *Sanctuary* and Gavin in "Knight's Gambit"). And, clearly, the reason that Faulkner needed yet another incarnation of the structure in Gavin Stevens was to explore the possibility that this figure might not end up a youthful suicide or middle-aged failure but eventually win through to some kind of qualified success in his personal and public life.

What I would like to focus on is Horace Benbow in his role as a transitional figure between Quentin Compson and Gavin Stevens and, specifically, center the discussion on a structural element shared by all three characters—the special relationship which each has with an only sister. For the most part I will be discussing Horace as he appears in *Sanctuary* (both in the original text and in the 1931 published version) and making digressions, as needed, into *Flags in the Dust* for further analysis of his character, as well as into other works in which Quentin Compson and Gavin Stevens appear, as comparisons between their characters and Horace's seem appropriate.

The first thing that one notices in comparing the 1931 published version of *Sanctuary* with Faulkner's original text is the major change that Faulkner made in the opening of the novel. The original version begins with the scene of the black murderer in jail awaiting execution; while the published version begins with the scene in which the runaway husband Horace Benbow, drinking from a woodland spring, sees first his own reflection in the pool and then that of Popeye's straw hat as Popeye advances soundlessly from his place of concealment to capture him. In the afterword to his edition of the original text, Noel Polk theorizes that the opening scene of the black murderer in jail is meant to produce a symmetry with the book's ending, which is to say that "the book concludes as it begins, by focusing on a murderer patiently awaiting his execution: the Negro at the beginning, Popeye at the end" (OT, 302). Faulkner was, of course, obsessed with symmetry, an obsession that underlies his interest in doubling and twinship, in mirror images and shadows. Indeed, there has probably been no writer since Racine who worked as hard as Faulkner to create symmetrical relationships of all kinds in his work.

Polk is, then, almost certainly correct in his explanation of Faulkner's choosing to begin the original version of the novel with the scene of the black murderer, but the difficulty is that the symmetry achieved by this opening isn't exact. For in both the original text and the 1931 published version, the last scene in the novel is not Popeye in jail awaiting his execution, but Temple Drake and her father sitting in the Luxembourg Gardens listening to a band concert while Temple examines her face in a compact mirror. Phrased that way, one can see immediately why Faulkner changed the opening of the 1931 version, for by beginning the book with Horace seeing his reflection in a pool, Faulkner creates an exact symmetry with the final scene of Temple looking at her face in a mirror. And Faulkner is able to extend this symmetry to include the next to last scene in the book as well, our final glimpse of Popeye. For since what Horace sees in the pool is not just his own reflection but the reflection of Popeye's hat, the presence of both images on the mirroring surface codes Horace and Popeye as mirror images of one another, as antithetical doubles. Small wonder then that our last glimpse of Popeye is a freeze frame that arrests him forever in a moment of ultimate narcissism:

> . . . they adjusted the rope, dragging it over Popeye's sleek, oiled head, breaking his hair loose. His hands were tied, so he began to jerk his head, flipping his hair back each time it fell forward again. . . .
>
> "Pssst!" he said, the sound cutting sharp into the drone of the minister's voice; "pssst!" The sheriff looked at him; he quit jerking his neck and stood rigid, as though he had an egg balanced on his head. "Fix my hair, Jack," he said.
>
> "Sure," the sheriff said. "I'll fix it for you"; springing the trap.[2]

Fixing one's hair is an activity usually performed in front of a mirror, and in effect Popeye, with his hands tied behind his back, tries to use the sheriff's gaze as a mirror for a final self-regarding gesture. But like the mirrored and mirroring gaze in Narcissus's pool, this one is fatal.

To the extent that our final glimpses of Popeye and Temple emphasize the narcissism of each, the two are assimilated in their self-absorption, a resemblance that evokes the physically impotent Popeye as a feminized male. And given the symmetry of the novel's beginning and end, this assimilation of Popeye and Temple at the close balances that other one at the start when Horace sees the reflection of himself and Popeye's hat in the pool. Faulkner's friend Phil Stone had certainly talked enough psychoanalysis to the author for him to know that a hat was a common dream symbol of genitalia, either male or female, so that this detail serves to reinforce our sense of Popeye as Horace's antithetical double, as a dark mirror image whose physical impotence reflects Horace's spiritual impotence. Of course, the key element in the Narcissus myth is that the object of Narcissus's love is a "being" (a reflected image) with whom he can never consummate that love, an object that renders him necessarily impotent. As Horace phrases his condition to Ruby Lamar, "You see, . . . I lack courage: that was left out of me. The machinery is all here, but it wont run" (16). What Faulkner's revision of the opening scene of *Sanctuary* achieves, then, is a symmetry in the novel's beginning and end (need I say, a mirror symmetry) that figuratively presents the narcissism of the three main characters as the book's central theme.

But narcissism is only what we would expect with Horace Benbow. After all, he has an only sister named Narcissa, and in the original text of *Sanctuary* his wife Belle says to him before they are married, "Dont talk to me about love . . . ; you're in love with your sister. What do the books call it? What sort of complex?" (OT, 16). A remark that provokes the following exchange:

> "Not complex. . . . Do you think that any relationship with her could be complex?" . . .
> "Call it what you like," Belle said. "How did she come to let you go to the war, even in the Y.M.C.A?"
> "I did the next best thing," he said. "I came back."
> "Yes," Belle said. "To her. Not to me."
> "Isn't one man at a time enough for you?" . . .
> She said: "So you hope one man is enough for her too, do you?" He said nothing. "That is, if you're the man, of course." . . . "Horace, what are you going to do when she marries? What will you do the night a man makes—" He rose quickly. . . .
> "Dont let that worry you. You know nothing about virginity. You've neither ever found it nor lost it."   (OT, 16–17)

This mention of virginity in the context of a brother's incestuous attachment to an only sister immediately recalls the situation of Quentin and Candace in *The Sound and the Fury,* and that relationship is explicitly imaged at one point in the novel in terms of the myth of Narcissus when Candace lies on her back in the stream and Quentin looks down at his sister as if she were his reflection. As Quentin remembers it, "I ran down the hill in that vacuum of crickets like a breath travelling across a mirror she was lying in the water . . . I stood on the bank I could smell the honeysuckle on the water."[3] Like the relationship between Quentin and Candace, that between

Horace and Narcissa, in its association of the sister with the brother's reflected image and thus in its consequent feminine coding of that image, suggests Faulkner's predilection for a special variant of the myth of Narcissus, a variant I shall call the myth of Narcissa. Recall that in the standard version of the story in Ovid's *Metamorphoses* Narcissus's is a "pride so cold that no youth, no maiden touched his heart" (149), including the nymph Echo who wastes away after Narcissus spurns her.[4] After one of the youths whom Narcissus has rejected prays to the gods for retribution, saying "So may he himself love, and not gain the thing he loves" (1: 153), the goddess Nemesis answers the prayer and brings Narcissus to a woodland spring where, in Ovid's words, as Narcissus "seeks to slake his thirst another thirst springs up, and while he drinks he is smitten by the sight of the beautiful form he sees. He loves an unsubstantial hope and thinks that substance which is only shadow" (1:153). At first Narcissus mistakes his reflection for another being living below the water's surface, but eventually he realizes that it is his own image he is in love with and that his love is hopeless. Narcissus wastes away for love of himself, and his body is metamorphosed into the eponymous flower.

In this version of the myth, though Narcissus at first mistakes his reflection for another being, once he has recognized it as his own there is never any sense that the image is oppositely gendered from himself. But in Pausanias's *Description of Greece,* there is a paragraph devoted to the spring of Narcissus in Boeotia in which the author gives a brief commentary on the myth, focusing specifically on a shift in the image's gender:

> They say that Narcissus looked into this water, and not understanding that he saw his own reflection, unconsciously fell in love with himself, and died of love at the spring. But it is utter stupidity to imagine that a man old enough to fall in love was incapable of distinguishing a man from a man's reflection. There is another story about Narcissus, less popular indeed than the other, but not with-

out some support. It is said that Narcissus had a twin sister; they were exactly alike in appearance, their hair was the same, they wore similar clothes, and went hunting together. The story goes on that he fell in love with his sister, and when the girl died, would go to the spring, knowing that it was his reflection he saw, but in spite of this knowledge finding some relief for his love in imagining that he saw, not his own reflection, but the likeness of his sister.[5]

For a variety of reasons Pausanias's gloss bears directly on the imagery of narcissistic doubling associated with Quentin and Candace in *The Sound and the Fury* and with Horace and Narcissa in *Flags in the Dust* and *Sanctuary*. First of all, Pausanias's version clearly links narcissism with the motif of brother/sister incest, suggesting that the object choice in incest is based on a narcissistic self-love which projects its own image on to a being that closely resembles itself because it is so closely related to itself. Second, it links the visual repetition of a mirror image with the visual repetition of twinship. Third, this version codes the narcissistic reflected image of the male figure as feminine. And finally, it associates the difference which prevents Narcissus's body from being physically conjoined with its reflected image with the difference which prevents Narcissus from being physically conjoined with his dead twin sister. Which is to say that in associating, as barriers to sexual union, the difference, on the one hand, between the body and its reflected image with the difference, on the other, between the living and the dead, this version of the myth suggests that the means to overcome the latter difference may serve as the means to overcome the former, indeed, suggests that Narcissus's actively taking his own life as a means of being united with his dead twin sister is preferable to that passive wasting away from unconsummated self-love which Narcissus endures in the standard version of the myth.

One is immediately reminded of the proleptic image of Quentin's drowning that we are given in *The Sound and the Fury* when he stands on the bridge the morning of his last day, sees his shadow on the water, and thinks, "if only I had something to blot it into the water, holding it until it was drowned. . . . Niggers say a drowned man's shadow was watching for him in the water all the time. It twinkled and glinted, like breathing" (90). Certainly Faulkner means for us to read this scene, in which Quentin describes his shadow-image as if it were a living person he intends to drown in the river, in relation to that other scene where Candace, lying on her back in the water, is evoked as a reflected image of her brother gazing at himself Narcissuslike in the stream. And it is especially clear that Faulkner means for us to read these two scenes in relation to one another given what occurs in the latter once Candace climbs out of the water and lies down on the bank. For Quentin proposes that he kill his sister with his knife and then kill himself, the knife serving as a phallic substitute to unite the two not in an act of physical love but in death, a *Liebestod* in which the two will be joined forever, because isolated forever, in their own private hell. It is precisely this scenario of a union in death with his sister-as-narcissistic-image that Faulkner means for us to see superimposed upon that earlier scene on the bridge when Quentin thinks about drowning his feminine-coded shadow-image, his narcissistic-image-as-sister. And the structural relationship of this scenario to that variant of the Narcissus myth found in Pausanias is made even plainer in yet another scene on a bridge when Quentin confronts Candace's lover Dalton Ames, tries to strike him, and, as he says, passes out "like a girl" (162). Thinking back on this episode later in his narrative, Quentin says, "I knew he wasn't thinking of me at all as a potential source of harm but was thinking of her when he looked at me was looking at me through her like through a piece of colored glass" (175), in much the same way that Narcissus in Pausanias's version looks at what he knows is his own reflection but sees the image of his dead twin sister through it.

The structural elements contained in Pausanias's version of the myth, which I have called the myth of Narcissa, clearly govern the relationship of Quentin and Candace in *The Sound and the Fury* but also that of Horace and his sister in *Flags in the Dust* and *Sanctuary*. We will discuss that relationship presently, but first we must consider for a moment the central feature in the myth of Narcissa—the linking of narcissism and incest, which is to say, the assimilation of an impossible sexual union (that of a body with its reflected image) to a forbidden sexual union (that of a brother with his sister) and thus the substitution within the myth of the latter for the former. Obviously, the associative link that allows the myth of Narcissus (in which a boy falls in love with his own image) to turn into the myth of Narcissa (in which a boy, in love with his identical twin sister, is reminded of that love after her death by his own reflected image) is the element of doubling shared by both mirroring and twinship. Had Narcissus's sister not been his mirror-image twin (even to the point of cutting her hair the same and wearing the same clothes), Pausanias's version of the story would make no sense.

Given that the visual duplication common to mirroring and twinship led Pausanias to associate narcissism with incest, one wonders whether his insight reflects an even deeper connection between the two, a connection rooted in the very constitution of the ego. Consider for a moment that stage in the ego's development occurring between the ages of six and eighteen months that Lacan calls "the mirror phase." As Laplanche and Pontalis describe it,

> Though still in a state of powerlessness and motor incoordination, the infant anticipates on an imaginary plane the apprehension and mastery of its bodily unity. This imaginary unification comes about by means of identification with the image of the counterpart as total *Gestalt*; it is exemplified concretely by the experience in which the child perceives its own reflection in a mirror.[6]

Lacan believes that the mirror phase in effect constitutes "the matrix and first outline of what is to become the ego" as the infant "perceives in the image of its counterpart—or its own mirror image—a form (*Gestalt*) in which it anticipates a bodily unity which it still objectively lacks," that is, as the infant "identifies with this image. This primordial experience is basic to the imaginary nature of the ego, which is constituted right from the start as an 'ideal ego'" (LP, 251).

Now one has a sense that infants between the ages of six and eighteen months don't spend all that much time looking at themselves in mirrors. Rather, they spend most of their waking hours with their mothers. Consequently, Lacan says that the image with which the infant identifies is that of "its counterpart" or of its own reflection in a mirror. In filling the role of the infant's counterpart at that age, the mother acts as the child's living mirror image. And it is from its interaction with this image of its self that the child learns the basic constituents of all human interaction—duplication (both visual and vocal) and reciprocity—indeed, learns the principle on which learning itself is based, mimicry. The infant discovers in the mirror of the mother's face that a smile begets a smile, a laugh a laugh, a frown a frown. It learns that the proper response to a hug is a hug, a kiss a kiss, and so on. In short the child learns from the mother through this process of mimicry, of visual and vocal doubling, the basic expressive elements in the vocabulary of human emotion. The principles of duplication and reciprocity would be reinforced by the child's reflected image in a mirror up to a point, which is to say, up to that point (remarked on in the original myth of Narcissus) when the child tries to make physical contact with his reflection. For then the child learns that though his reflected image, like his mother's face, can respond with a smile to a smile, his image, unlike his mother, cannot respond to a hug with a hug. At some point the child also notices a further difference between his reflected image and the image of the counterpart: the fact that his reflected image is under his control in a way that the image of the counterpart is not, that his image always reciprocates those gestures of affection which the child initiates while the image of the counterpart may or may not. So that one theorizes that the child, in seeing this difference between his mirror image and the image of the mother, longs to control his mother's gestures of affection as completely as he does those of his reflection.

What this suggests, then, is that since the mother usually fills the counterpart's role by acting as the child's mirror image during this formative period of the ego when the vocabulary of human emotion is acquired, the mechanism of narcissism is attached almost from the beginning to that mirroring love of the mother for the child and the child for the mother, that what narcissism means, in effect, is to love yourself in the way that you imaginatively desired your mother love you. Which is simply to say that narcissism and an incestuous desire for the mother are joined at the root.

But there is implicit in this linking another lesson that the child must eventually learn—the lesson of substitution. For just as the desire to be physically united with the other is a central part of the myth of Narcissus, so the child learns that that desire, which is impossible to consummate between a body and its reflected image, is possible with the mother as counterpart but forbidden. And the fact of that substitution of a possible but forbidden union for an impossible one points to a further substitution of a possible and unforbidden union as the solution to this problem, points to a substitute who is not a member of one's immediate family but who either physically resembles the mother or whose love recalls one's own narcissistic image of the mother's love for the child. But there are, of course, other possibilities within this array of substitutions, possibilities that lie between the forbidden union of the son with the mother and the unforbidden union of the son with someone unrelated, the most obvious of these being the forbidden union of brother and sister.

As I suggested earlier, this discussion of an original link between narcissism and an incestuous desire for the mother provides a model for understanding Faulkner's manipulation of elements in the myth of Narcissa in creating the relationship between Horace Benbow and his sister. The first thing to note in this regard is that though Candace and Narcissa are both described at various times in language that evokes them as their brothers' mirror images, neither Caddy and Quentin nor Narcissa and Horace are actually twins. However, Faulkner does incorporate the element of twinship into the Horace-Narcissa structure by displacing it onto Narcissa's choice of a mate, which is to say that though Narcissa substitutes for a forbidden union with her brother a union with someone unrelated to her, she chooses a figure specifically coded as "a twin brother"—young Bayard Sartoris. And if that isn't enough of an evocation of Pausanias's version of the myth, Faulkner makes Bayard a twin whose sibling is dead, a surviving twin obsessed with death as the means of being reunited with the only person he ever loved. As Miss Jenny tells Narcissa in *Flags in the Dust,* "Bayard love anybody, that cold brute? . . . He never cared a snap of his fingers for anybody in his life except Johnny."[7]

Faulkner describes the relationship of Bayard and Narcissa in details clearly drawn from Pausanias's version of the myth. At one point in a kind of symbolic foreshadowing of his grandson Bayard's fate, a fatality embodied in the alternation of given names from generation to generation, old Bayard remembers a scene from his youth when he was escaping from a Yankee patrol through the woods and stopped to drink at a woodland spring: "As he leaned his mouth to it the final light of day was reflected onto his face, bringing into sharp relief forehead and nose above the cavernous sockets of his eyes and the panting animal snarl of his teeth, and from the still water there stared back at him for a sudden moment, a skull" (97). Old Bayard recalls this scene as he sits in the attic inscribing the date of young Bayard's twin brother John's death in the family Bible. And, appropriately enough, Narcissa first seems to become attracted to Bayard when he is convalescing from having almost drowned in the creek. Narcissa is, of course, associated throughout *Flags in the Dust* with the image of water, as one would expect, given her connection with Narcissus's water-reflected image interpreted as that of his sister. At one point Faulkner says that with Horace's return to Narcissa after the war, "he let himself slip, as into water, into the constant serenity of her affection again" (183). And with Horace back, Narcissa "thought of Bayard, but briefly, and without any tremor at all. He was now no more than the shadow of a hawk's flight mirrored fleetingly by the windless surface of a pool, and gone; where, the pool knew and cared not, leaving no stain" (188–89).

But if Narcissa's union with Bayard is a substitute for a forbidden union with her brother, then the incestuous attachment of brother and sister is itself, as Faulkner implies, a substitute for that between son and mother. Though Narcissa is seven years younger than Horace, she is represented throughout *Flags in the Dust* (and only to a slightly lesser degree in *Sanctuary*) as being a mother-figure for him. When Miss Jenny challenges Narcissa on her mothering of Horace, saying "Why don't you get married, and let that baby look after himself for a while?", Narcissa's only reply is "I promised mother" (33). And as Faulkner makes clear, Narcissa, after her mother's death, had filled the role of mother-figure not only for Horace but for Horace's father as well, suggesting that the sister-brother attachment is also a substitute for the incestuous desire of the daughter for the father: "Narcissa acquired two masculine destinies to control and shape, and through the intense maturity of seven and eight and nine she cajoled and threatened and commanded and (very occasionally) stormed them into concurrence. And so through fourteen and fifteen and sixteen. . . . Then Will Benbow's time came, . . . and the current of her maternalism had now but a single channel. For a time this current was dammed by a stupid mischancing of human

215

affairs, but now Horace was home again and lay now beneath the same roof and the same recurrence of days, and the channel was undammed again" (188).

Now if the main reason that Faulkner makes young Bayard Sartoris a twin obsessively attached to his dead sibling is to code Narcissa's choice of a mate as a narcissistic brother, then it seems equally clear that the principal reason for Horace's involvement with Belle Mitchell's sister Joan Heppleton in *Flags in the Dust* is to provide a roughly parallel situation in which Horace's choice of a mate is coded as a sister. Recall that when Belle is in Reno getting her divorce from Harry Mitchell, Horace meets and has a brief affair with Joan. As if to underline by antithesis the parallel between Narcissa's marrying a twin brother and Horace's having an affair with his future wife's sister, Joan says, in response to Horace's remark on their first meeting that he should have known she was Belle's sister, "How? Nobody yet ever said we look alike. And you never saw me before" (343). The implication is that just as Narcissa has chosen a husband who looks exactly like his dead brother, Horace has chosen a wife who resembles her sister not in physical appearance but in character and instinct. For what Horace learns about Joan Heppleton during their brief affair is that she is a woman of predatory sexuality and unparalleled commonness. In short, he learns the truth of what Narcissa in a mixture of rage and despair had said to Miss Jenny about Joan's sister Belle, "But that woman. . . . She's so dirty!"

On the one occasion when Joan stays all night at Horace's, she prowls about the house looking into dark rooms, at one point opening the door to Narcissa's bedroom and asking whose it is. When Horace tells her, Joan replies,

> "Oh, your sister's. The one that married that Sartoris." She examined the room quietly. "I'd like to have known that man," she said in a musing tone. "I think I'd be good for him. . . . Yes, I'd have been just the thing for him." (347–48)

Uneasy about this intrusion into his sister's privacy, Horace repeatedly asks Joan to come away, and the scene ends with her inquiring tauntingly whether Horace feels that her presence in his sister's bedroom is a "sacrilege" and a "desecration." And that, of course, is precisely what he feels. Faulkner says that the next day Horace experienced "revulsion" over the incident: "he thought of his sister and he felt unclean" (348).

Clearly, the whole point of the scene in Narcissa's bedroom lies in Joan's remark that she would have "been just the thing for" young Bayard Sartoris, an identification of Joan and Bayard implying that the position within this structure of substitutions that is filled by the Sartoris brothers in relation to Horace's sister is filled by the sisters Belle and Joan in relation to Narcissa's brother. The only asymmetry in these relationships being that while in the first group it is Bayard who is married to Narcissa but in love with his brother, in the second group it is Horace who is married to Belle but has made love to her sister.

The scene with Joan and Horace in Narcissa's bedroom is also meant to remind us of another scene described earlier in the novel when young Bayard, returned home after the war, sits

> quietly in the room which he and John had shared in the young masculine violence of their twinship, on the bed where he and his wife had lain the last night of his leave, the night before he went back to England and thence out to the Front again, where John already was. Beside him on the pillow the wild bronze flame of her hair was hushed now in the darkness. . . .
>
> But he was not thinking of her then. . . . He was thinking of his brother whom he had not seen in over a year, thinking that in a month they would see one another again.
>
> Nor was he thinking of her now. . . . He was thinking of his dead brother. . . . (48–49)

In the scene with Horace and Joan, a brother is in his sister's bedroom with a woman to whom he will make love later that night (though almost certainly not in that room) and yet all he can think of is his sister's reaction to this affair, while in the scene which Bayard remembers, a brother is in bed with his first wife (Narcissa's predecessor) in the room which he and his twin had shared growing up and all he can think of is rejoining his brother. And just to make sure that we don't miss the parallel between these two scenes Faulkner gives Bayard's first wife the same striking physical feature that he gives Joan Heppleton and describes that feature with exactly the same phrase in each case—"the wild bronze flame of her hair" (48, 406). Indeed, the phrase evokes a sculptural quality to the female form that, when combined with the color bronze, may be meant to remind us of that "almost perfect vase of clear amber" which Horace had fashioned, a vase "chastely serene" which Horace "kept always on his night table and called by his sister's name in the intervals of apostrophising both of them impartially in his moments of rhapsody over the realization of the meaning of peace and the unblemished attainment of it, as Thou still unravished bride of quietude" (190–91).

In structurally coding Narcissa's mate as a narcissistic brother and Horace's mate as a sister, Faulkner never for a moment implies that there is any actual resemblance between Bayard and Horace on the one hand or between Belle and Narcissa on the other. Indeed, on several occasions in *Flags in the Dust* Narcissa compares the Sartoris twins to her brother much to the twins detriment, leading her at one point "to thank her gods he was not as they" (77). And, of course, one of the ongoing topics of conversation between Horace and Narcissa in *Flags in the Dust* is how different Belle is from Narcissa, how much she represents in character, appearance, and conduct everything that Narcissa is not. It is as if the structural coding were a kind of template superimposed on Horace's and Narcissa's relationships to reveal the incestuous desire for the opposite-sex sibling that represents their ideal of an object-choice but that seems to operate in reverse in the actual choice of a mate. Which is to say that either because they despair of finding someone who resembles the beloved brother or sister, or because they don't want to find someone who resembles them too closely and thus competes with them, or simply in reaction to the forbiddenness of their idealized object-choices, they choose a mate who, while bearing a structural resemblance to the sibling, bears virtually no resemblance in terms of personality.

Which brings us to the next link in this chain of substitutions. For if, as we have suggested, the child's desire for an impossible union with its own image is linked to the forbidden incestuous desire for the mother-as-mirror-image during the stage of ego formation, and if the only slightly less forbidden desire for union with the opposite-sex sibling is a substitute formation for this, then we would expect to find, as the chain of substitutions progresses, that a parent's attachment to an opposite-sex child substitutes for that parent's incestuous desire for its opposite-sex sibling. And something very much like that is what happens with Horace and Narcissa. On the day that young Bayard is killed in a plane crash, his and Narcissa's son is born, a son that Miss Jenny had decided should be called John. But when it comes time to name the boy, Narcissa rejects the name John (and presumably all the Sartoris doom which the name's alternation with that of Bayard over the generations evokes) and gives him her family name instead, calling him Benbow. But more interesting still is the nickname which Narcissa chooses. One would expect a child named Benbow to have as his affectionate diminutive either Ben or Bo, but in *Sanctuary* Narcissa calls her son Bory. And I would argue that as Narcissa took her son's given name from her family, so she also took the form of his nickname from the same quarter. Which is simply to say that the reason Narcissa's nickname for her son in *Sanctuary* is Bory is that her nickname for her brother throughout *Flags in the Dust* is Horry.

What this rhyming suggests is that in giving her son her own family name Narcissa was, unconsciously or not, naming him after her brother, an intention that becomes even plainer in her choice of a diminutive. Indeed, in Faulkner the figure of Echo (a figure of aural doubling) haunts the myth of Narcissa just as surely as in Ovid she haunts the myth of Narcissus, a myth of visual doubling.

This naming of the son after the brother is only what we would expect given what happens with that other, earlier brother-sister pair who share this same structure of incestuous desire for a sibling. For Caddy names her daughter after her dead brother Quentin, just as Miss Jenny had suggested that Narcissa name her son after her husband's dead brother John. No doubt, Caddy had meant to memorialize her brother by this naming, to bring him back to life in a sense through the namesake child. And certainly her brother would have been dearer to her than the child's father (particularly since Caddy says she doesn't know who the father is, though readers generally assume it is Dalton Ames). But it is no distortion of the text to suggest, given how clear a sense Faulkner conveys of the incestuous attachment between Quentin and Caddy, that part of the reason for Caddy's naming her daughter after her brother is as an expression of her desire for Quentin to have been her child's father. Or at the very least, to give the impression that Quentin was its father and thus, by a simple act of naming, to accomplish that incestuous deed which her brother had contemplated but been unable to achieve, a deed that, as Quentin imagined it, would have left them forever damned in their own private hell but forever wed in their isolation. And I would suggest that a similar dynamic governs Narcissa's echoic naming of her son, the nickname serving as an unconscious expression of Narcissa's desire to have a child by her brother. Indeed, Bory immediately becomes the object of that same overpowering "current of maternalism" which his uncle had been the sole object of till then, so much so that by the time of the 1933 story "There Was a Queen" Narcissa has her ten-year-old son sit in the creek with her as she symbolically purifies herself for spending the night in Memphis with the Federal agent, then has Bory sit next to her at dinner that evening because, as she says, "I got so lonesome for you last night in Memphis,"[8] and finishes by making him promise that they will never leave each other again. Clearly, this is a queen who means to turn her son into the kind of lifelong consort she had hoped her brother would be. And just as clearly the scene in which mother and son sit fully clothed in the creek is meant to recall the scene of Quentin and Caddy at the creek in *The Sound and the Fury*.

Just as Faulkner balanced the coding of Narcissa's choice of a mate as a "narcissistic brother" against the episode of Horace's involvement with Joan Heppleton and the resultant coding of Horace's future wife as "a sister," so he balances this subsequent link in the chain of substitutions by drawing a parallel between Narcissa's relationship with her son Bory and Horace's relationship with his stepdaughter Little Belle. Indeed, it is this latter relationship that in some sense forms the hidden center of Horace's character in *Sanctuary*. Faulkner alerts us to this early on in the narrative when he has Horace, after being captured by Popeye at the spring and brought to Lee Goodwin's, describe an incident that had occurred just before he left home, describe it to the listening Ruby Lamar in imagery whose psychological import we are already familiar with. Horace begins by telling Ruby about the grape arbor and hammock that he sees from his window at home, remarking that "we know nature is a she; because of that conspiracy between female flesh and female season" (13). In his rambling monologue Horace associates the grape blossoms with the image of his stepdaughter blossoming into womanhood and the memory of her trysts with young men in the arbor hammock. Little Belle never introduces her boyfriends to Horace but simply explains away his intrusions into the arbor by saying, "It's just

Horace": "Just, you see; in a little white dress in the twilight, the two of them all demure and quite alert and a little impatient. And I couldn't have felt any more foreign to her flesh if I had begot it myself" (13). On the day of the incident in question, Horace and Little Belle are home alone. Horace scolds her for picking up a college boy on the train and bringing him to the house, and Little Belle retorts, "You're a fine one to talk about finding things on the train! . . . Shrimp! Shrimp!":

> "Then she was saying 'No! No!' and me holding her and she clinging to me. 'I didn't mean that! Horace! Horace!' And I was smelling the slain flowers the delicate dead flowers and tears, and then I saw her face in the mirror. There was a mirror behind her and another behind me, and she was watching herself in the one behind me, forgetting about the other one in which I could see her face, see her watching the back of my head with pure dissimulation."
> (14–15)

Just as Horace's narcissism is evoked in the novel's opening scene when he sees his reflection in the spring and Temple's emblematized at the novel's close as she sits in the park looking at her face in a compact mirror, so Little Belle's place in this structure of proliferating narcissism is figured in a scene where she and Horace embrace between facing mirrors.

As we said, the opening scene in the novel also evokes Popeye as Horace's distorted mirror image, and as critics have noted, it is precisely the parallel between Horace and Popeye that forms the book's core. The revelation that begins when Horace embraces Little Belle between the facing mirrors, a revelation that causes him to run away from home, continues through the rest of the novel as Horace sees, as if through a glass darkly, that what the physically impotent Popeye does to Temple with a corncob is an image of what the spiritually impotent Horace would like to do to his stepdaughter. And this dynamic of proliferating narcissism, this double mirror structure in which one pair of narcissists (Popeye and Temple) mirror another pair of narcissists (Horace and Little Belle) is only what we would expect within that larger structure in which incest mirrors narcissism, in which the desire for an impossible union with one's own image is reflected into the son's desire for a forbidden union with the mother-as-mirror-image, and then reflected in turn into the brother's incestuous desire for the sister, and finally mirrored by the stepfather's desire for the stepdaughter.

Faulkner makes clear the nature of Horace's feelings for Little Belle in a subsequent scene in which Horace is preparing to take the train to Oxford to look for Temple. On the bureau in his room are Horace's "watch, his pipe and tobacco pouch, and, propped against a book, a photograph of his stepdaughter. Little Belle. Upon the glazed surface a highlight lay" (162). As Horace stands looking at "the sweet, inscrutable face . . . out of the dead cardboard," he thinks of "the grape arbor at Kinston, of . . . the murmur of voices darkening into silence as he approached, who meant them, her, no harm; who meant her less than harm, good God; darkening into the pale whisper of her white dress, of the delicate and urgent mammalian whisper of that curious small flesh which he had not begot" (162). He moves suddenly, and "as of its own accord the photograph" shifts, "the image" blurring "into its highlight, like something familiar seen beneath disturbed though clear water; he looked at the familiar image with a kind of quiet horror and despair, at a face suddenly older in sin than he would ever be" (162–63). Horace gets ready to leave for the train, "putting his watch and his tobacco pouch into his pocket," and it is only when he reaches the station that he realizes that "he had forgot his pipe" (163), that it is still lying on the bureau next to the photograph of Little Belle.

As we said, Phil Stone had certainly talked enough Freud to Faulkner for us to be fairly sure that Faulkner knew the psychoanalytic significance of standard dream symbols, such as Popeye's hat and in this case Horace's pipe, the pipe being identified in *The Interpretation of Dreams* as a common symbol

223

of the male genitals. What is remarkable about this scene, then, is not only how explicitly Faulkner symbolizes Horace's incestuous desire for Little Belle through the business of the pipe left on the bureau with the picture, nor how clearly he links this incestuous desire to narcissism by showing that it is aroused specifically by a lifeless image out of "dead cardboard," an image that seems to be immersed in "disturbed though clear water," but rather how exactly this scene recapitulates the structure of the one in which Quentin stands above Caddy lying on her back in the branch as if she were his reflected image and then, holding his knife to her throat, offers to join them both forever in death only to drop his knife and lose it when Caddy says "yes push it" (152). As the lost phallic knife figures Quentin's psychic impotence, so the forgotten pipe figures Horace's. And just so that there will be no mistaking the way in which his spiritual impotence mirrors Popeye's physical impotence, Faulkner tells us that during his unsuccessful search for Temple in Oxford Horace bought himself another pipe, a corncob pipe: "He returned to the station an hour before the train was due, a filled but unlighted cob pipe in his hand. In the lavatory he saw, scrawled on the foul, stained wall, her pencilled name. Temple Drake. He read it quietly, his head bent, slowly fingering the unlighted pipe" (168). This scene in the lavatory, with Horace looking at Temple's name and fingering his pipe, is completed by a later scene in a lavatory when Horace, having returned to Jefferson after finding Temple at Miss Reba's, looks again at Little Belle's photograph and finds that "the small face seemed to swoon in a voluptuous languor, . . . leaving upon his eye a soft and fading aftermath of invitation and voluptuous promise and secret affirmation" (215–16). Suddenly Horace becomes ill and rushes to the bathroom: He "plunged forward and struck the lavatory and leaned upon his braced arms while the shucks set up a terrific roar beneath her thighs" (216). As the image of Temple lying on the corn shucks merges with Horace's feelings for Little Belle, Horace's vomiting becomes a kind of perverse ejaculation, expressing at once his forbidden desire and his self-revulsion at this desire.

Horace's last encounter with Little Belle in the novel bears the subtle but unmistakable imprint of the myth of Narcissa. After Lee Goodwin has been lynched, Horace returns to his wife in Kinston and finds that Little Belle is away at a house party. Horace phones her long distance and while he waits for the connection to be made, he keeps repeating "something out of a book he had read:'Less oft is peace. Less oft is peace'" (293). The line is from the ending of Shelley's poem "To Jane: The Recollection." In 1821 Shelley met Jane Williams in Pisa. She had been married, but her husband had left her and she was now living abroad with Edward Ellerker Williams and their two children. The Shelleys and the Williamses were much in each other's company, and Jane seemed to Shelley "a sort of spirit of embodied peace in our circle of tempests."[9] Indeed at one point Shelley and Jane Williams seem to have become amorously involved. The poem memorializes a day the two spent in the Pine Forest near Pisa, a day of such sublime calm that it becomes in the poem an objective correlative for that "spirit of embodied peace" that is Jane. No doubt, Horace Benbow's attraction to the poem stems from the Narcissuslike imagery of its fifth section. Shelley says that so calm were the winds that day that the surfaces of the forest pools were un-ruffled mirrors reflecting the sky and trees and, one assumes, reflecting as well the images of the poet and the woman who is the subject of this "recollection." He concludes,

> Sweet views which in our world above
>   Can never well be seen,
> Were imaged by the water's love
>   Of that fair forest green.
> And all was interfused beneath
>   With an Elysian glow,
> An atmosphere without a breath,
>   A softer day below.

> Like one beloved the scene had lent
>   To the dark water's breast,
> Its every leaf and lineament
>   With more than truth expressed;
> Until an envious wind crept by,
>   Like an unwelcome thought,
> Which from the mind's too faithful eye
>   Blots one dear image out.
> Though thou art ever fair and kind,
>   The forests ever green,
> Less oft is peace in Shelley's mind,
>   Than calm in waters, seen.[10]

As the woodland pool mirrors the beloved's face, so the mirroring pool of Shelley's mind reflects the image of that peaceful day when he saw Jane's reflection in the water, and rare as such calm days are, rarer still is the woman who could create for a day such peace in Shelley's restless spirit.

Now if this poem meant something to Horace, as his remembering the line "Less oft is peace" would suggest, it was undoubtedly because Shelley's memorializing of a woman who seemed a "spirit of embodied peace" reminded Horace of his sister, whose tranquil nature is the subject of frequent comment in *Flags in the Dust*, a quality that causes her brother to address her as "O Serene" (187) on several occasions and to apostrophize the vase which he calls by his sister's name as "Thou still unravished bride of quietude" (191). Faulkner probably also meant for us to register the resemblance between Horace's own situation and that of the poet whose line he quotes, for Shelley was obsessed with a beloved sister (Elizabeth) and was rumored to have had a sexual relationship with his wife Mary's half-sister, Claire Clairmont, a situation that evoked Southey's famous remark about a "league of incest." (Southey's remark also alluded to the fact that Byron had fathered an illegitimate child by Claire Clairmont and was rumored to have had an affair with Shelley's wife Mary, and that Byron had hinted widely about an incestuous affair with his half-sister Augusta. If Faulkner does mean for us to compare

Horace's situation [in love with his sister and having made love to his wife and her sister] to Shelley's, then we can see why, in that incident from *Flags in the Dust* evoking Narcissa's own repressed sexual nature [her keeping the obscene letters sent by an anonymous admirer], Faulkner chose to make the author of those letters *Byron* Snopes.)

That Horace quotes the line "Less oft is peace" while waiting to say goodnight to Little Belle on the phone makes clear the substitutive nature of his desire for his stepdaughter, makes clear that it is her purely structural resemblance to Narcissa (i.e., her status as an incestuously forbidden object-choice, even though Little Belle is only related to Horace by marriage) that unconsciously fuels Horace's desire. For as with Horace's choice of a mate, Little Belle is, in terms of personality, the antithesis of Narcissa.

The line of poetry "Less oft is peace" is, as we mentioned earlier, one of several links between Horace Benbow and the third avatar of the character-structure we have been examining, Gavin Stevens—a line that Gavin quotes in the novella "Knight's Gambit." The main difference, of course, between Gavin and the two earlier characters is that while Quentin's and Horace's special relationship with an only sister is both the major event in their personal lives and the central action in each of their stories, Gavin's relationship with his only sister, though it may be the major event in his personal life, is clearly *not* the most important event in his story. Whatever Gavin's feelings are for his sister Margaret, they are never presented in any of the works in which he appears as being the principal aspect of his character, as being as intensely, incestuously tragic as the feelings of Quentin and Horace are for their sisters. Which is simply another way of saying that Gavin seems to make his way through a structure of substitutions to achieve, late in life, something like success in his eventual choice of a mate. And yet, though Gavin is able to prevent his personal life from being overwhelmed by his relationship with his sister, we can still see traces of the myth of Narcissa in his story. From what we have seen of this structure in the characters of Quentin and Horace, we know why, for instance, Faulkner gives Gavin not just an only sister but a twin sister, why Gavin lives most of his adult life with his sister's family, why the most significant relationship in his life is his love for another man's wife (Eula Varner Snopes) and his love for her daughter (Linda Snopes), and why, though Margaret Mallison doesn't name her son after her brother, Gavin serves as a father-figure for Chick in all the stories in which they appear, reducing the character of Charles Mallison Sr. to a cipher.

Of the several links between the characters of Gavin and Horace, the one most relevant to our present discussion, as well as the one most clearly distinguishing their characters from Quentin Compson's, is that both men marry and, more significantly, that both choose, structurally speaking, the same kind of mate. Which is to say that both marry women who have been married before, and that the fact of a previous marriage must be faced by Gavin and Horace on a daily basis because each of their wives comes to her second marriage with children from the first—Belle Mitchell with Little Belle and Melisandre Backus Harriss with her son Max and her daughter Miss Harriss. It is significant, then, that the line of poetry which Horace Benbow quotes while waiting to say goodnight to Little Belle on the phone ("Less oft is peace") is the same line quoted by Gavin Stevens in "Knight's Gambit" when he happens to meet his childhood sweetheart Melisandre one day on the street after a separation of many years. Gavin congratulates her on what he assumes is her impending marriage to the Argentine fortune hunter Captain Gualdres, and Faulkner describes the blush that spread across her face at this remark in imagery reminiscent of the fifth section of Shelley's "To Jane: The Recollection." As she looks at Gavin, the blush covers her face "as the moving shadow of a cloud crosses a patch of light. Then it even crossed her eyes too, as when once the cloud-shadow reaches the water, you can not only see the shadow, you can even see the cloud too."[11] As the woodland pools in Shelley's poem reflect the sky whose tranquillity is a figure of that "spirit of embodied peace," Jane Williams, so Melisandre's eyes are imaged as two watery pools that reflect the cloud lying over the relationship between her and Gavin. And in some sense, of course, the principal mystery solved in "Knight's Gambit" concerns this relationship.

What the reader learns over the course of the story is that Melisandre, who was a close childhood friend of Gavin's twin sister, was secretly engaged to Gavin when she was sixteen. Gavin left to study at Heidelberg; there was a misunderstanding, and Melisandre broke off the engagement. She married a stranger named Harriss, had two children, and after the bootlegger Harriss's death she returned to Jefferson as the wealthiest widow in the county. Gavin enacts during the course of the story a kind of displaced Oedipal scenario in which he must prevent Melisandre's son from murdering his would-be stepfather Captain Gualdres in order to demonstrate his paternal authority over the young man, and not just that, but have Max Harriss accept that authority, thereby acknowledging Gavin's fitness to become his stepfather by marrying Melisandre.

We might note in passing that the emotional center of the story for Faulkner as he was writing it, the point of empathy that gave him a firm grasp on the characters' feelings and motivations, was undoubtedly the relationship of the prospective stepfather and stepson, Gavin and Max. For like Gavin, Faulkner had lost his childhood sweetheart Estelle Oldham to another man (Cornell Franklin), and when she returned some ten years later as a divorced woman with two children (Victoria and Malcolm Franklin), Faulkner won her back. Moreover, Faulkner had a favorite and devoted nephew, Jimmy Faulkner, who, like Chick Mallison, saw air combat in World War II. This is not to suggest that in "Knight's Gambit" Faulkner was

simply writing veiled autobiography, but rather that in imagining the emotions of a stepfather trying to establish his authority over a stepson and using the fact of an adoring nephew's
willing acceptance of that authority as a lever to bring this
about, Faulkner clearly had analogues in his own life to draw
on. For like Gavin, Faulkner knew that the successful winning back of the childhood sweetheart depended to a large
extent on his relationship with her children.

What the story accomplishes, then, is the coding of Gavin's
choice of a wife as a childhood sweetheart who is the wife of
another man (as made evident by the existence of that other
man's children), a sweetheart who must be rewon after the
other man's death. But then doesn't every boy have a childhood sweetheart who is married to another man, a fact made
evident by the boy's very existence, and doesn't the boy fanta-
size that his sweetheart loves him more than she does the other
man, indeed, loves him more because in some odd way she
loved him before she loved the other? At least that's the way
Chick Mallison phrases it in *The Town*. He remembers asking
his mother when he was twelve what the relationship was
between Eula Snopes and Manfred de Spain, and his mother
telling him to ask his Uncle Gavin. He says his mother couldn't
tell him that Eula and Manfred were doing the same thing in
bed that she and his father had done when he was conceived,
couldn't tell him because he was her child and because a child
wouldn't believe it: "Because to a child, he was not created by
his mother's and his father's passion or capacity for it. He
couldn't have been because he was there first, he came first,
before the passion; he created the passion, not only it but the
man and the woman who served it; his father is not his father
but his son-in-law, his mother not his mother but his daugh-
ter-in-law if he is a girl."[12] Chick thinks that his mother didn't
tell him because, as he says, she had to guard his and his uncle's
innocence both, "since maybe she was my mother but she was
Uncle Gavin's twin and if a boy or a girl really is his father's

and her mother's father-in-law or mother-in-law, which would make the girl her brother's mother no matter how much younger she was, then a girl with just one brother and him a twin at that, would maybe be his wife and mother too" (305).

That a man's twin sister "would maybe be his wife and mother too" sums up the myth of Narcissa about as succinctly as it can be put, unless one were to add "and maybe his daughter as well." The coding of Gavin's mate as a childhood sweetheart formerly married to another man with whom she has had a child presents Melisandre, in structural terms, as a figure of Gavin's mother. But what distinguishes Gavin's object choice of a previously married woman with children from Horace's, or for that matter, distinguishes it from what Gavin's choice would have been if he had been able to convince Eula to take her daughter Linda, leave her husband Flem Snopes and her lover Manfred de Spain, and marry him, is that Gavin's choice of Melisandre is clearly one that has the complete approval of Gavin's sister, the kind of approval that Horace never had from Narcissa when he married Belle and that Gavin would never have had from Margaret if he had married Eula.

Indeed, there is a strong implication in "Knight's Gambit" that since Melisandre had been a schoolmate of Gavin's sister, it was Margaret who originally introduced the two. And it was certainly Margaret who kept in touch during the years Melisandre and her children were living in Europe and South America. So that one gets the feeling that Margaret had picked her friend Melisandre long ago as an ideal wife for her twin brother. Which of course makes Faulkner's decision to have Gavin quote Shelley's line "Less oft is peace" when he meets Melisandre again especially appropriate, for the quotation, evoking the poem's imagery of narcissistic mirroring and the recollection of a beloved woman who embodies peace, is Faulkner's way of indicating that Gavin's choice of Melisandre as a wife, this figure of the childhood-sweetheart-as-mother, is a substitute for the twin sister that carries the sister's approval, a substitute that, unlike Horace's choice of a wife, draws the sister closer to her brother rather than driving her away. Certainly, in having Gavin quote the same line of poetry as Horace, Faulkner means for us to notice the similarities in their characters and gives us a reference point for comparing his inflections of the structure of narcissism and incestuous desire in these two. For clearly that structure, as it is embodied in Quentin, Horace, and Gavin, is the backbone upon which Faulkner's most intriguing fiction is constructed.

Notes / Index

NOTES TO THE INTRODUCTION / 1. Ernest Jones, *The Life and Work of Sigmund Freud* (New York: Basic Books, 1955), 2:343–44.

2. Frederick L. Gwynn and Joseph L. Blotner, eds., *Faulkner in the University* (New York: Vintage Books reprint, 1959), p. 268.

3. James B. Meriwether and Michael Millgate, eds., *Lion in the Garden: Interviews with William Faulkner, 1926–1962* (New York: Random House, 1968), p. 251.

4. H. Edward Richardson, *William Faulkner: The Journey to Self-Discovery* (Columbia: University of Missouri Press, 1969), p. 210.

5. Mark Twain, *The Writings of Mark Twain*, ed. A. B. Paine (New York: Gabriel Wells, 1923), 16:208. All subsequent quotations from *Pudd'nhead Wilson* are taken from this edition.

6. Twain, *Writings*, 19:382–83.

7. Henry James, *The Complete Tales of Henry James*, ed. Leon Edel (Philadelphia and New York: J. B. Lippincott, 1964), 12:194. All subsequent quotations from "The Jolly Corner" are taken from this edition.

8. Robinson Jeffers, *Roan Stallion, Tamar, and Other Poems* (New York: Random House, Modern Library, 1953), p. 115. All subsequent quotations from "Tamar" are taken from this edition.

NOTES TO THE TEXT / 1. William Faulkner, *Absalom, Absalom!* (New York: Random House, Modern Library College Edition, 1964), pp. 357–58. All subsequent quotations from *Absalom, Absalom!* are taken from this edition.

2. Richard Poirier, " 'Strange Gods' in Jefferson, Mississippi: Analysis of *Absalom, Absalom!*," reprinted in *Twentieth Century Interpretations of Absalom, Absalom!*, ed. Arnold Goldman (Englewood Cliffs, N.J.: Prentice-Hall, 1971), p. 14.

3. Frederick L. Gwynn and Joseph L. Blotner, eds., *Faulkner in the University* (New York: Vintage Books reprint, 1959), p. 71. All subsequent quotations from Faulkner's university conferences are taken from this edition.

4. Otto Rank, *The Double*, trans. and ed. Harry Tucker, Jr. (Chapel Hill: University of North Carolina Press, 1971), p. 77. All subsequent quotations from *The Double* are taken from this edition.

5. William Faulkner, *The Sound and the Fury* (New York: Random House, 1946), pp. 100–101. All subsequent quotations from *The Sound and the Fury* are taken from this edition.

6. Otto Rank, *Das Inzest-Motiv in Dichtung und Sage* (Leipzig and Vienna: Franz Deuticke, 1912), pp. 443–65.

7. Sigmund Freud, *The Standard Edition of the Complete Psychological Works of Sigmund Freud,* trans. and ed. James Strachey, et al. (London: Hogarth Press, 1953), 20:106–7. All subsequent quotations from Freud are taken from this edition, which will be cited hereafter as S.E.

8. Lucy Menzies, *The Saints in Italy* (London, 1924), pp. 153–54.

9. William Faulkner, *As I Lay Dying* (New York: Random House, Modern Library, 1967), p. 26. All subsequent quotations from *As I Lay Dying* are taken from this edition.

10. William Faulkner, *The Unvanquished* (New York: Random House, 1938), p. 222. All subsequent quotations from *The Unvanquished* are taken from this edition.

11. William Faulkner, *Light in August* (New York: Random House, 1932), p. 321. All subsequent quotations from *Light In August* are taken from this edition.

12. Ernest Jones, *Papers on Psycho Analysis* (Boston: Beacon Press, 1948), p. 407. All subsequent quotations from Jones are taken from this edition.

13. Søren Kierkegaard, *Repetition,* trans. Walter Lowrie (New York: Harper and Row, 1964), pp. 15, 18, 23, 126.

14. Wallace Stevens, *The Collected Poems of Wallace Stevens* (New York: Alfred A. Knopf, 1954), p. 440.

15. Friedrich Nietzsche, *Thus Spoke Zarathustra,* in *The Portable Nietzsche,* trans. Walter Kaufman (New York: Viking Press, 1954), pp. 249–54. All subsequent quotations from *Zarathustra* are taken from this edition.

16. Erwin Panofsky, *Studies in Iconology* (New York: Harper and Row, 1962), p. 74.

17. Friedrich Nietzsche, *Philosophy in the Tragic Age of the Greeks,* trans. Marianne Cowan (Chicago: Henry Regnery Co., 1962), pp. 52–53.

18. Malcolm Cowley, *A Second Flowering* (New York: Viking Press, 1974), p. 143.

19. Wilhelm Stekel, *Compulsion and Doubt,* trans. Emil A. Gutheil (New York: Washington Square Press, 1967), p. 474. All subsequent quotations from Stekel are taken from this edition.

20. Guy Rosolato, *Essais sur le symbolique* (Paris: Gallimard, 1969), p. 63. All subsequent quotations from Rosolato are taken from this edition.

21. Julian of Norwich, *Revelations of Divine Love,* trans. Clifton Wolters (Harmondsworth, Middlesex, England: Penguin Books, 1966), pp. 164–70.

22. William Faulkner, *A Fable* (New York: Random House, 1954), p. 68. All subsequent quotations from *A Fable* are taken from this edition.

23. William Faulkner, *Mosquitoes* (New York: Liveright, 1927), p. 46. All subsequent quotations from *Mosquitoes* are taken from this edition.

24. Joseph Blotner, *Faulkner* (New York: Random House, 1974), 1:511.

25. William Faulkner, *Soldiers' Pay* (New York: Liveright, 1926; Liveright reprint, 1970), pp. 91–92.

26. William Faulkner, *Sartoris* (New York: Random House, 1956), p. 182.

27. William Faulkner, "An Introduction to *The Sound and the Fury*," in *A Faulkner Miscellany*, ed. James B. Meriwether (Jackson: University of Mississippi Press, 1974), pp. 158–59. Unless otherwise noted, subsequent quotations from the introduction are taken from this edition.

28. William Faulkner, "An Introduction for *The Sound and the Fury*," ed. James B. Meriwether, *The Southern Review*, n.s., 8, 4 (Autumn 1972):710.

NOTES TO APPENDIX 1 / 1. Joseph Blotner, *Faulkner: A Biography*, 2 vols. (New York: Random House, 1974), 2: 1201. All subsequent quotations from Blotner are taken from this edition.

2. Edgar Allan Poe, *Collected Works of Edgar Allan Poe*, ed. Thomas Ollive Mabbott, 3 vols. (Cambridge, Mass.: Harvard University Press, 1969–78), 2: 551.

3. William Faulkner, "An Error in Chemistry" in *Knight's Gambit* (New York: Random House, 1978), 113. All subsequent quotations from "An Error in Chemistry" are taken from this edition.

4. William Faulkner, "Knight's Gambit" in *Knight's Gambit* (New York: Random House, 1978), 137. All subsequent quotations from "Knight's Gambit" are taken from this edition.

5. Raymond Chandler, *The Big Sleep* (New York: Random House, 1976), 144. All subsequent quotations from *The Big Sleep* are taken from this edition.

6. Raymond Chandler, *The High Window* (New York: Random House, 1976), 161.

7. William Faulkner, *The Town* (New York: Random House, 1961), 45, 181, 302, 305.

8. Reuben Fine quoted in Alexander Cockburn, *Idle Passion: Chess and the Dance of Death* (New York: Simon and Schuster, 1974), 42.

9. Cockburn, 101.

NOTES TO APPENDIX 2 / 1. William Faulkner, *Sanctuary: The Original Text,* ed. Noel Polk (New York: Random House, 1981), 299. All subsequent quotations from the original text of *Sanctuary* are from this edition which will be cited in the text as OT.

2. William Faulkner, *Sanctuary* (New York: Vintage, 1958), 307–8. All subsequent quotations from the 1931 published version of *Sanctuary* are from this edition.

3. William Faulkner, *The Sound and the Fury,* New, Corrected Edition (New York: Random House, 1984), 149–50. All subsequent quotations from *The Sound and the Fury* are from this edition.

4. Ovid, *Metamorphoses,* 2 vols. (Cambridge, Mass.: Harvard University Press, 1977), 1:149. All subsequent quotations from Ovid are from this edition.

5. Pausanias, *Description of Greece,* 4 vols. (Cambridge, Mass.: Harvard University Press, 1929), 4:311.

6. J. Laplanche and J.-B. Pontalis, *The Language of Psycho-Analysis* (New York: Norton, 1973), 250–51. All subsequent quotations from Laplanche and Pontalis are from this edition which will be cited in the text as LP.

7. William Faulkner, *Flags in the Dust* (New York: Vintage, 1974), 57. All subsequent quotations from *Flags in the Dust* are from this edition.

8. William Faulkner, "There Was a Queen," Collected *Stories of William Faulkner,* (New York: Vintage, 1977), 742.

9. Percy Bysshe Shelley, *The Complete Works of Percy Bysshe Shelley,* 10 vols., ed. Roger Ingpen and Walter E. Peck (New York: Gordian Press, 1965), 10:346. I would like to thank my colleague Jerome Christensen for his help with the Shelley/Byron material and an old friend, David Vanderwerken, for pointing out the source of the quotation "Less oft is peace."

10. Percy Bysshe Shelley, *The Complete Poetical Works of Shelley,* ed. Thomas Hutchinson (Oxford: Oxford University Press, 1904), 751.

11. William Faulkner, *Knight's Gambit* (New York: Vintage, 1978), 164. All subsequent quotations from *Knight's Gambit* are from this edition.

12. William Faulkner, *The Town* (New York: Vintage, 1961), 305. All subsequent quotations from *The Town* are from this edition.

INDEX /

Compson, Mrs. (great-grand-mother of Quentin and Candace) (*The Sound and the Fury*), 56

Compson, Quentin (*Absalom, Absalom!* and *The Sound and the Fury*), 54, 56, 64, 82, 83, 84–85, 88, 93, 141, 144, 162, 166, 171, 172, 204, 220, 227, 232; attitude toward blacks of, 36–37, 209–10; as brother avenger, brother seducer, 25, 37–40, 41, 43, 97; compared with Narcissus, 35–36, 41–43, 151–53, 207–8; death of, compared to death of Christ, 52–53, 124–25, 147, 150, 154, 155; and interchangeability of roles, 28–29, 30–31, 47, 49, 50, 52, 67–70, 74–80, 121–22; linking of incest and death by, 41–49, 51, 53, 58–59, 91, 153, 224; as narrator, 1, 8, 20, 21, 26–27, 61, 73, 114, 166; relationship with father, 187; as surrogate of Faulkner, 158–59, 171; temporal dilemma of, 63–64, 80, 109–11, 119–20, 123; and virginity, 37–38, 39, 41, 74, 111, 112–14, 130, 203, 207. *See also* Freud, Sigmund; Jones, Ernest; Kierkegaard, Søren; Rank, Otto

Corporal, the (*A Fable*), 156, 166; as Christ, 135; relationship of General to, 136, 145, 147–48; resistance of, to authority, 135, 137, 138, 141, 143, 144–45, 147–48, 150; reversal of roles and, 139–40, 142–43

Cowley, Malcolm, 112

Crane, Hart, 8, 20

"Damuddy" (*The Sound and the Fury*), 44–45

David (Old Testament), 25, 148–49, 150

"Delta Autumn" (1942), 59, 60

Driscoll, Thomas à Becket (*Pudd'nhead Wilson*, Twain), 12–13

Driscoll, Judge York (*Pudd'nhead Wilson*, Twain), 12

Dupin ("The Murders in the Rue Morgue," Poe), 11, 175–76, 188, 190

Edmonds, Roth ("Delta Autumn"), 59, 60

Emerson, Ralph Waldo, 11

"Error in Chemistry, An" (1946), 175, 177–79, 181, 184, 185

"Encounter with an Interviewer, An" (Twain), 13–14

Essex, Colonel Cecil Burleigh (*Pudd'nhead Wilson*, Twain), 12

Fable, A (1954), 135–48, 156, 166; significance of Christ's death in, 125

Fairchild, Dawson (*Mosquitoes*), 161, 163, 164, 164–66, 167

"Fall of the House of Usher" (Poe), 11

Farewell, My Lovely (Chandler), 189

Faulkner, William, 17, 27, 57, 88, 112, 136, 149, 155; ambivalence of, to the South, 21; on castration complex, 6, 58–59; genealogy of works of, 11, 20; and image of death, 91, 124–25, 150, 157; and narcissism, 6, 59, 159; on relationship between narrator and story, 8, 28; and relationship between

Irwin, John T.
    Doubling and incest/repetition and revenge : a speculative reading of
Faulkner / John T. Irwin.—Expanded ed.
        p.   cm.
    Includes bibliographical references (p.   ) and index.
    ISBN 0-8018-5231-5 (pbk. : alk. paper)
    1. Faulkner, William, 1897–1962—Criticism and interpretation.
2. Doubles in literature.   3. Revenge in literature.   4. Incest in literature.   5. Repetition (Rhetoric)   I. Title.
PS3511.A86Z854   1996
812'.52—dc20   95-40638